# Dr Harry Barry

## Beneath the Surface
*A Memoir*

An Irish Doctor's Journey of Resilience, Empathy and Self-Discovery

HACHETTE
BOOKS
IRELAND

Copyright © 2025 Dr Harry Barry

The right of Dr Harry Barry to be identified as the Author of the Work has been asserted by him in accordance with the Copyright, Designs and Patents Act 1988.

First published in Ireland in 2025 by
HACHETTE BOOKS IRELAND

1

All rights reserved. No part of this publication may be reproduced, stored in a retrieval system, or transmitted, in any form or by any means without the prior written permission of the publisher, nor be otherwise circulated in any form of binding or cover other than that in which it is published and without a similar condition being imposed on the subsequent purchaser.

Some names and details have been changed within this book.

Cataloguing in Publication Data is available from the British Library

ISBN 9781399740913

Typeset in Adobe Caslon Pro by
Palimpsest Book Production Ltd, Falkirk, Stirlingshire

Printed and bound in Great Britain by
Clays Ltd, Elcograf S.p.A

Hachette Books Ireland policy is to use papers that are natural, renewable and recyclable products and made from wood grown in sustainable forests. The logging and manufacturing processes are expected to conform to the environmental regulations of the country of origin.

Hachette Books Ireland
8 Castlecourt Centre
Castleknock
Dublin 15, Ireland
(email: info@hbgi.ie)

Authorised representative in the EEA

A division of Hachette UK Ltd
Carmelite House, 50 Victoria Embankment, London EC4Y 0DZ

www.hachettebooksireland.ie

'An exceptionally beautiful book – a blend of memoir, medicine and meditation. In *Beneath the Surface*, Harry brings us on a compelling odyssey that weaves his own life story with empathetic reflections on the lives of others.'
Ryan Tubridy

'Harry's incisive, empathetic and good-humoured commentary on life is turned to the seasons of his own life – to moments of joy, of grief and the days of calm in between ... It is a real pleasure to join him for a tale well told.'
Dr Anne-Marie Creaven, Associate Professor in Psychology, University of Limerick

'A beautifully inspirational and thought-provoking book which ... provides unique insights into the life and work of one of Ireland's most influential doctors. It is quite simply a remarkable story of a remarkable man.'
Sr Stan Kennedy

'A luminous, powerful exploration of becoming, *Beneath the Surface* reminds us that the richest stories are often the quietest – and that understanding ourselves and listening to each other are the greatest adventures of all.'
Brendan Kelly, Professor of Psychiatry, Trinity College Dublin

'*Beneath the Surface* is a testament to a life lived with courage and care. It reminds us that our greatest insights often come from our hardest moments, and that love, service and connection remain the truest guides in uncertain times.'
Dr Sabina Brennan, neuroscientist and author

'A deep and powerful memoir, *Beneath the Surface* illuminates Harry Barry's sheer depth of knowledge and awareness of the human condition. It explores his wisdom and guidance that have been a shining light for so many people over the years.'
Cathy Kelly

Dr Harry Barry is a highly respected Irish author and medic, with over three decades of experience as a GP. With a keen interest in the area of mental health and suicide prevention, Dr Barry is the author of numerous books addressing various aspects of mental health including anxiety, depression and toxic stress. His previous bestselling books include *Emotional Resilience*, *Anxiety and Panic*, *Emotional Healing*, *Self-Acceptance* and *The Power of Connection*. *Beneath the Surface* is his first memoir.

*This book is dedicated to Brenda, my soulmate and fellow dreamer, and to my guide and mentor, Sr Kieran Saunders MMM (1909–1997)*

Some names and identifying details have been changed within this book.

# Contents

| | |
|---|---:|
| Introduction | 1 |
| Part One: Growing Up | 9 |
| Part Two: College | 45 |
| Part Three: The Apprentice | 99 |
| Part Four: Africa | 137 |
| Part Five: Donegal | 211 |
| Part Six: Coming Home | 239 |
| Reflections | 303 |
| Appendices: Blueprints | 317 |
| Acknowledgements | 321 |

Had I the heavens' embroidered cloths,
Enwrought with golden and silver light,
The blue and the dim and the dark cloths
Of night and light and the half-light,
I would spread the cloths under your feet:
But I, being poor, have only my dreams;
I have spread my dreams under your feet;
Tread softly because you tread on my dreams.

    'Aedh Wishes for the Cloths of Heaven'
          – W.B. Yeats

# Introduction

Picture the scene. It was summertime and the sun was splitting the rocks. My wife Brenda and I were clambering over the grassy knolls down onto the rocks in Clogher Head, County Louth. We finally arrived at our destination, a depression set in the rocks facing out over the Irish Sea. Spreading out a blanket, we opened our picnic basket. There is nothing more satisfying than savouring a sandwich and a mug of tea out in the open air.

I felt so much at peace. I had the person I loved most in the world beside me, and in one of my most favourite spots in the country. With our picnic over, Brenda settled down with her book and I lay back against a rock. I saw a seal pop its head out of the water to gaze at us, before suddenly diving under the waves.

Those who know and love me constantly chide me for 'living in my head'. They despair of those moments when I look off into the distance, musing about new concepts or ideas, or problem-solving some issues. On occasion, it can take some time for me to exit such reveries. Out on the headland that day I found myself entering this meditative space, reflecting on the fact that I had been on the earth for over seven decades.

Questions flooded my mind: where had those seventy-years-plus gone? They seemed to have passed by in the blink of an eye. What had I achieved during this time?

Who was I? Husband, lover and soulmate? Father of three wonderful children? Grandfather to three beautiful grandchildren? A doctor and healer? A mental health advocate? An author? A media commentator? How did all of these come to pass?

What had become of my dreams? Had I been able to fulfil them? Was it time to reset them?

What of the future?

It also came to me on reflection that day that I had been on a lifelong quest over the decades, seeking answers to a number of questions.

What was the essence of *healing*? Did it involve the whole person?

What was *wisdom* and how did one acquire it?

Most of all, how did one find *meaning* in a world so broken and splintered? Was I searching for the essence of being?

So many questions filled my mind. If I was to answer them honestly, it would mean revisiting various periods of my life. Each one of us has a story, a life less ordinary. Mine was no different. It was time to explore it further.

I had to face the reality that I was getting tired, mentally and physically. It was as if sharing the burdens of so many people for so long was finally catching up with me. Maybe now was the time to tell my story, especially while I still had the energy to do so.

And so my journey of rediscovery began.

In retrospect, what an amazing roller-coaster of a life it has been. Filled with adventure and romance. Soaked in the tears of grief and loss. There have been periods of joy and laughter, intermingled with those of sadness and pain. So many wonderful players who appeared regularly on the stage during the last seven decades have now left us. Most of what I have been fortunate to achieve has been built upon the shoulders of those giants who have gone before me.

Revisiting my life story brought me into the world of *memories*. What amazing, mysterious entities our memories are. Modern neuroscience has shed light on how every detail of our lives, both emotional and contextual, is being continuously formed, shaped, reshaped and encoded in our brain, often when we are asleep. Memories are always there for instant retrieval, ready to be brought back into our conscious minds, if required. Like it or not, we *are* our memories, whether joyful, painful or traumatic.

Our personal memory of a situation, as I was to discover, may fundamentally differ to that of others. In this sense, our memory banks are unique to each one of us. There is also the question of space. The brain has a limited storage capacity so prioritises some memories over others. Some of our earliest memories are often subsumed under the many layers of new memories formed since.

I have found revisiting so many memories to be an emotionally challenging experience. There were many times when I found myself in tears. On other occasions, I found myself uplifted, borne on the wings of those wonderful human beings who carried me when all seemed hopeless. I frequently found myself emotionally lost in the letters and documents from past times and in the many fact-checking interviews and conversations with family members, friends and colleagues. It was like revisiting a different world, and yet, increasingly, I felt it was important that the many voices that enriched my life with their wisdom and knowledge be heard. For this is not just my story, but the story of generations who have gone before me.

When I sat down to write, I discovered that some fascinating threads weaved their way through my rediscovery of the past. Here are just a few.

## *Dreams*

I found myself reflecting on the idea, and the importance, of dreams as I wrote my story. Not so much the night-time ramblings of our subconscious mind, beloved of Freud and Jung. Rather, those conscious dreams all of us have, often beginning in childhood, that motivate and guide us in our lives, and help determine how our lives might evolve. The dreams that signify hope and potential: the romance and love we will find, the adventures we will have, the places we will visit, the people we will meet, the lives we will lead. Such dreams are like clouds, floating over the landscape of our lives. Earthbound, we experience the peaks and valleys of life with its joys and sorrows. Above, oblivious to these happenings, float our dreams. They may constantly change as we age, but without them and the sense of hope that they bring, our lives can become grey and meaningless. It was one of the great insights I had when writing this book. How all of us must have the courage to follow our dreams, no matter what others might think or say, no matter the cost or where they bring us to. In doing so, we are following our hearts.

## *The Outsider*

I have always believed myself to be an outsider – standing on the periphery, looking in. This encouraged me to remain fiercely independent throughout my life, refusing to allow my mind, in particular, to be pigeon-holed into any formal or fixed viewpoint or within the strait-jacket of conformity. I view myself as an observer, like a bird sitting high up in a tree, looking out over the landscape below.

Being an outsider has afforded me the opportunity to see a broader picture of life, with its many different colours and hues. This is especially the case in my approach to mental health, where my objectivity and curiosity have allowed me to observe and analyse others, giving me a deeper understanding of issues and a strong desire to help. The outsider by nature will often be a loner – as I am – but this was a price I was happy to pay as long as it allowed me to help others.

## *Empathy*

I now realise that I inherited the gift of empathy early on in my life – of being able to sense the emotional landscape of another person and to make deep human connections with them as a consequence. This gift became honed and polished with the assistance of others and as the decades progressed. It became the cornerstone of my life of healing.

## *Resilience*

This is one of the most important life skills that any of us can develop – the ability to constantly adapt to whatever life throws at us. My story is a story of resilience and, at times, of pure survival. The fact that I am still here striving and thriving is a testimony to the power of resilience. It continues to form a fundamental part of my whole approach to mental health and wellbeing.

## *Service*

It may seem an old-fashioned concept in our busy individualistic modern world. This idea of being there for each other. To go beyond ourselves for the betterment of others. To share our hearts and minds with each other. To be there for those who are most in need. Is this not love in its purest form?

## *The Feminine*

On this journey of self-discovery, I have found that I am most comfortable in the feminine nature of being. All of us have a masculine and feminine side and I have come to realise that I am much more attracted to the latter. It represents a softer, warmer, empathetic, nurturing, pragmatic and often more intuitively deeper understanding of the human condition.

## *Healing*

I have been searching my whole life for a holistic understanding of both physical and mental health, where each is seen as interchangeable and essential for our optimal wellbeing.

We have made such strides in the treatment of physical health, and I have been fortunate to witness the giant advances in combating sickness and disease throughout the decades. Advocating for such strides in mental healthcare is an ongoing battle, and there is still much to do. It lags significantly behind physical healthcare, but its importance to overall health and wellbeing should not be underestimated.

## *Meaning*

What is life all about? Where do we come from? Where are we going? These are the questions that I have been asking throughout my life. This story tells of how I finally came to my understanding of the essence of meaning. What a journey of discovery it has been.

These are just some of the threads running through this story. It is a tale of hope, of joy, of sorrow, of the deeper side of what it is that makes us human. It's a story of an enduring love that wrapped up so many, including me, in its warm embrace. Everything has flowed from this fountain of nourishment.

To think that none of this might ever have happened.

For this is where my story begins.

# PART ONE

## *Growing Up*

CHAPTER 1

## *It Might Never Have Been*

Deep down, at the core of our being, we all search to understand how we became the person who looks back at us in the mirror. Why have we developed certain traits? Why do we think and behave the way we do?

Why have I always felt like an outsider? I have always been fiercely independent and an observer of others and life. Where did these traits come from? The answer to these questions, as I would discover, lay in my childhood.

But maybe we should start at the beginning. For all of us, our origin stories are based on chance encounters and unforeseen circumstances. For me, I keenly remember how sobering it was to discover that I might never have been. Did the revelation of my origins lay the groundwork for what was to come? Maybe the seeds were sown from that moment onwards.

The story of my beginnings is a typically Irish story, and of course was shaped long before my birth. It is my mother and father's story, and shows how simple twists of fate led to my existence. It's a story full of romance and love, sadness and loss. It was told to me by my maternal granny when I was a medical student.

It all began when a vibrant young woman met a dashing doctor, and they fell in love. She had grown up in Glasnevin, Dublin, and was no stranger to tragedy, having lost her father to cancer when she was eleven. After she left school, she joined the bank. As evidenced by photos of the time, she was attractive and loved a good party. At her family home, it was routine to roll up the carpet and for the dancing to begin.

The doctor was involved in the radiological diagnosis of the dreaded illness tuberculosis, which was rampaging through Ireland at the time. He worked from the same rooms in Harcourt Street as Dr Noël Browne, who would later become minister for health. The couple were deeply in love. They got engaged and were busy organising their wedding. Rings were purchased, the wedding venue chosen, wedding outfits bought and a future house picked out.

Then life intervened to shatter their plans. One fateful night, the woman was minding her fiancé's surgery, waiting for him to arrive. He was late. When he finally appeared, he fell in through the door, covered in blood. He had been involved in a motorbike accident on the way to work. She accompanied him to the Mater Hospital in Eccles Street, where he was whisked off for routine tests, which included a chest X-ray. Little did they know what was in store.

Her fiancé's X-ray revealed the classic snowy pattern of widespread miliary TB. Nowadays it's considered to be a serious condition, but in the 1940s it was frequently a death sentence. As TB was a highly infectious disease, the doctor was immediately confined to a sanatorium for total isolation. On investigation it was discovered that the woman herself had early signs of pulmonary TB.

What followed was a nightmare. She spent a significant time convalescing at home. Her fiancé, isolated in the sanatorium, alone and afraid, was pining for the woman he loved. On one occasion he even absconded from the sanatorium and made his way to his fiancée's home. A terrible scene occurred on the doorstep, where the mother of the girl, with tears in her eyes, refused to let him in. He returned to the sanatorium in despair. Despite the best efforts of the medical and nursing teams, the doctor died.

His death tore a hole in the young woman's heart. Her grief was all-consuming. Eventually she returned to work, where she endured the numbing routine of the job, only to go home every evening and head straight to her room to cry tears of pain and loneliness. Her whole world had imploded. She was not only grieving the loss of the person she loved, but also her future. The woman in question was my mother, and without doubt I would not be here if this unspeakable tragedy had not happened. She experienced so much loss for one so young.

Bit by bit, my mother picked up the pieces of her life. She was now working as a personal secretary in the head office of the old National Bank of Ireland in College Green, opposite the Bank of Ireland building, near Trinity College. There she met a man called Harold Dominic Barry, who was doing relief work, covering for people who were off sick, at the time. He was from Limerick city and came from a large family of eight. He was a keen sportsman, playing rugby at junior level for Munster. Harry was no stranger to sadness and tragedy himself, having lost his younger sibling Jack to leukaemia in 1936, at the age of twenty-six, and his own father in 1941. Although he never spoke about the loss of his brother, it would haunt him for the rest of his days.

Like my mother, he loved to socialise and was a great dancer. He was extremely charming. Charming enough to win the affections of my mother, and they began to date, before finally marrying in 1950. They had their reception in the Gresham Hotel in Dublin. To this day it remains one of my favourite places. They honeymooned in Wales, and in 1951 my brother Gerald was born. Two years later, my mother gave birth to a second son under the care of Professor Éamon de Valera at a clinic in Hatch Street in Dublin – me: Harold Patrick Peter Barry. She was determined that I was to be always known as Harold rather than Harry to distinguish me from my dad. I had arrived and our story begins.

•

For the first three years we lived in Moate, County Westmeath, where my parents had moved just after they married due to my father's job. I have little memory of the time. I am reliably informed by some sources, including Gerald himself, that from the beginning my brother considered me a threat. He decided that putting a cat over my face might solve the problem, but alas this strategy failed. It did, however, leave me with a lifelong aversion to cats.

In 1956, my father was transferred to the bank in Dundalk and the family moved into a house on Faughart Terrace on St Mary's Road. The house is still there, a lovely red-brick three-storey building with a large back garden. Across the road, behind an imposing stone wall, lay St Mary's College, a school that was run by the Marist Fathers, which I would subsequently attend. This house would play a pivotal role in my early childhood years, and would be our family home for the next five. With two small children, it was a chaotic period of time for my parents, but they loved Dundalk and its people and settled in quickly to their new abode.

My memories of that time are fragmented. However, I do recall that my mother always seemed to be unwell, and this had a profound impact on me and our relationship. She had a number of serious medical issues, in particular a chronic peptic ulcer which concealed a more serious underlying gallbladder condition that remained undiagnosed for a considerable time. She had two difficult births with Gerald and myself, with resultant gynaecological issues. My recollection is of her being in hospital for significant periods of time, and this led to a struggle to bond with her emotionally. In 1958, despite her gynaecological difficulties and her illnesses, my mother became pregnant with my brother David. There was no contraception available at that time, so women had little control over their fertility. She apparently had a horrific birth. Her gynaecologist, Professor de Valera, informed her that she would never again have children.

My mother, in retrospect, must have been deeply traumatised by these births and the seismic events which had occurred up to this stage in her life. She was also trying to care for my granny in Dublin. The accumulation of these life-altering experiences made it difficult for her to emotionally bond with us in a maternal way. This absence of natural nurturing must have impacted on us as children. Was it one of the reasons that I would assume my outsider status? She did her best to care for us all, but I never experienced that warm maternal affection, so vital and nourishing for each one of us. When she was well she looked after all of our practical needs. She was always a wonderful cook. What was missing were those hugs, those gestures of affection and security that all of us as children crave. She clearly loved us all deeply, but struggled to demonstrate this emotionally. Was this a symptom of the time, or was it the legacy of such difficult births, or was she scarred by her own traumatic past? It was probably a mixture of everything.

My father was very frazzled during this period and was extremely tough on Gerald and myself. His own mother, Marian, had died in 1955 and she had been of great assistance to both my parents. It was hard for my father. He had to look after my mother when she was unwell, while rearing two small unruly boys and also holding down a new job in an unfamiliar town. There must have been little time for any real form of emotional nurturing of us.

Tough love was also the order of the day, especially for men and boys. Real men did not show their feelings. Real men 'manned up', did whatever was necessary for their families and reared their children, especially boys, to behave in a similar manner. My father, for all of these reasons, struggled to emotionally bond with us, but made up for this in so many other ways. I am immensely grateful to him for the many gifts he has left me. This did not mean that our relationship did not go through rocky periods.

My overriding memories of St Mary's Road relate to my experiences of childhood asthma. In those days there were no magic inhalers or nebulisers available, and the condition was poorly understood. I recall having to ingest ephedrine tablets, the only treatment available. I hated the taste, and would gag and retch whenever I attempted to swallow them. The asthma led to persistent shortness of breath and a dry, irritant cough. This was exacerbated by the usual childhood infections, sore throats and upper respiratory tract infections, routine for a small child under eight but infinitely worse for an asthma sufferer like myself. Looking back on it now, this was another contributory factor to my lifelong feelings of being an outsider. Illness separates us from others, and childhood asthma certainly did so in my case.

I spent a substantial amount of time in bed following a serious bout of double pneumonia, which we now call bronchopneumonia. I passed the time reading books and listening to an old radio. These lonely times helped to cultivate my great lifelong love of reading. Once introduced, I never looked back. Books allowed me to escape into my head and to visit so many wonderful places. They fostered my curiosity and creativity. I became a voracious reader.

However, I fell behind in my schooling. The superior of the Marist College used to visit me. He was very kind and on one occasion brought me over to the school, giving me some treats when I was feeling a little better. He encouraged my parents to involve me in playing sport as much as possible to manage my asthma. This was a turning point. I slowly recovered and began to take part in regular sports activities.

Despite everything, I was happy in St Mary's Road. We were close to the port and my father would often bring me down to see the ships docked there. I remember also those Christmas stockings, filled with many wonderful toys and games that were so exciting to a small child.

At the age of seven, I made my First Communion. I remember there was a simple mass followed by a communion breakfast at the school. There is a photo, which I cherish, of myself and two other classmates, resplendent in our shorts, school blazers and ties, looking very holy indeed on the day. This picture was taken sixty-five years ago.

I vividly recall playing with other boys on the street, building go-carts from bits of wood and castor wheels. The fun we had, racing one another with our home-made, rickety vehicles. Then there were those two wonderful trees in the back garden, which my friends and I delighted in climbing.

I took away some life lessons from these early days of childhood into my older years. I'm a believer that if you want small children to thrive and become resilient, give them plenty of time and space to play. Let them take risks. Teach them how to read. They will do the rest themselves.

When I was eight years old, we moved from Faughart's Terrace to a new home on the Demesne Road in Dundalk. As a child, I actually moved house three times between 1956 and 1965 in Dundalk alone. If you include the move from Moate, we moved six times between 1953 and 1970. This constant movement made it difficult to set down roots anywhere.

If you watch a bird, they are constantly flitting from branch to branch, from tree to tree, always watching, always observing, always on the move. This is how I felt from the beginning. There was never any feeling of constancy. I was already a very quiet child and socially shy. I feel that it was during this period that I developed my observational traits. However, I was also very stubborn, and coupled with a strong independent streak, I regularly got in trouble in school for speaking my mind. My competitive nature also began to shine through. These elements of my personality meant that I struggled to fit in socially, further enhancing my outsider status.

Why so many moves over such a short period of time? The answer lies in my father's occupation. He worked initially in the family business in Limerick, but then joined the National Bank of Ireland, which at the time was regarded as the gentleman's bank. Life was not easy for the bank official at that time. You were at the mercy of the bank's head office. It was common for the bank official to be regularly uprooted and sent to a new village, town or city. It was not particularly well paid, especially for those on the bottom rung of the ladder. Few could afford to buy a home until much later in their lives, so rental and continuous movement were the norm.

The bank was a fickle place to work. Depending on the economic circumstances of each era, it alternated between requiring their managerial staff to be outgoing extroverts and pull in new business, to being technocratic introverts, tasked with ensuring that every 't' was crossed. My father belonged to the former group of bankers. As a result, he would find himself frequently trapped between these shifting tectonic plates.

During the period spent on the Demesne Road, my parents seemed happier and more settled. My father loved to potter around in his shed, making things and tending to the garden, while my mother was busy rearing us. We became a more cohesive family unit, and both my parents enjoyed spending time with us. All of us became much closer as a result.

This was a time when Gerald and I were allowed to roam free during school holidays. I used to spend time with other local lads, clambering over wood piles in a local timber yard or playing and swapping marbles. I have vivid recollections of autumn and the great conker battles we would have. It was also a time when my father taught me how to ride a bicycle, as I was always afraid of falling off. I now realise, many years later, that I suffer from dyspraxia, which might explain my balance issues at the time – think Paddington Bear and you get the picture. Then one evening he quietly took his hand away and I was off. It was my first real taste of freedom.

Now that I could cycle, the world was at my feet. Gerald and I used to ride down the back roads into Faughart, the site of St Brigid's Shrine. And then there was Halloween! In those days, fireworks were only available in Northern Ireland, so Gerald and I would cycle the thirteen kilometres into Jonesboro, a small rural village in County Armagh, to buy bangers, rockets, sparklers and Catherine wheels. Despite living in a border town, there was at this stage no real tension between North and South, and I always felt safe. Nevertheless, these roads were well patrolled, so on occasion the fireworks had to be dumped at the side of the road for pickup later. It was all part of the excitement. Then there was the barmbrack, with the ring inside, the hanging apples, the treasure hunts and the community firework displays.

I always loved the puppet shows we put on for our friends and family. We would use old curtains and lots of imagination to create a show, where friends would have to pay an entrance fee. It was such innocent fun. My parents allowed us much latitude and put up with all of our antics, something for which I am eternally grateful to both.

At other times, they would bring us to the sea, sometimes

to Shelling Hill outside Dundalk and at other times to Clogher Head near Drogheda. It's still one of my most favourite places to visit. These trips would include a picnic, the best part for any child. The soggy bananas (ugh!) from an old biscuit tin were standard, as were other goodies with the flask of tea. My father had a deep love of the sea and was a powerful swimmer. He developed this affection from his childhood days in Limerick, where the family would decamp to Kilkee for the summer. He was happiest when he was beside the ocean, and passed on this love of the sea to me. There is something elemental and wild about the ocean that seeps into our souls. He used to love walking the beach, and I also have fond memories of heading down with him to Greenore, close to Carlingford Lough, on summer evenings to watch the fishermen, rods embedded in the sand, busy reeling in their catch, with the big waves rolling in. Another favourite trip, often made with my mother, was to the woods in Ravensdale. There our attention was taken up with trying to dam a small stream with pieces of wood.

Music played an integral part in our growing up; it was a constant and enduring presence in our home. My parents loved classical music. My mother's eyes would often fill with tears on listening to Gounod's 'Ave Maria'. The music seemed to resonate deeply with something inside her. I was gifted as a child with a powerful soprano voice. It meant that I was asked for years to sing solo at Christmas midnight mass in the Marist church, which I loved. I felt free when I sang, as if some inner force was being released. It is the same sense of freedom I feel when encountering Mother Nature: wild, raw, untamed and uncontaminated.

When I was ten my maternal grandmother, Granny Murray, who was affectionately known as Nellie and our only living grandparent, became ill. Her diagnosis was angina, and she stayed with us when she was recovering. I believe now that she (as did my own mother) suffered from Prinzmetal's angina, a spasmodic form of chest pain, most likely triggered by anxiety and quite benign. This was a difficult period for my mother. She felt responsible for my granny, but found taking care of her quite challenging as she spent much of her time in bed. I remember my mother being more irritable during this period. Granny's presence didn't impact much on us as children, however; we simply accepted it as normal. She soon recovered and returned to life in Dublin, and order in our household was restored.

Glimpses of my mother's rebellious nature would come through at times, and one of these was when she was smuggling goods across the border. I think she loved the romance and adventure of it all, and these days brought out her mischievous character. It is hard to imagine how different a relationship we in the Republic had with Northern Ireland at that time. I was completely au fait with the Northern lilt, as I sauntered down the main streets of Dundalk. Dundalk was a prosperous town and had two big industries – Carroll's cigarette factory and the Harp Lager brewery. Newry was also a wealthy town, but there always seemed to be a different feeling when we visited there. The people spoke differently, though they were always very friendly, even if they were more business-like in their dealings. There was an unspoken connection between both regions as the Troubles had yet to come.

At that time, butter, tea, bacon, eggs, clothes and tobacco

were much cheaper in the North. My mother would regularly pack us into the car and head into Newry for a day of shopping, usually on a Thursday. Dilly, as my mum was affectionately known to her peers, was a madcap driver and remained so all her life. She never took a driving lesson or passed a driving test and was only given a full licence under an amnesty agreement in 1979. As kids we never noticed her lack of driving skills, and luckily, she never had an accident.

On our surreptitious shopping expeditions to Newry, we had to pass through two border posts, one on the Irish side, another on the Northern Irish side. One got accustomed to the inconvenience and, for us children, it was great fun. Having completed the relevant shopping in Newry, goodies such as Opal Fruit sweets often bought in Woolworths were the highlight of our visit.

The real fun began on the return journey, where the customs officials on the Irish side were on high alert for the 'butter smugglers' who dared to attempt to bring cheaper food back from the North. My mum was simply hilarious. She just had a way with people, and managed to escape, time after time, with the goods hidden in every possible corner of the vehicle. The poor officials were in the presence of a master, but never realised it!

Newry wasn't the only place my unlicensed mother frequently drove us to. She also brought us to visit Granny Murray in Dublin, once she got better and moved home, and we were frequent visitors.

Dublin played an integral part in my younger life, and I still hold a huge affection for the city. Even though so many memories of my childhood are patchy, lost in the annals of time, recollections of those magical trips to Dublin with my mum and Gerald are forever embedded in my mind.

The final destination for these trips was 91 Botanic Road, Glasnevin. What a road trip for a small child. In those days, there was no M1 motorway clogged with lorries and cars. This was a more interesting journey along winding country roads, through Castlebellingham, into the town of Drogheda. The latter stood out, for two reasons. The first was that we had to crawl through narrow, busy streets which seemed to go on forever. These streets were jammed with cars and people. The second was the sight of buckets filled with limestone and shale, high up in the air, passing over the tops of cars and into the cement factory. To us as children these were endlessly fascinating.

As we got closer to Dublin, I can recall the wonderfully ornate lamps that lined the streets. On arriving at Botanic Road, we had to then negotiate the back lanes to park. We were so excited to see Granny. She was a larger-than-life character to us as children and always so kind. Out would come the frying pan in the scullery and the pot of tea and, of course, the goodies. The second Gerald and I entered the house, we would scatter to explore the many rooms.

The main living space was the kitchen, where all of the food and conversations between Granny, uncle Paddy, if he was around, and Dilly would ensue. The front room and dining room were connected by a double door and this was usually my first port of call. This was where all of the dancing had taken place when my mother was a young girl. In the front room lay an old gramophone record player, with a few records. There was a broken record by the tenor John McCormack and

I played it endlessly, fascinated by the scratchy needle and his wonderful voice. Upstairs at the top of the landing lay uncle Paddy's room. He suffered from chronic asthma and was always slightly hoarse. I can still remember the musty odour that emanated from his room. It had an air of sickness about it, and I recall all the different devices used to manage his illness scattered on the bedroom table.

Gerald and myself would frequently find ourselves in the back garden on the steps, busily playing shop. This serious game could go on for hours, providing endless entertainment. If uncle Paddy was around, we were in business. He would walk down with us to the local shop to buy some sweets. Then he would bring us into the Botanic Gardens, which were so exotic and exciting. The highlight was the glasshouses, with their hot tropical palms and earthy, floral smells. We had great fun running up and down these buildings. On other occasions he might bring us to see Glasnevin Cemetery, close to where they lived and where Grandfather Murray was buried. What a special place it was, and still is. Finally, some tired little lads would pile into the car and head back to Dundalk, our minds filled with the wonderful experiences of the day.

CHAPTER 2

*The Promotion*

My parents had made many friends in Dundalk by this stage and were gradually becoming natives. My mother was a great bridge player and a wonderful networker, happiest when socialising and mixing with others. Then the unthinkable happened. Assured that a further pregnancy was unlikely, even impossible, my mother became pregnant again. She delivered her fourth son, my brother Kevin, in 1964. She was just coming to terms with this latest arrival being yet another boy, when life once again intervened. The bank manager at the time, a lovely gentleman, retired, and my father was appointed to take his place.

Becoming a bank manager was a major step up for a bank official at that time. You were now a very significant player within the community; you had the say on whether someone would get a loan or not. You also lived in the local bank house. This is how we found ourselves as a family uprooted again, and we moved into our third house in Dundalk, namely the National Bank of Ireland house in Roden Place. This was situated opposite the main parish church in the town, which locals called the cathedral. One unexpected consequence, however, of my father's promotion was that it immediately set us apart as a family from the rest of the community. You were now treated differently, adding to my emerging feelings of being an outsider.

The rooms in the bank house were large and spacious and there was a lovely garden. The house was perfect for entertaining, and my mother loved to throw a party. There was a bank porter to help with maintaining the garden and other aspects of the building. For me personally, the move brought me closer to the local newsagent shop, Tempests, where I bought my weekly comic. I lived in the world of the *Dandy*, *Beezer*, *Beano*, *Topper* and other wonderful comics. As a child, that shop was a wondrous place. Every week I would head over to collect the latest edition. I can still remember the pulley system between the shop office and the floor, where money and receipts passed back and forth. It was the highlight of the week.

My consumerism didn't stop there, and I loved visiting the Saturday afternoon markets, where the fastest-talking men, usually from up North, would pull down packet after packet of tools or some other fascinating materials to a child, and arrive with the 'price of all prices' for the lot. I was learning the art of the salesman at the feet of the masters!

I remember wonderful summers, cycling out to the seawater pool in Blackrock, outside Dundalk. It was the place for young people to hang out, with the pop music hits of the summer blaring. I was initially afraid of getting out of my depth in the pool. I owe a lot to my dad, who was determined that I would learn to swim. He kept holding me afloat until one day he removed his hands and there I was, swimming and keeping afloat on my own. It was a joyous moment. I have never looked back, and I feel more at home in the waves of the sea than in chlorinated swimming pools. I loved that seawater pool in Blackrock and recall my bitter disappointment, many years later, on my return to County Louth to find it gone. I associated it with the happiest period of my childhood.

But life has a way of throwing the unexpected into our path, and in 1965 when David was seven, he had a terrible accident that had lifelong consequences. He was a beautiful-looking child with blond curls and blue eyes. One day he was playing and swinging from the upstairs banisters in our house when he slipped and fell, landing with great force on the stone floor below. His face was badly damaged and his teeth were smashed in. I was not in the house at the time of the accident but I remember arriving home to the aftermath. David was bleeding heavily from his face and was extremely traumatised. The local GP had been called and organised for him to go to the accident and emergency room of the local hospital. He was fortunate not to sustain any severe head or spinal injuries in the fall. Although the physical injuries were to have lifelong effects, I wonder whether the trauma of the event left even greater psychological scars.

My mother was devastated by the event, likely blaming herself for it as all mothers tend to do when something tragic happens to their child. This accident bound David and my mother together for life. After the fall, he made her promise that she would not send him away to boarding school. She agreed and was true to her promise. He was the only one of the four of us to avoid this awful fate. Sadly, the fall was not the last trauma David was to endure.

Nothing would ever be the same after this accident. Life never stands still, and we were soon caught up in its swirling vortex.

•

The powers that be in head office in College Green decided that my father's trajectory was upwards. He was an old-fashioned banker, with the knack of attracting business from the wider community. A vacancy for a bank manager came up in Wexford in 1964. My dad agreed to leave Dundalk, and moved himself and his family to Wexford. It was a large, wealthy town at the time, and this role was seen as a major promotion. Such a move would completely disrupt everything my parents had built up in Dundalk. They had many friends, and we as children had settled in at school and socially. All this was about to change. For me, this move could not have come at a worse time developmentally. I was thirteen years old and entering that difficult phase of adolescence. Within a few months, everything I had known would be up in the air.

Gerald was just about to enter the Leaving Certificate cycle and I was about to enter the Intermediate Certificate (now known as the Junior Certificate) cycle. Big decisions had to be made. As was normal for the time, my parents did not consult either Gerald or me; they simply informed us that we would return as boarders to St Mary's College in Dundalk. We had no say in the matter. I remember being upset that I would be away from home for the first time, but I was also relieved that Gerald would be with me. David was only eight years old, and my mother had a promise to uphold. It seemed only sensible that he would remain with my parents and Kevin and go to school in Wexford. This enforced separation may partially explain why I never became as close to David as I did to Gerald.

I was sad to leave Wexford and return to St Mary's after only just arriving in our new town. The Wexford people were warm and friendly. I felt at home very quickly, despite the town itself being so different from Dundalk. The bank house that we lived in was situated on the quay, overlooking the port. Wexford was a prosperous town, but less action-packed than Dundalk. I never really had a chance to gel with students my own age there, as I wasn't attending the local school. I remember being lonely in Wexford for that reason. Adolescence is a time when we need our peer-group friends to help us grow and develop as human beings, and I was missing this connection. I believe that the destruction of such possible connections in my new home town consolidated my feelings of being an outsider. I simply did not feel that I fitted in anywhere any longer. I was emotionally anxious about all of these moves, so withdrew further into myself.

There were some benefits to the move. The weather was warmer in Wexford, with less of the east wind that whipped up during the spring months in Dundalk. There were wonderful beaches close by, including Curracloe, where my father, when he was single, used to rent a mobile home during the summer months. We grew to love Rosslare beach, with its unusual wooden palisades embedded into the sand. We swam on this beach many summer evenings. Beside the beach was the iconic Rosslare Golf Course, where Gerald and I would train it out from Wexford to play. I lost so many balls in those dunes that they must still be picking them up! Then there was the wild beach at Carne, where we would sometimes picnic. The event that stood out from this time was the Wexford opera festival. My parents were so excited during the weeks of the festival. They would be out every night with their new friends. One of the most frequent visitors to our home was Paddy Fitzpatrick, who was managing the Talbot Hotel in Wexford at that time. He became a very close friend of my parents and always expressed a desire to open his own place. Years later, when he opened Killiney Castle Hotel in Dublin, they were among his first invited guests.

But those halcyon days of our first summer in Wexford could not last forever, and Gerald and I had to leave the safety and security of our family and return as boarders to the Marist College in Dundalk. It is hard to explain the level of trauma of this upheaval, just as I was entering adolescence. This was one of the most difficult periods of my life.

In the Ireland of the fifties and sixties, church and state ruled with an iron fist. Children were to be seen, not heard. Discipline in the form of corporal punishment was viewed as the correct way to shape young men. Emotional and physical abuse were the norm. Parents assumed that getting into trouble at school meant that *you* were the problem, and not the school. It was a time of tough love.

I entered St Mary's College as a four-year-old and remained there until I was fifteen, so it played a major role in my childhood. The college was founded in 1861 by the Marist Fathers and was a sister school of the Catholic University School (CUS) and Chanel College in Dublin. It had a long, proud tradition. The school was run by a combination of Catholic priests, brothers and lay teachers. Many of them were decent teachers, whilst others filled us with absolute fear and terror. I had one wonderful lay teacher, Mr Flanagan, who inspired us all. He was a classics scholar. I developed a great love of English and Latin from him.

For the first nine years, up to the age of thirteen, I was a day pupil, and I had a great group of friends, and still count them as such to this day. I was happy at school, even if corporal punishment was a frequent by-product. Canes and straps, often tipped with embedded strips of metal, were standard forms of chastisement for any minor or major perceived misdemeanour. Some teachers preferred the use of the strap and cane as teaching methods, rather than assisting us to love the subjects they taught. That was the way of the time. We lived in a state of permanent fear that we would make some mistake and end up on the receiving end of a drubbing.

What made school exciting for me personally was the huge range of sports available. I loved playing every sport, even if I was not particularly good at anything. I loved running, especially sprinting, which made me feel as free as a bird. I also enjoyed basketball, tennis, Gaelic football, badminton and the long jump. I regularly represented the school in inter-school competitions.

All changed when Gerald and I were enrolled as boarders rather than day pupils. The two years which followed were hard on both of us. We were removed from our family. We felt trapped, unable to roam freely as before. The level of corporal punishment meted out to boarders was much worse. The level of bullying between students was also horrendous. Was there an underlying grudge towards day pupils, who had freedom, versus boarders, some of whom may have felt abandoned by their families? I believe there was. I lived in a state of constant fear and anxiety and only survived by throwing myself into academic studies, debating and every type of sport. I felt unmoored, lonely, missing my family and friends, and wondering if I would ever get out of jail.

Matters came to a head when, following a row over the distribution of food at the table, I was savagely head-butted by a psychopathic student who rejoiced in destroying the face of a fellow pupil. I sustained injuries to my nose, which over the years have led to four major surgeries. My front teeth were smashed in, with the loss of one tooth in particular, and my confidence was shattered. The superior asked me to reveal the name of the culprit, but in those days there was an omertà. If you broke this, you would be bullied even further. I believe that my brother and some friends had a quiet word with the culprit. I was learning first hand that life is not fair. On my next visit home I begged my parents not to send me back to St Mary's when my brother Gerald was finished with his Leaving Cert, and thankfully they listened.

There were some highlights during this period. Irene Quinn, who owned Ballymascanlon Hotel at the time, was very good to Gerald and me, and brought us out on a few occasions to feed us up. The McGuinness family were also very kind to us, often taking us out of the school for breaks. It was on a visit to see them that I decided to become a doctor. The father was a GP who cared deeply for his patients, and I was very affected by his obvious dedication. I have often reflected on what drove my decision to become a doctor. Was it because of my own experiences of childhood asthma? Was it because of my mother's experiences with illness? But there is little doubt that my visits to this family were pivotal. The father was a quiet, caring man who was clearly devoted to his patients. He did not necessarily speak much about them, but something was triggered in me during my interactions with him. Maybe it prompted the first rustlings of an inner desire to help other people? Whatever the reason, he inspired something inside of me where I suddenly knew for certain that this was the path I wanted to follow.

Looking back now, despite the hardships that I endured within its walls, I realise that St Mary's College was a great school, especially for day pupils. It provided me with a solid educational base and a lifelong love of all sport. Academically, it helped me to achieve decent grades in the Inter Cert. However, the bullying, the physical and emotional abuse, and living in a constant state of fear has left trauma and psychological scars that remain with me to this day. I made one promise to myself: no child of mine would ever set foot in a boarding school. I have fulfilled this promise.

I was busy trying to settle in to life as a boarder, and with my family in a new town, when in 1966 further tragedy arrived into the life of my mother. I had a small bedroom in the bank house between two larger reception rooms and in November of that year was at home for a few days. My mother came into the room ashen-faced. Her eldest brother, Peter, her closest sibling, had been involved in a serious road traffic accident after dropping his father-in-law home. Peter was a swashbuckling character who had previously walked away from two small-aeroplane crashes. He was secretary of the Irish Sugar Company at the time and was getting ready to welcome Tony

O'Reilly, who was arriving to take over Erin Foods the following day. For a week he lay in a coma before succumbing to his injuries. He was fifty-five. The previous May my mum had lost her eldest sister, Mary, who died of cancer at the age of fifty-four. Her body was brought home from the States where she had been living and was subsequently interred in Glasnevin Cemetery, alongside her dad. Within six months she had lost her eldest sister and brother.

Peter's death in particular was a further devastating blow for someone who had already lost her dad, sister and fiancé at a young age. My mother was an amazingly resilient woman, despite this stream of tragedy. She would never again speak of the deaths of Peter, Mary, her father or fiancé. Silence about such tragic events was the norm at the time. It was as if you were meant to be stoical and simply accept whatever life threw at you. I often wonder if such silences bred in me a passive acceptance of difficulties and traumas that I have experienced throughout my own life.

## CHAPTER 3

## *Once More Untethered*

We were finally adjusting to our new domestic situation in Wexford when our world shifted again. We had been resident in the town for barely two years. It was 1968 and I was fifteen. My father, so successful at bringing in new business, now found himself in the hands of the new breed of banking technocrats who required all borrowing to be secured, and if not, the manager would find himself in trouble. He belonged to a dying group of gentlemen bankers now facing a novel world of systems and protocols. He agreed to move to a new branch, this time in Thurles, County Tipperary.

It was a difficult time for the whole family. I was struggling to recover from the trauma of my assault. Gerald had finished his Leaving Cert and had applied for the bank. David continued to bear the emotional scars from his accident. Kevin, the youngest, was only a small child and so was probably impacted the least. For my father, there was the added loss of the sea he loved so much. We were a family adrift, isolated in our own experiences and traumatised by so much upheaval over a short period of time.

If I had felt an outsider while living in Dundalk and Wexford, that paled in comparison to how I felt now. It was inevitable that I would feel like this. If you take a young teenager and transplant him from the east coast into the midlands, to a new school in an unfamiliar town with a whole new group of peers who had likely known each other their whole lives, then that teenager will inevitably feel like an outsider. I was enrolled in the local Christian Brothers school, where I would spend my final two years leading up to the Leaving Cert. I found myself becoming increasingly introverted and threw myself into my studies, using reading as a coping mechanism. By then I had told my parents that I wanted to study medicine. My mother was immediately supportive. It must have been difficult for my father, what with my mother's previous romantic history, but he agreed to back me and never tried to dissuade me. All I had to do now was attain sufficient grades in the various subjects to achieve my goal.

That proved to be extremely difficult as the local school didn't have some of the subjects required for entry into medicine on their curriculum. My Irish was terrible, as the brother teaching us was quick to point out. I vividly remember him holding up my first essay, destroyed by red slashes, commentating on the absurdity of the idea of me being in an honours class. The school didn't do pure physics, so I had to study this myself with the help of a lovely brother who took pity on me. I was thrown out of the Latin class early on for allegedly talking. I was never allowed back into that class for the duration of the two years, so I had to study this on my own.

At the same time, I was really missing the various sporting activities that were so much part of my childhood. I was forced to take up hurling and was, of course, useless. Gradually, I made some friends, but I never really felt like I belonged. I also missed the sea. I am at my happiest within the radius of the seashore, the beach, the waves, the sand dunes, the cries of the gulls.

There were to be some positives, however, to the move. One of those was a once-in-a-lifetime trip to a city in the heart of East Germany.

Old passports tell such a story and can trigger strong emotional memories of certain periods of time in our lives. I got my first passport at sixteen, and the first stamp was from the German Democratic Republic (GDR), as East Germany was known at that time. The year was 1969 and Europe was a different place to what it is now. Established in 1949, East Germany styled itself as a socialist republic, but was of course a communist puppet state under Russian rule. So how did an innocent sixteen-year-old find himself crossing the border into this extremely hostile territory?

A cousin on my father's side, Teddy, was studying to become a priest in the local seminary in Thurles. I was a regular visitor. He was a lovely person, full of laughter and good humour. As I was finishing fifth year, word came down that the students were planning a trip to West Germany to take part in a work camp rebuilding ruins during the summer months. This was organised by the seminary, and there were two spaces left. My parents were happy to see me busy during the holiday period, so they agreed to let me go. I happily joined the group.

We landed in Dusseldorf in West Germany and arrived at the work camp near Koblenz, where we met young people of our own age, male and female, from all over Europe. The clerical students were a wonderful bunch, full of mischief. Music and laughter were the order of the day. We were under the watchful eye of the Captain, who had fought in the Second World War. Interestingly, none of us ever inquired as to the role he played or the side he fought for. We were busy every day, repairing and renovating a bombed-out site. At night-time the students would take over the local hostelry and music would belt out, disturbing the local townspeople, who tended to opt for an earlier bedtime. We even took some boat trips down the Rhine.

For a naïve sixteen-year-old, it was exciting to mingle with the different nationalities. There were the moody French guys, smoking their Gauloises cigarettes and covertly sipping Armagnac from their flasks. Then there were the German, French and Scandinavian girls, who seemed like a rare species, with their modern clothes and general air of confidence. I still have nightmares about the food. Black rye bread, lemon tea and fatty frankfurters were not my idea of a good meal, but I survived. I remember one date in particular, 20 July 1969, when we all gathered around an old TV set to see the first astronauts landing on the moon. What an amazing experience, and one embedded in my mind forever. We had reached the moon!

Towards the end of this amazing adventure, we were rewarded with a week-long trip to Berlin. We boarded a bus to begin the long trek from West Germany, which was part of the original EEC, into East Germany. Much has been written about the reign of terror carried out by the Stasi, the secret police at that time. We spent six hours on the border, trying to cross into East Germany to reach our final destination, Berlin. It was at the border that I received my first passport entry.

Berlin was situated in the heart of East Germany. It was divided into West Berlin, run by the British, American and French, and East Berlin, run by the East Germans on behalf of the Russians. The various armies had all reached Berlin around the same time towards the end of the war, and each grabbed a piece of the city.

I cannot describe my sense of wonder and awe on arriving into West Berlin. Money was pouring into this part of the city. The people were well dressed, and the shops were so modern. The Kurfürstendamm, or main street, seemed to go on forever and was like something from outer space to a young person from Ireland. Thurles seemed like the ultimate backwater in comparison.

In the middle of the city, however, stood that awful wall. In place since 1961, it was built by the communist government of the GDR to prevent its population from escaping into West Germany. Barbed wire, machine guns, barking Alsatians and concrete barriers were the order of the day. It was awful seeing people and families torn apart by this monstrosity. It cast such a pall over the whole city.

We were shown places where people had bravely tried to escape and died, and where others had made it through. We were also brought to the room where Hitler had allegedly ordered the filming of the slow hanging from meat hooks of those brave souls who had attempted to assassinate him during the war. All of this created my lifelong hatred for autocratic regimes, whose only desire is to conquer and control the lives of ordinary people for their own personal and political objectives.

Then there was that visit into East Berlin. I will never forget the sense of menace experienced when passing through

Checkpoint Charlie. With hatchet-faced East German officials, male and female, all in uniform, attack dogs straining at the leash, soldiers with machine guns at the ready, it was truly terrifying. When we did cross into East Berlin, it was like retreating fifty years in time. The cars were so old and everything was decrepit in comparison to West Berlin. The people were browbeaten and the whole place seemed so quiet.

It was with relief that we retreated from this part of Berlin, but the memory stayed with me. This is where we might find ourselves once again if we allow democracy to be taken over by autocratic fascist regimes.

The wall fell in 1989 with both Germany and Berlin uniting. I revisited Berlin, over forty years since that first trip, to find a much-changed city. I had an animated chat with a Berliner, a survivor of that terrible time. He explained to me sadly that the fall of the wall and the reintegration of both peoples of Berlin came at a high cost, financially and socially, with many suicides following in its wake. There is little doubt that there was an enormous amount of emotional distress experienced by people in Berlin at the time of the city's reunification. It must have put an intolerable strain on the mental health of those affected. Some simply struggled to cope with the suffering caused by the change in their lives, and for them, suicide became the only way they felt they could handle this distress. It was one of the key learning points of my own journey into mental health – that emotional distress rather than pure mental illness was often the precursor to such a drastic, tragic decision.

•

With a summer well-spent, I returned home to embark on my final year – and the much-dreaded Leaving Certificate. I spent too much time studying for my exams. I got panicky, around Christmas, and fearing that I might fail Latin, I took up French as well, borrowing the notes from the local girls' school. The year passed in a blur of studying, but finally the great day arrived when I completed my final exam. I had just turned seventeen.

While anxiously awaiting my results, I decided that the best thing to do to take my mind off things was to spend my summer holidays working in a hotel in Kilkee, County Clare. The link between Limerick folk and the seaside town of Kilkee is legendary and begins in the cradle. Many of my father's relations would relocate to the town for their annual holidays. Where else would I go for the summer, to get out of my parents' hair and make a few bob? I believe that students can learn as much, if not more, from their holiday jobs as from their studies. When I reflect on this time in Kilkee, I realise that it was a great training ground for life.

My first impression of Kilkee at the time was how sprawled out the town was. It seemed to consist of a never-ending line of guesthouses and hotels. The beach was vast and wide, and I have a distinct memory of the grey sand. There was no throbbing centre to the town; instead young people used to hang out in groups close to the beach. So, it was with a sense of optimism that this hapless student rolled into the thriving town. I had secured a job as a live-in waiter at the Hydro Hotel, which would have been considered a luxurious hotel at the time. If they had realised just how much chaos I would introduce into their orderly business, they might have demurred.

It's fair to say that I was not a natural when it came to the hospitality industry. This became increasingly obvious when the crash of broken dishes and glasses and the clatter of cutlery hitting the ground became familiar sounds in the restaurant. But I persevered and became a passable waiter in their main restaurant. It did teach me much about people and life. I loved the spit-and-polish bit, in terms of setting tables properly, acquiring self-discipline and being in uniform. It was people who were the most surprising. Some guests were lovely, warm, appreciative and generous. Others were argumentative, rude, demanding and ungrateful. This was a microcosm of life. It was valuable to learn this message early on.

There was only one golden rule in the hotel: the customer is always right. One quickly learnt how to massage egos, go with the flow, read people and act accordingly. Not only did I learn how to carry several plates on one arm while passing through a swinging door with the other, but more importantly, I learnt how to manage and cope with difficult social situations. I also had to live with the unsociable hours, poor pay and general discomfort which came with the job. A chaotic student became a half-decent waiter.

When I was off-duty, I tried to hang out with my cousins and the other young people spending the summer in Kilkee. I found myself wanting to be like them, but I struggled to fit in. As always, I experienced a sense of disconnection from my peers, and I often felt lonely and unmoored. They all knew each other from previous summers and were there to hang out and have a good time. I, on the other hand, was working long hours at the hotel and also found it difficult to be fully accepted as part of the clique. I wanted to be like them, and liked by them, as all young people do at that age, but I simply was not part of their world.

I did love the sea and found great solace in nature. I would sneak off to visit the Pollock Holes, which are seawater pools that would fill with the tide. I even tried jumping off the lower diving board set into the cliffs, but this was not one of my better decisions. It is hard to believe that my father's brother David used to dive off the road, way above the two diving boards, into the sea. Bravado or madness, I am not sure which.

By the end of the summer, I had a much greater appreciation of how hard people in the service industry work, and how poorly paid and unappreciated they often are. I try, as a consequence, to always treat people who work in service industries with respect and gratitude.

Soon, it was time to return home to Thurles and receive my Leaving Cert results, which would hopefully lead me onto the next step on my journey to become a doctor. My results? As I often comment to young people coming to see me, I have never since been asked by anyone, 'How did you do in the Leaving Cert?' Because in the end, it was, and is, only an exam – a means to an end. When the results did arrive, I had done enough to be accepted into UCD to study medicine. That was all that mattered. It was now time for this outsider to venture forth and begin to embrace his dream. Dublin beckoned.

# PART TWO

## *College*

## CHAPTER 4

## *The Journey Begins*

Opposite the kitchen window of my current home in Drogheda lies an area of the garden with poor soil. No matter the bush or shrub planted, it was usually rejected. In despair, we decided to throw down a pile of wildflower seeds. They took some time to germinate, but then something extraordinary happened. One by one the seeds gave way to wild, uncultivated flowers of every colour and description. I was witnessing resilience in action. These humble seeds survived, when all else perished.

Emotional resilience. Two words that have shaped my life. The ability to adapt, to roll with the punches, to surf the waves of life. I now realise that the seeds of resilience were laid down during my college years. I have often said to parents that what really matters is how resilient and adaptable your child is by the age of twenty-five, not their academic achievements. And so it was with me. The greatest seed of resilience is that of unconditional self-acceptance. I would love to say that I managed to achieve this during those turbulent years of college.

In reality, it would come later, when someone much greater than me, a 'gardener of the soul', would help germinate this seed and bring it to fruition.

Little did I realise this in 1970, when I first arrived in Dublin aged seventeen to begin my six-year odyssey to become a doctor. I was destined to become one of those countless penniless students populating the streets of the capital at that time. In my case, it really did feel as if the country boy had finally come to town. I recall a mixture of emotions. On the one hand I was excited about arriving in the city, but I was also anxious and filled with a natural trepidation as to what the future would hold for me. It all felt so new and so raw. Gone were the usual supports from home. Up here in the city I was on my own, with few people to rely on.

It didn't feel too exciting, in particular, when I began my year of pre-med in Belfield. I hated this suburban campus and held a special dislike for the science building. I can remember the airless nature of the place. At the time, it was not the extraordinary campus it is today; it was more like a big building site on the outskirts of Dublin. It felt out of the action. But at least it had a science and an arts block and a student restaurant.

As for the class of 120, I was overawed and immediately felt a complete outsider. There were a number of clear divisions. You had the townies versus the ones up from the country. You had the brilliant students, and then the rest of us. You had those who came from the northside of the city versus the southside, and the general misconceptions and stereotypes that came with that divide. A lucky few had cars or motorbikes, but the majority had to contend with the vagaries of public transport. But the biggest rift was between those who came from a medical family background, and those of us who didn't. Irrespective of our origins, we were all simply young people trying to find our way in the world.

Looking back, though, it's easy to see why I felt out on the periphery. I was the first in my family to go to college. Money was scarce. I had no family history of medicine. When it came to my knowledge of Dublin, I had wonderful childhood memories of visiting my granny in Glasnevin and a few trips at Christmas to see the exciting store windows in Switzers on Grafton Street, but was otherwise lost. The southside of Dublin was a foreign country to me. How was I ever going to cope with my brilliant, moneyed, ostensibly better-educated, often sophisticated student colleagues? The impostor syndrome was alive and well.

My parents, in their wisdom, decided that I would spend the first few months with my cousin Pam and her husband out in Shankill. They were lovely people, and I enjoyed being near the sea, but it was a long journey each day for a first-year student.

I struggled with the jump in educational standards from school to college. I had never done zoology at school and hated it. Try and dissect the mouth parts of a cockroach and find it inspiring! Physics was a real struggle, as I had never had formal classes on the subject and was hopeless at maths. I was extremely fortunate with botany as I was able to get assistance from one of my lecturers, Fr Martin Brennan SJ, who managed to vividly convey his sense of wonder about the natural world and the universe. I finally got the hang of chemistry without blowing up the lab. It was an inauspicious start to my college career.

How did I survive that first year? I am still unsure. This was my first taste of resilience in action. Maybe it was sheer stubbornness, a will not to give in. Or perhaps it was a determination that, no matter what, I would achieve my goal of becoming a doctor. I was already forming friendships with some people in my class and this really helped. It was a relief to get home at Christmas and Easter to see my family. It was not possible to get home at weekends, which did add greatly to my feelings of isolation. They were not so sanguine about seeing me dissecting a rabbit in the shed, however, as I readied myself for exams.

I managed to sit and pass my pre-med exams. In those days, you had to get through the initial year of science subjects first before being considered suitable to continue on to do the full medicine curriculum. I cannot adequately describe my relief and my excitement at the prospect of moving closer to town. My studies would now continue in Earlsfort Terrace, the home of medicine in UCD.

A student colleague then recommended to me a famous student digs situated in a residential area off Leeson Street. Even by the standards of the time, it was relatively cheap. On a day towards the end of my last term, I found myself ringing the doorbell of what would become my home for the next five years and which played such a role in my college life. A stern but motherly soul answered. Her name was Kitty and she would become my de facto mother in Dublin for the years to follow. Following an extensive interview on the doorstep, she took pity on this earnest eighteen-year-old struggling medical student and agreed to hold a place for him for the following term. The outsider had found his new home.

•

My first year in UCD had flown past in a whirlwind of new experiences, people, subjects and places, and now the freedom of the long summer break was fast approaching. My parents were introduced to an American nun who was visiting her relations in Thurles. She suggested to them that I might work as a student in a hospital in Texas during the summer holidays.

It was a rite of passage in those days, and still is, for Irish students to make their way to the States during the summer months, and my parents were agreeable to me doing just that. They paid for my flights and visa, and I was off to America.

I left for New York in June 1971. I was overawed and initially terrified by this raw, noisy, dirty, crowded city, a gateway for so many Irish emigrants in the past. I was lucky in that my great-uncle, Peter Dolan, was working and living there at the time. I had the privilege of staying with him at his home in the Bronx for a week before flying down to Texas. Peter was an official tour guide at the Empire State Building. He proudly brought me on a complete tour, stopping off on many floors to introduce me to his colleagues. He was a wonderful wisecracking, larger-than-life character.

He was married to a long-suffering Irish American woman, Kathleen, a lovely lady, who put me up for the week. They had no children. The apartment they lived in was heavily secured with multiple locks and bolts. At that time, New York was a dangerous city with rampant crime, especially on the subway. The city was filthy and the people were noisy. The cops on the beat often sent tourists, including me, in the wrong direction for their own amusement. I vividly remember the yellow taxis, which seemed to be everywhere. Most of all, I can remember the pulsating energy to the place. It felt worlds away from Dublin.

After a week braving the mean streets of New York, I flew down to Houston, Texas. I was met by a lovely lady, a nurse, with whom I stayed for the duration of my time in the States. She lived in Port Arthur, a city about ninety kilometres from Houston, where the hospital I would be working in was based. She had a tragic history in that her husband, who had been a consultant, died from cancer at a young age. She was now sole provider for her son and three daughters, all of whom were in their teens.

I received a major shock on my arrival in Texas when I discovered that I had misplaced my passport and visa. I frantically rang my great-uncle. He explained that passports were like gold dust, so I was unlikely to see it again. I would have to contact the Irish embassy. Then a few days later, he rang me with news. The taxi driver who drove me to the airport, and with whom I had chatted, had discovered the passport in the back of his cab. He retraced his steps to my uncle's apartment to return it. This was apparently unheard of, but I think he took pity on this poor Irish stray. There are still good people in this world.

From the beginning, I struggled in Texas. The heat and humidity were crippling, with every garment I wore soaked through with sweat within minutes. It took weeks for me to understand the Texas accent, where everything was said with a slow drawl. 'Hi y'all' translated to 'How are you all?'

My landlady and her kids were pleasant and hospitable people, but I struggled to connect with them. I especially couldn't understand their approach to food. They came together at 7.30 in the morning for a full breakfast that included orange juice, pancakes, eggs and bacon, but there were no formal meals for the rest of the day, with everyone wandering in and making sandwiches from the fridge. They also loved to order in large pizzas and other takeaways, which was unheard of in Ireland at that time. I also struggled with their sense of humour – it was so different to Irish humour. They seemed immersed in the past, with John Wayne and the Alamo on constant repeat on the TV. They never walked anywhere. Three of the family were adolescent girls, whom I could not relate to. I did, however, spend a good bit of time chatting to their dog. But I could not complain – they were very welcoming people.

I began to work as an aide in the large local hospital. It was foreign to everything I was used to. My job was to attend to individual patients with a mobile nebuliser-type machine and dispense a course of medication to those with respiratory problems. I found some of the patients to be very demanding, and I was often treated by them as an orderly. I quickly realised that without medical insurance you did not exist. By 1971, Medicare had been introduced to help those over the age of sixty-five with the cost of medical care. However, many were still uninsured at the time. Different hospitals had different policies as to whether or not they would treat those without insurance. There was also a deep-seated racist element evident in the wider community of Port Arthur. There were many gang-related rapes and violent incidents between white and black groups. All of this was foreign to an innocent eighteen-year-old student from Ireland.

Northern Ireland was in the throes of the Troubles at the time, so it was often in the news. I was regularly asked if

Dublin was burning, as it was assumed in Texas that the whole island was up in flames. I stopped trying to explain that the Troubles were most active in the northern cities of Belfast and Derry, not Dublin. They couldn't understand the nuances of the political situation.

I was also seen as a bit of a freak. I liked walking to get some exercise. Passing cars took a delight in beeping their horns at me. Was I mad? Nobody walked in Texas. You drove everywhere. A teenager was driving by sixteen. I tried to play some tennis, but the heat and humidity made this impossible at any hour of the day.

The family took me on an amazing journey into Houston. It was a concrete jungle, surrounded by a vast elevated highway system that took an hour to breach. I visited the now-defunct Astrodome made famous for its baseball and football. Next door was AstroWorld, a sprawling theme park akin to Disney World. We also visited Austin, a most beautiful city with its Ivy League college. There I had the largest steak I have ever eaten.

It was with some relief, however, two months later that I said goodbye to my host family, thanked them for their kindness and scarpered back to New York. My great-uncle brought me on some further trips, including to one of the largest emergency departments in the city. It was like a war zone, but I found it fascinating. Finally, I left to fly back home, not realising that I would never see him alive again. It would be forty years before I set foot once more on American soil.

But it was a new college year, and time to begin my medical studies in earnest.

CHAPTER 5

## *City Life*

With a mixture of excitement and apprehension, this medical student and his baggage approached the front door of a large Victorian terraced house in a leafy residential area off Leeson Street in September 1971. This was to be my home for the next five years. For those of us who came to love the place, despite its many idiosyncrasies, it was referred to simply as Thirty-Six.

The door was answered by Kitty, the housekeeper, who quickly made me feel at home. I was fortunate that I was sharing a room with only one other person. This was special treatment, as some rooms had four beds or more. My roommate was called Murdoch and we became great friends over the years. He was studying electrical engineering, and the bedroom fireplace mantelpiece was permanently piled high with evidence of his work.

It was a classical Victorian house over two levels, both massive, with multiple rooms and a huge basement. It was packed to the hilt with students and a few workers, maybe between twelve and fifteen of us at any one time, who came from every part of the country. There was a small patchy back garden that was never used and a driveway to the front with steps leading to the front door. It was old at the time, and I mean *old*. All the windows were of a sash type and insulation was never high on the agenda. The house was always cold, and in winter there was usually frost on the inside of the bedroom windows. The standard joke was that we had to open the front door on a cold frosty morning to let the warm air in! I spent winters with all of my coats stacked up over the bedclothes to stay warm. It was bracing, to say the least.

I remember clearly my initial checking out of the upstairs bathroom. The toilet was an old-fashioned model with a high wall cistern. I turned my attention to the bath. The taps were so ankylosed, it was obvious they were last used in Victorian times. This was worrying; how could you take a bath or shower? I checked the sink to discover that only the cold-water tap worked. I was reliably informed by my new housemates that of course there was no hot water and the bath had not seen any use for decades. But how, I asked, were we supposed to wash our hair? I was relieved to hear that there was hot water for one hour in the downstairs bathroom every Friday evening, as the lads would be heading out on the town. Problem sorted!

I checked out the living room on the ground floor to see if it was feasible to study there in the evening. This was a large draughty room with a big wooden table. Then there was the fire. As I was to learn quickly, heat was not considered a priority. The fire would be lit every evening with great gusto, but the second it took hold it was slacked, which meant smothered in a very fine type of coal, ensuring that the fire would last for the night but would generate almost no heat. Water was also added to the slack to guarantee its longevity. No wonder the warm, comfortable library of Earlsfort Terrace beckoned me every evening and would become my home from home.

The house was owned by two spinster sisters, who lived in a large room at the front. They were traditional in their views on how young male students should behave. Any student who had the temerity to bring a lady home late at night would be faced with immediate eviction. Being under the influence was also frowned upon and sometimes considered a reason for ejection. A tough ask with this rowdy crew of male students occupying the space at that time.

Kitty lived downstairs and kept the whole show running. How I loved this special lady who was so kind to us, even if she was sometimes stern. She took an active interest in each one of us and would always be on our back if we weren't studying or fully engaging with our courses. She patiently put up with the two mistresses and the madcap crew of students who invaded the house every September. I owe her huge gratitude. Kitty is long gone, and I pray she is being rewarded for her efforts.

Down in the bowels of the basement, where Kitty had her own private room, was the kitchen where we had our breakfast, evening meals and a hot lunch on Sundays.

The fry in the morning was filled with grease, so I learned to avoid it. The evening meal consisted of minute slivers of cold meat left over from the roast on Sundays and brown bread which got harder as the week progressed. The joke was that by the end of the week the bread would bounce back off the wall to meet itself. There was no question of any waste occurring. In the middle of the hall on the way down to the basement was the payphone. If only that phone could talk, what stories it would tell.

Students had stayed in the digs since time immemorial, even back to war times. There had been a period when both males and females had resided there. There was something about this mad, nutty building that inspired us. One might suggest good-humouredly that we were determined never to return, and this drove us onwards! It was to be a major foundation stone on my journey towards becoming a doctor.

For all of its deprivations, Thirty-Six was a wonderful place for an outsider like myself. It provided a readymade community of lads from all over the country, all of us in the same boat. Within its walls, I felt accepted. No wonder I felt at home. Fun and laughter were the order of the day. It was cheap, and most of us were constantly broke. It was wonderfully placed, close to Leeson Street and up the road from Earlsfort Terrace. It was also close to the centre of town. I had found a new mother figure in Kitty, who protected and cared for me during the years that followed. I had a new friend in Murdoch and over time would make many more. When I reflect on the sterile nature of college life for many young people nowadays, I would wish such experiences for them.

•

It started out so well. On one of my first days at Thirty-Six I found myself leaving the comfort of my new digs and walking down the bustling surrounds of Leeson Street to orient myself with my new neighbourhood. I passed by the residence of my botany lecturer, Fr Brennan SJ. I took in Hatch Street; the premises where I was born was by then a student hostel for the moneyed classes. On the right-hand side of Leeson Street, on the way to Stephen's Green, I passed by CUS, a sister school of St Mary's College, Dundalk. Then there was the Leeson Lounge, a typical student hangout which would become the scene of drunken escapades. I could see the entrance to what looked like a big park in front of me. If I turned left, I would arrive at Earlsfort Terrace, my new academic home, but I was keen to reach Grafton Street, so I crossed the road and entered St Stephen's Green.

I immediately fell in love with the Green, and to this day I feel at home in this place of peace and tranquillity. It was teeming with visitors, students, workers and families; many were simply sitting on benches or on the grass, admiring the wonders of Mother Nature. But I was on a mission, so I followed the crowd and found myself exiting opposite Grafton Street. I wandered down this lovely old street, drinking in the sights, listening to the buskers, gawping at the passers-by, checking out restaurants and shop windows, especially Switzers (now Brown Thomas). It was a feast for the eyes. I made it as far as the entrance to Trinity College and then decided it was time to head back. I returned to the Green. A simple journey back, out through the gates and down Leeson Street, back to my student digs. What could be easier?

But then the fun began. The paths seemed labyrinthine and I found myself lost in St Stephen's Green. I struggled to find the Leeson Street exit. I remember getting panicky. This was ridiculous, and I was too ashamed to ask anyone. What would they think? I wandered around and located an exit, but I knew this wasn't the right one. Back I returned to the centre, to try a different route. No joy there either. There were no smartphones with GPS in those times! I was stuck in this maze of a park.

Eventually, I had to bite the bullet and ask for directions. That didn't work out either as the person was a tourist and just as confused as I was. Finally, I found someone who directed me towards the correct exit. With burning cheeks, this disoriented student found himself back on Leeson Street, heading with some relief towards Thirty-Six.

This inauspicious beginning to my interactions with St Stephen's Green did not change my deep love for it. It became an important refuge during my student days, especially when times were difficult or when loneliness crept in to steal my heart. Despite wonderful friendships and camaraderie with my fellow Thirty-Six inmates, student colleagues and good friends, I remember this period as a lonely time. I was missing a soulmate. There were few opportunities and little money to socialise. I still couldn't shake off that feeling of being an outsider in the Dublin scene. Many of my class spent time with each other in pubs like Hartigan's or O'Donoghue's, standing around and chatting for hours with pints in their hands. I did not feel comfortable in this milieu. I simply did not belong.

I missed my family, especially my brother Gerald with his wonderful wacky sense of humour. I missed the sea and I wasn't familiar with the coastal towns and villages, so I was grateful to one of my new friends, Anthony, for introducing me to Howth Head, where I felt instantly at home.

The city is a lonely place for a young student. And as a result, I often sought refuge in the safe embrace of St Stephen's Green. Once I had finally discovered how to exit this beautiful space, I felt very much at home. My favourite spot was a bench directly facing the pond, where I would watch the ducks swimming back and forth over to the banks. On that bench I would contemplate life and where I was going. The dreams I had for the future, the direction my life might take. I missed having someone to open up my heart to. A combination of attending boarding school and having an 'outsider' status meant limited opportunity. In retrospect, this self-reflection by the pond was a form of mindfulness, and I would feel refreshed and at peace after spending some time there.

I occasionally spotted, but never interacted with, my uncle Con, sitting quietly on one of the benches in the centre of the park. He was always alone and seemed lost in his own world of thoughts. Like everyone in my mother's family, he too had experienced trauma and tragedy, having lost his father and first wife, both at a young age. Maybe I should have seized the moment and empathised with him, but I was young, immature and struggling with my own loneliness. I'm not sure that I would have had the language to open up any deep conversation. Maybe, in retrospect, my silence was for the best.

I passed by the pond with the ducks recently and was saddened to see that the bench upon which I sat was gone, as is my uncle Con, who died aged sixty-eight in 1981 from cancer. I am now at peace and pray that he is too.

## CHAPTER 6

## *Blame It on the Bones*

And now, finally, a new term was about to begin and I was no longer confined to the soulless Belfield campus. I had made it to the medical faculty at Earlsfort Terrace. I cannot describe the emotions I felt on first climbing the steps, passing between those pillars and entering the front door. It was with a mix of pride, excitement and nervousness – and a sense of accomplishment – that I arrived in the building that was to be my academic home for the rest of my student days. The Great Hall or Aula Max, as it was known then, was where I would take my exams. The Great Library, with its quiet dignified spaces, was where I would spend much of my time, studying.

The medical faculty, an integral part of the building, had been situated in Earlsfort Terrace since 1931. The whole place was steeped in history. I felt the weight of this history, and hoped to add to it, in my own small way, in the time I would reside there.

How I loved this ancient building. From those very first few days, I knew that this was where I was meant to be.

Our medical education began with the study of anatomy. This involved learning the names of all the bones in the body, and the muscles and tendons that are attached to them. Then we had to memorise all the nerves which supply them, and finally the different organs and tissues in the body. It was also the first time I was introduced to the dissection room with its overwhelming smell of formaldehyde. I found the experience of dissecting human bodies initially quite daunting. It was hard to comprehend that each body had once been a live human being. After a while, one learned to adjust to the situation and we students were very grateful to the families who had allowed their loved ones' bodies to be dedicated to science.

However, I have to admit, I found the subject uninspiring. Unless you were planning to become a surgeon, it was monotonous and boring to memorise all the information required. But since everything began and ended with anatomy, the two years had to be endured, if not enjoyed. I did, however, like James B. Coakley, who was professor of anatomy. He was a kindly man who had quaint quarters in Earlsfort Terrace. With pipe in mouth, he would often be found reading or correcting papers in his rooms beside an open fire. What a lovely academic life he had.

One might ask what kept me going during this period. I did not particularly enjoy the subjects we were studying. But part of life's learning is that sometimes, in order to achieve a goal, we must accept such things as part of the journey. We cannot exclude the dull and boring aspects and just seek out the exciting parts. This attitude of taking the rough with the smooth was to become one of the bedrocks of building my resilience.

The other subject studied over the first two years in Earlsfort Terrace was physiology. Before discussing how illness and disease affected human beings, we had to understand how the living body worked, from cellular mechanisms up to whole bodily functioning. I found this subject more interesting, as it was laying the foundations for the rest of the medical course.

Neither of these subjects got my juices flowing, but those two years were crucial in establishing my foundation as a medical student and helping me to grow and mature as a young adult in 1970s Dublin.

From the beginning of my academic career in Earlsfort Terrace, we were divided into small groups for the purposes of tutorials and experiments. I still find it astonishing how important it is where your name comes in the alphabet, and how this can have a significant impact on who comes into your world, and how it influences the direction your life can take. The tutorial groups were one such example, as they were put together on a strictly alphabetical basis. As my surname began with B, I was to spend most of the following five years in the presence of small groups of fellow students with surnames ranging from A to K. What a lovely group of people they were. Many of them became good friends and remain so to this day. Thrown together from the widest variety of backgrounds, we learned to work with, and implicitly trust, each other.

Intermingled within this group were mature students Ignatius and Jimmy, who along with some dentists had returned to college to study medicine. Ignatius and Jimmy, who came from a science background, brought with them such wisdom and maturity and took this immature student under their wings.

There were many others too whose friendship I valued greatly during this time.

There is one person who stands out from this group, and that's Anthony, my friend who introduced me to the delights of Howth Head. As he was close to me on the alphabet, we were thrown together on a regular basis. We often studied together, especially at exam times. We became good friends over the course of our first two years in Earlsfort Terrace. His family came from the northside of Dublin and he brought me to visit them on occasion. His mother was a lovely lady and was very kind to me. His father had a number of jobs, one of which was film critic for one of the newspapers of the time. This meant that he received regular invites to the opening nights of new films. Boy, did Anthony and myself avail of these invitations. It also meant that we got into the cinema to see some movies for free. I have some fond memories of the Regent Cinema on Findlater Place, now sadly gone, where we were regular visitors.

Anthony also loved music and was a member of a loose group of musicians, one of whom was called Declan. Another was Carl, who was amazingly talented on a number of instruments. I spent my time listening to these talented musicians perform as a group. We also had some madcap times with Cormac, another musical talent out in Belfield. It was a time of ideas, music and revolution for students, not only in Ireland but throughout the world.

One of my most vivid memories of this period is of being a pillion passenger on the back of Anthony's beloved motorbike. When coming up to traffic lights he would begin to chant, 'Give me a green, give me a green.' Inevitably it would be a red!

I was greatly saddened when Anthony decided at the end of his second year in Earlsfort Terrace to transfer from medicine to a different course. I really did miss his support and camaraderie.

•

Meanwhile, life was continuing as usual in Thirty-Six. Nothing can describe the level of mischief that occurred there. There was a wonderful camaraderie and bonhomie. There are many wonderful stories, some of which I will relate, others best left unspoken.

One of my favourites involved a student called Mac. Mac was what we would call an eternal student and an almost permanent resident. Every evening, the younger of the two sisters would climb the stairs, knock on the door of each room, peer in and shout, 'Tea is ready.' Mac resided in one of the larger bedrooms with multiple beds. Every night on hearing the sister's steps on the stairs he would hide in the wardrobe. The sister, on entering an empty room, would then exclaim, 'Where is that fellow Mac?' and head back down the stairs. By the time she got to the basement he was always just behind her. The poor woman never really understood how he did it.

On other occasions, 'visitors' would be smuggled in and all concerned would have to creep by the bedroom where the two sisters resided. If one of the students, as occurred regularly, was 'locked', they too would have to be carried quietly up the stairs, for fear of being discovered and evicted. I am absolutely sure that Kitty was completely aware of what was going on, but wisely chose to ignore the shenanigans as much as possible.

On another occasion, following the ejection of one particularly notorious student, the post box for the following few weeks was found to contain ladies' clothes, apparently last seen on a line at the back of the house.

Then there were those times when the young nephew of the two sisters arrived. We gave him the nickname 'Little monster'. He took a devilish delight in waking us up in the morning with the sound of a football clacker device that would have awakened the dead. He also used the same device to call us for tea. Fiendish!

Then there was the scramble on a Friday evening. Imagine, if you can, not having a shower or bath from one end of the week to the other. We must have been a smelly lot. There was the inevitable rush on a Friday evening to wash our hair in warm water and look presentable for our date – those of us who were lucky enough to have one. It was worse than a rugby scrum. But the fun and laughter continued, and somehow we all managed to survive and thrive.

My other home from home in Dublin was 91 Botanic Road, Glasnevin, the house where my granny (Nellie Murray) and uncle Paddy lived. I would visit there regularly and always received a warm welcome from Granny, who was now in her eighties and still going strong. Granny Murray was a big-boned, stout woman who always wore her hair coiled up in a bun. Out would come the frying pan any evening I visited, as she fussed around making sure that this poor student was properly fed. She usually cooked up a fry for me, with sausages, thick rashers and an egg. We always ate in the living room, which was just off the small kitchen. I remember it being a really relaxing, informal room. She was such a hospitable woman, and I would try to visit her at least once every term, so I saw her around four or five times a year.

She was also a mine of information, allowing me to develop a unique insight into my mother's family. It was she who revealed the tragic circumstances surrounding the death of my mother's original fiancé, a subject never broached at home. Originally a Dolan, whose family came from Balla in County Mayo, her father was an RIC officer. She was also able to recall the Black and Tans, and the fear they instilled in the people of Dublin, and was full of stories about the civil war and how some of her own family had to go on the run, including one of her brothers who had to be secreted out of Ireland. He eventually arrived in the US and married his brother Peter's sister-in-law. It was not uncommon at the time for two brothers to marry two sisters.

Nellie was working as a postmistress when she met her husband Cornelius, manager of one of the oil-importing businesses at the time, who died tragically young. She described how devastating his death had been for herself and her children. My mother, who was only eleven at the time, and her youngest sister, Sheila, were especially traumatised by the early death of their dad as they had been the apples of his eye. Peter, the eldest boy, had to leave the Jesuit novitiate where he had been studying for a year to look after the family. Any money Nellie had was put into buying her house. Each year she bought clothes at sale time and kept them in a large wooden box at the end of her bed, to be handed out as they were needed to each member of the family. It was a hard time, but she ensured that they all had a good education. TB, or consumption, as she always said in a whisper, had devastated not only her life but the lives of so many of her friends, family and neighbours.

She spoke of her sadness when her son Con's first wife May died, and of the death of her eldest daughter Mary and eldest son Peter, all in the same year. She was a force of nature. She even revealed to me on one occasion that when my mother was younger and first working, she was transferred to Waterford. It seemed that she was living the high life down there, and she was constantly asking my granny to send her extra funds. The only way Granny Murray could stop the requests was to have her transferred back to Dublin. So she made her way to head office in College Green to insist that my mum be brought back to Dublin, and actually got her way. She must have been formidable. I decided not to tell my mother this piece of information!

Granny Murray had always been a religious person and felt it was her faith that brought her through the tough times. The house was full of religious symbols, with the Sacred Heart picture with the lamp in front of it prominently displayed.

Then there was my uncle Paddy, who worked in insurance, but I got the impression that he never really valued what he did. He would keep up a running commentary on how it was only the professions that really survived the hard times and encouraged me to study hard to get there. He was a great man for the horses and the whiskey.

I was privileged to spend this rare quality time with Granny and developed a better insight into my mother and her siblings as a result. I cherished this period, and even now, decades later, still remember it with fondness.

I learned much from my visits to Granny in terms of resilience, and how quickly life can change for each one of us, in her case with the sudden death of her husband. How often tragedy is part of life, as was the case with my mother, and how sometimes we have to battle to get through the tough periods, as she did so admirably, rearing six children without their father. It is not how we cope when everything is going well which matters, rather how we manage when things, as they are wont to do, go pear-shaped. The seeds of resilience were being sown, even at this early stage of my life.

CHAPTER 7

## *A Lesson in Life*

It should have been a moment of great celebration of an amazing achievement, but sadly it turned out to be an unmitigated disaster. The worst thing was, it happened so easily. One of my classmates whose dad was in the know informed me that I had won the Ethics Prize. I found the subject interesting, and I was delighted, as this was the first prize that I had won since starting college. My friend insisted that we had to celebrate and, like an innocent abroad, I agreed. We found ourselves in the Leeson Lounge. I had a few pints, but forgot that alcohol is a powerful substance. Normally a pint of shandy was enough for this weakling. But I was on top of the world and a good night was had by all.

Back I returned to Thirty-Six, feeling very pleased with myself. I lay down on the bed, when suddenly the room began spinning out of control. I felt sick and barely made it to the bathroom, where I proceeded to empty my stomach contents. Eventually it settled and I was able to get to sleep.

The following morning, I realised with horror that the plate with my front tooth (due to the assault when I was a boarder) was gone, obviously flushed down the toilet. It was later, when I received the bill for my new plate and tooth, that I truly got the message. The money received for the Ethics Prize just about covered the cost. A much-chastened medical student resolved to be more careful, and future celebrations were to be more subdued affairs. It was a valuable life lesson.

Before I knew it, the end-of-year exams were upon us. One of my favourite scientific principles is the uncertainty principle, one of the core concepts underlying quantum mechanics. It suggests that at sub-atomic level, nothing is ever certain or fixed. I have applied this principle of uncertainty to assist people who have come to me with anxiety. Many people who struggle with this condition are craving certainty. In real life, uncertainty is king. This became crystal clear to me on entering the exam hall to sit my biochemistry exam, the study of the building blocks for life itself. I often quote my experiences during this exam to young people as an example of how uncertain life can be.

The exam was meant to be a breeze. We had studied the papers and prepared for the usual questions to appear. However, when I read the questions on this exam paper I immediately broke out in a cold sweat. I noticed that the room was gradually emptying, with many gone long before the allocated time was up. For the first time in three decades, the examiners had changed the questions. They were also couched in such vague language that I struggled to answer them. What was meant to be a certainty turned out to be a nightmare of uncertainty.

By this stage, I was more resilient in relation to exams, and indeed life itself, and understood that I had to adapt. If I had a shot at every question and tried to apply what I did know, I might survive. I started with what seemed like the easiest questions and worked my way down.

Whilst many of my classmates panicked and left early, I dug in and did my best to find solutions. I passed. More importantly, it taught me to never assume, to accept the uncertainty of life and most of all to adapt to whatever situation it presents. It was to be a core principle of my whole approach to resilience. Life is innately uncertain and we have to be able to roll with whatever it throws at us. In this case it was simply an exam. Later, I would be faced with much more significant challenges. But being able to adapt is what will save us, as it did me. I was soon able to put such concepts into practice on my first visit to London.

• 

I have always loved the Bagatelle song 'Summer in Dublin', released in 1980. I remember more vividly my infamous summer of 1972. One of the many characters in Thirty-Six was Eddie. He, like most of us at the time, was off for the summer holidays as he didn't have any studies or exams. He had previously been to London and prevailed on me to join him there that summer.

And so it was with great excitement that we headed off. From the second I arrived in this teeming metropolis at the ripe old age of nineteen, I was hooked. The city was a magical place in the 1970s, especially when coming from Dublin, which seemed so tame in comparison. My first impression was that it was so big, so multicultural and diverse; it was incredibly exciting for a young student. There was a great sense of freedom in the air. I loved the marvellous old buildings, the wonderful parks, the huge department stores filled with luxurious goods and exotic foods, and the buzzing theatres of the West End. I was mesmerised by the underground system and how efficiently it worked. There was so much to see and do, I didn't know how I would fit it all in.

Our first task was to find a place to stay. In those days, there were some great student accommodation hostels in different parts of the city, which were leased out to foreign students during holiday periods. Eddie knew just the place, ideally situated in the heart of the city. After Thirty-Six, it felt like we had arrived at the Hilton. Clean beds, lovely shower rooms, communal kitchens and facilities – it was too good to be true. We quickly made friends with students of all different nationalities. But despite getting caught up in all the excitement, reality soon hit. We had to find work to pay for all of this. Eddie managed to find us a job working in a factory, packing plastic bottles into boxes. It was back-breaking and mind-numbingly boring assembly-line work, but we were earning decent money.

When we were not working, we enjoyed much of what this great city had to offer. We went either individually or as groups to musicals, live performances, recitals in the Royal Albert Hall and many other events. Eddie especially loved simply to sit and watch people. From him, I realised just how much we can learn from such observation. I punted on the river in Cambridge and visited Brighton with its seaside charms. Eddie eventually fell for a red-haired beauty, but this didn't turn out so well – another story the details of which I cannot fully reveal. Think of a thriller novel involving an Eastern Bloc country, a drug cartel, an unlikely mob boss and a tempestuous love affair and you get the gist. It's a book in itself.

Then, trouble began to brew. Whispers started that many of us were about to lose our jobs. This was a potential disaster for Eddie and me, as we were relying on the job to keep us going financially for the summer. However, one day the CEO's secretary asked us to assist in moving furniture in head office.

There is something about the Irish! We really are rogues. Eddie went on a full charm offensive with the poor secretary. He explained that I was a destitute medical student, desperately trying to raise enough money in the summer months to fund my place on the course. Losing my job would be catastrophic. The unfortunate lady didn't have a chance as we bombarded her for the day. Later, on returning to the factory, word came down detailing the people who were to be laid off. Strangely, two Irish students somehow managed to escape the fall of the axe. We had survived.

Finally, it was time for us to depart and return to dear old dirty Dublin, to our mouldy digs and real lives as students. How can you put a price on the life lessons I learned during this summer? A few more bricks had been added to my wall of resilience. I had learned to adapt to whatever situation presented itself, to read people, to take responsibility for myself as a young adult, to problem-solve situations and, most of all, to accept myself and others as I found them.

# CHAPTER 8

## *Words of Wisdom*

At the beginning of Third Med, frustration set in. I had studied hard for the first three years, but never performed as well in exams as other students. I spoke to my mentors, Ignatius and Jimmy, and aired how I felt. It was Ignatius who uttered words of wisdom which were to change everything.

He explained that most students fall into the trap of trying to memorise and regurgitate large amounts of material in a bid to overpower exam correctors with their extensive knowledge. The real trick was to pick out key findings in what we studied and to keep returning to the subject in question until you fully grasped them. Then study exam papers to practise how to put these findings down. It was one of the great eureka moments of my life. In retrospect, with new neuroscientific information, he was advising me to *interrogate* and not *memorise* information. He was so far ahead of his time: what words of wisdom.

I realised then why I had struggled for the previous three years. I developed a new approach, which I called *the skeleton*.

This is where, following intensive interrogation of the data, I would create a skeleton picture of the five key findings for each topic studied and reproduce this skeleton at exam time. I never looked back.

I have shared this insight, to positive effect, with many young students over the years. I was fascinated to read recently that when we approach learning in this way, our hippocampus, the part of the brain that helps us to remember and recall data, is particularly active, much more so than when we try to memorise. While I had been focusing solely on the concept of knowledge, per se, I really should have been focusing on the application of information. This was my initiation into understanding the critical difference between knowledge and wisdom.

This understanding is what I took with me when I embarked on new subjects. From the second I picked up that large pathology tome in my third year, I was hooked. Pathology is the study of illnesses and what happens in the body as a result. It was about how things worked: what was going on in the cell? How did illness affect the different organs in the body, especially at cellular level? I found it so exciting. I could almost visualise in my mind what was occurring at both a macroscopic and microscopic level with each illness.

What had been a slog now became a joy to study. Helped by the words of wisdom from Ignatius, I began to apply the skeleton to everything. I was especially interested in areas like immunology, which many in my class found challenging.

We had to prepare a thesis in pathology. I picked a little-known organ called the thymus to focus on, and explored what would happen if our T-cells, which are the heavy-duty white cells critical to our immune response, were wiped out. Little did I realise at the time that I was actually writing about what would happen in the AIDS epidemic that would subsequently follow, where these cells were destroyed by a sexually transmitted and blood-borne virus.

At the same time, I was introduced to the world of microbiology. We had a wonderfully engaging professor at the time, Professor Patrick Meenan, who made the subject interesting and funny and whose lectures were always packed. Once again, I was fascinated by the world of viruses and bacteria and how they worked.

This new insight into how to study, combined with my love and fascination for these subjects, ensured that when the exams took place around Easter 1974 I was awarded the Memorial Prize in Pathology. That was the year when I finally felt I had arrived. I knew this was the case when, during my oral, the external professor of microbiology was having a row with my own professor as to which department I would come to work with on graduation. The reality was that I had no interest in joining either. More importantly, my exam results allowed me to win three student prizes in total, which meant that valuable money came into the account of this penniless student to help him survive in Dublin. Hard work and perseverance had finally paid off.

My sense of arrival was based on a combination of being externally validated for all the hard work I had put into my studies and a deep inner sense of achievement. I hadn't come from a medical background, yet I had two professors looking for me to join them. I had also been offered the chance to do an extra year in pathology, at the end of which I would receive a degree in the subject of pathology. I declined the offer, but did agree to assist the class behind me with pathology slides, and was paid for the privilege. Also, I had already made up my mind at that early stage that I would be going into general practice. I did not like the whole hospital environment and felt that I would enjoy the work of, and thrive as, a general practitioner.

Following the highs of pathology and microbiology, I found myself, in the summer and autumn of 1974, studying pharmacology. The task seemed insurmountable. We were faced with memorising a bewildering number of drugs, their usage, interactions and side-effects. The tomes were massive. I found myself firmly back on terra firma. Failure was staring me in the face. There had to be some way of cracking this nut.

Years of graft, together with the wise words from Ignatius, came to the fore. I developed the insight that if I applied the same approach used with pathology to the study of this ostensibly impossible subject, I might survive. Instead of trying to memorise vast amounts of information, I focused on trying to understand and interrogate how each individual family of drugs worked in the body. This meant that I could accurately predict side-effects and interactions. The relief was huge and I was able pass the exam with distinction.

Little did I realise then that I was creating a blueprint for the future – a way of breaking down large amounts of information into simple, manageable chunks, easy for anyone to engage with. This insight was to be life-changing, not only for myself but for countless others whose mental health I have been able to assist with. This insight was crucial in helping me draw up the blueprint discussed later which would be so helpful in assisting patients to manage all forms of anxiety, especially panic attacks, phobias, general anxiety and social anxiety.

There was also the added bonus of a few more scholarship prizes and more funds deposited into my account.

•

A critical decision had to be made by each individual student at the beginning of Third Med, namely which of two hospitals they would attach themselves to in the fourth and final med years: the Mater on Dublin's northside, or St Vincent's on the southside. This was to be another significant dividing moment. Half of the class, who lived in or had attachments to the southside, would head to Vincent's. The rest of us, a motley crew of northsiders and country bumpkins, would go to the Mater.

This split had long-reaching consequences that continue to this day. We naturally became closer to student colleagues who attended the same hospital and lost track of others who didn't. Some of us would later go on to work in the hospital chosen and build up long-term relationships with each other. In my case, I began to spend increasing time with three colleagues: Jimmy, Ignatius and Paddy. Myself and Paddy became known as the paediatrics in view of our younger age profile, while Jimmy and Ignatius, older and wiser, were known as the geriatrics. We became firm friends outside of the classroom and hospital, and played regular tennis matches. The four of us visited patients together and examined each other clinically. They helped me feel less isolated and I remember those times with fondness.

How I loved the Mater. It was a very old hospital, founded in 1851 by the Sisters of Mercy, who were very much still in charge during my time there. I remember the long wards, the high ceilings and the sense of history contained within its walls. It was the only hospital my mother would ever talk about, and if unwell she would always attend there. In those days, the consultants were like gods and we looked up to them in awe. We were finally beginning our clinical journey where we would observe illness in real life and how it affected patients.

In Third Med, we mainly attended lectures and tutorials in the Mater. By Fourth Med, called Res Year (as in the past, students would reside in the hospital when developing their clinical skills), we were each assigned to particular teams in the Mater, dealing with areas such as cardiology, GIT (gastro-intestinal tract), diabetes, respiratory illness and so on. Each consultant would have a long retinue of students, hospital doctors and nurses following them from patient to patient in the wards every morning on their rounds. Later, we would learn how to take a history from individual patients and examine them, especially if they had interesting physical signs such as a heart murmur, an enlarged liver or some other evidence of pathology.

I was notoriously late for consultant ward rounds. The 46A was the main bus going from Leeson Street to the Mater, and I was at the mercy of the timetable and traffic. Dr Drury, a leader in his field and a stickler for punctuality, took me aside one day following his rounds. In an exasperated tone he chided this poor outsider: 'Harry, you will have to try to be on time for these ward rounds.' I remember being frustrated at being reprimanded about something that was so often out of my control – it was touch and go whether a bus would show on time, or at all. The poor man, I must have been a nightmare to deal with. I greatly respected him, however, and did my best to be punctual.

Most of our time was spent in the area of physical medicine, but we were occasionally exposed to the world of mental illness. This was not an experience I remember fondly. Back in the seventies, psychiatry was still in the dark ages. We were over those awful times where procedures such as lobotomies had turned many mentally ill patients into vegetables, and we were fortunate in having lectures from the great Professor Ivor Browne, but I can recall never being interested in pursuing a career in the area of mental health. This was despite Professor Browne being one of the leading experts in his field. He had the vision to challenge many of the controversial procedures carried out at the time and to promote the importance of psychotherapy as an alternative route. However, with the limited knowledge available and before modern neuroscience had come into being, some of his theories did not sit well with me. It was thought then that depression was anger turned in, and that one of the best ways to prevent further relapses of psychosis was for the afflicted person to live well away from their mother. None of this made any sense to me. Modern neuroscience has now shed a scientific light on the real causes of many of these conditions.

The final nail in the coffin for me was our visit to the inpatient care unit in Grangegorman in Dublin. I can still remember the long-locked wards, the lost souls wandering up and down, many there for so long that they had become completely institutionalised. I was both horrified and angry. Surely there had to be other ways of helping people struggling with mental illness? Maybe deep down, however, this visit was laying seeds that would later come to fruition. When I look at where we are now in relation to mental health I often think back to those terrible times and how far we have travelled in the intervening years. Yet how far we still have to go. We still have a poor understanding of emotional distress, depression and anxiety and how best to manage them. We also lack properly resourced and manned mental health community teams to deal with serious mental illness.

•

It was not all work and no play, however. Life continued on in Thirty-Six as usual, and it was a welcome relief given the long, intense days at the Mater. One of the Thirty-Six inmates somehow landed a once-off job in the Bank of Ireland on College Green shifting furniture. We were all drafted in, and a fee of five pounds per person was agreed: a fortune for an impoverished student. On the Saturday morning in question we all trooped into this wonderful old building and the fun began. Our furniture-shifting skills were sadly lacking, to say the least, but for five pounds we attacked the task with enthusiasm. I didn't realise it at the time, but across the street was the original head office of the old National Bank of Ireland, where my mum and dad met all those years before. To this day I am not sure how we succeeded in turning the place around, but by the end of the day a group of happy students trooped out and headed for the nearest pub to celebrate our proudly earned wealth. When I now pass this iconic building I remember with fondness those wonderful times.

The family banking tradition had been continued by my brother Gerald, who, like many young men at that time, left home at the age of seventeen. He began working in the bank in 1968. In those days, nobody stayed at home beyond eighteen at the latest. You got your Leaving Cert and you departed, to either work or, in a small number of cases, go to college. Gerald passed his banking exams. He had a great sense of humour and loved chatting to people, which made him ideal for such a career. He was posted initially to Fermoy and then onto Miltown Malbay in County Clare, close to the beautiful beaches of Spanish Point and White Strand, which he really loved. It is a part of the world that has remained close to my own heart. Stories of how his landlady couldn't feed him are legendary and true. He would consume loaves of bread and pounds of cheese following a full dinner. It was hard to feed the monster.

Time moved on and in 1974 he purchased his first car and was as proud as punch. That summer we decided to christen the car by heading off to Kerry for a two-week camping trip. It would be a bonding session for both of us, separated as we were by distance, studying for me and a full-time job for him. At least, that was the plan! We spent some time camping in Ventry, a village outside Dingle, on the scenic Slea Head peninsula. Everything was going swimmingly until, literally, everything went swimming. We decided, in our innocence, to pitch camp on a clifftop overlooking the sea. That night a storm came rolling in and almost took us and the tent over the cliff edge. Everything was totally soaked, as were we. The following day was spent trying to dry out the tent on Ventry Strand.

We moved on to further pastures in Kerry, to Derrynane and Caherdaniel, where we visited the house where Daniel O'Connell had lived. I was awed by the architecture and interior design. Out in the beautiful gardens, Gerald struck up a conversation with one of the gardeners, who spoke in what I thought was a foreign tongue. This conversation went on for about fifteen minutes. Subsequently, he patiently explained to me that they had been conversing in the Kerry dialect and had a most interesting discussion. It was my first introduction to the Kingdom. I can now understand this melodic language whenever I return, as my ears are fully attuned.

For Gerald, the most embarrassing moment of the trip occurred when he decided that the two of us should visit a local pub, to have a drink and soak up the atmosphere. We sat at the bar and Gerald ordered a pint of Guinness. Then both the barman and Gerald turned to me. 'Could I have a glass of shandy?' I asked innocently. There was a stunned silence. Gerald gave me a dig and whispered furiously, 'Could you at least order a pint?' Red-faced with embarrassment, I upped my order to a pint. We downed our drinks and quickly left. Alas, it was soon time for us to depart, me back to Dublin to continue with my studies and him to his banking job. I treasure that time we spent together; it was a wonderful experience and never to be forgotten.

CHAPTER 9

## *The Night the Lights Went Out*

It was written in the stars. One evening in April 1975 when I was in Fourth Med, I returned home from my nightly studies in the college library to be met by Murdoch. Had I heard that Jamie Stone was going to be playing the Aula Max in Earlsfort Terrace that night? The Aula Max was the vast room where we all sat our exams while studying in the Terrace. It was also occasionally used for concerts and small dances.

I remember being tired that evening and reluctant to go. The only reason I went was because Jamie Stone, the stage name for Carl, one of Anthony's musician friends from years before, was playing. He was now a rock star. I felt that I should support him. So, after a quick brush of the hair, off we went. The concert was in full flow when we arrived, with a small dance taking place at the same time. It was great to see Carl performing and we were enjoying the music.

Then, out of the corner of my eye, I saw her. A dark-haired stunner, with the most beautiful eyes. I headed over to ask her to dance. She described me later as 'an intense guy with lovely brown eyes, a mad mop of hair, shiny pants, a blue jumper with holes in both sleeves, thick shoes and two left feet when it came to dancing'. In retrospect I must have seemed like someone from another planet or down from the mountains. What a catch! Luckily for me, she agreed to dance, so we made our way on to the floor.

Then, suddenly, the lights went out. A power cut. By the time they came back on, she was gone. Murdoch began pulling on my shoulder. He had seen and heard enough and wanted to head back to Thirty-Six. I remember telling him that there was something about that girl, and I headed off to find her in the crowd.

I often reflect on how simple it would have been to have let it go, and how differently our lives would have turned out if I had. But I have always trusted my instincts.

Fortune was on my side, and I did find her and asked her to dance again. I discovered that her name was Brenda. There was an immediate chemistry. Her brother was also there that night, and he must have wondered how she ended up dancing with this trainwreck of a student. Aside from that instant connection, both of us found it incredibly easy to talk to each other. I remember going home that night with my head in the clouds and my heart filled with joy. Love had made its first appearance into my life.

Anybody normal would have proposed a movie or a meal for the first date. This romantic dreamer, however, suggested that we go for a walk in the Dublin mountains the following weekend. To my surprise, she agreed. I remember that first date so clearly. Brenda was from Galway and studying social science in UCD. She was staying in a hostel in Dundrum run by French nuns, and the nun in charge, Sr Hawkins, made her a lovely picnic. I think Kitty did likewise for me. These wise women knew that affairs of the heart might be brewing.

That Sunday we took the bus out to the Dublin hills. I remember telling Brenda on the walk about the fascinating world of bees and her listening patiently to my ramblings. I also remember the perfect picnic we had. We are both happiest when we are out in the wilds of Mother Nature enjoying a picnic. We also got totally lost, as I was navigator-in-chief. Given my experience in St Stephen's Green, this was not surprising. Somehow, we found our way back home in one piece, and I can still remember our overwhelming relief at boarding the last bus back to Dublin. Yet something beautiful was born that day, and both of us departed with hearts filled with the excitement of finding that special person.

Over the next couple of months, we spent every weekend together. We went out for meals, to the movies and took trips to Howth, and during the week we did our best to keep in contact by phone. There was a powerful physical and emotional connection between us. But summer holidays were fast approaching and I would be heading home for that period. Brenda would be spending the summer in Dublin as she was due to sit her final exams in the autumn. It seemed so unfair that we would be separated so soon after finding each other.

Love always finds a way, and that is what happened. In our case, it was through the power of the written word in the form of letters and occasional lines of poetry. Back then, there were no mobile phones, emails or social media. Even connecting with someone by phone was difficult. And so, letters were the order of the day. As part of my research for this book I re-read some of those letters. They were so intense and emotional that they brought tears to my eyes. They were the letters of lovers and remain private to us both.

In the midst of those beautiful days, I occasionally wrote lines of poetry to share with Brenda. One such poem was 'Moments' and I feel it is very prescient. It was written in mid-1975 and captured how I felt at the time.

*Moments*

>Wispy glances – soft and timeless,
>Dreamy hours of Time grown still,
>The gentle hush of a shadowy eve,
>And the loving softness of a woman's touch,
>The chorus of a thousand joy-filled hearts,
>And the swirling magic of a ghost-like dew.
>Moments – precious, wondrous gifts,
>Snatched from the clutching arms of Time,
>Free from the numbing cares of life,
>Untouched by the ceaseless hum,
>And the soulless, mindless chaos
>Of a dreary far-off world,
>Fleeting glimpses of elusive Peace,
>For the helpless victims of merciless Fate,
>Draughts of air for dying embers.

•

The summer of 1975 was a time of personal and family upheaval. Back home in Thurles, my father sensibly decided to retire from the bank, which meant leaving the bank house, our home for so many years. My parents moved into rented accommodation, but my father didn't stay idle for long and headed up a new branch of the First National Building Society. He was happy in his new role and grateful that the people of Thurles supported him in his move. Former customers of his at the bank switched to the building society. The bank's loss became the building society's gain. People never forgot how good my father was to them when they needed assistance.

I spent much of this summer at home in Thurles, and took time with Gerald to visit our brother David in Waterford, who was in the bank there at the time. I was, however, missing Brenda, who was busy preparing for her own final exams in the autumn. We were both busy and public transport was expensive. It was just the way of the time. I spent a month on placement in Nenagh Hospital to improve my clinical skills and found it very interesting. I was working under the auspices of the county physician, Dr Brian Lemass. He looked after a wide variety of medical illnesses, so it was a pleasant change from the Dublin hospitals where everything was more specialised. I felt that the clinical experience gained here was of great assistance later when I was doing my final exams.

During this summer, I prevailed upon Gerald to give me some basic driving lessons. The plan was simple: we would find a quiet back road with little traffic near our home in Thurles, I would get behind the wheel, and he would allow me to disengage the clutch and drive the car forward.

Everything was going wonderfully until we had to slowly go around a corner. I exuberantly over-corrected the steering and, to my horror and his absolute dismay, managed to drive his lovely little car halfway up a telegraph pole. Needless to say, his language was unrepeatable, so I sheepishly allowed him back into the driving seat to extricate us from our predicament.

I prevailed upon him one more time for another spin behind the wheel. I had just taken my place behind the wheel on a stretch of the same quiet road, when behind us arrived a garda squad car with lights blazing. A most embarrassing interlude took place, with the guards examining every part of the car for any defects and also checking out the paperwork. We got off with a warning. Our father was not amused and I found myself grounded in relation to further exploits. Sadly, my brother Gerald never brought me out driving again.

I arrived back in Leeson Park in the autumn of 1975, excited that the end was near. I could sense a nostalgia in Kitty that this was going to be my final year in Thirty-Six. There was also a certain young lady who had stolen my heart waiting for me in Dublin. What love can do to our memories! To this day, I have only hazy recollections about the months that followed from an academic perspective, but I have much clearer ones of the whirlwind times spent with Brenda. All I can remember of the former is how hard I worked, day and night, to ready myself for the plethora of exams, written and clinical. It was an exhausting year. We spent much of our time in hospital, where we would carry out examinations of cases that would often appear in our clinical exams. Then there was the mental exhaustion of studying for the actual written exams. There just never seemed to be enough hours in the day to prepare adequately.

We sat the exams in two batches. The first included paediatrics, psychiatry and obstetrics and was finished by Christmas. The second set, and the most important, medicine and surgery, were completed by the summer of 1976.

I remember that myself, Ignatius, Jimmy and Paddy spent hours helping each other clinically and sharing notes. There was this great sense of camaraderie. Like the four musketeers, we were 'all for one and one for all'.

How did we do? All would be revealed.

More importantly, Brenda was back in my life again from when I returned to Dublin in the autumn of 1975 for my final year of college. She had finished her final exams in the autumn and was mentally drained, but she now had her degree. Having toyed with town planning, she opted for the civil service, landing up in the Department of Finance as an administrative officer. She also had to leave her beloved hostel and had moved into a flat on her own in Morehampton Road.

It was lovely to reconnect with her. She brought love into my life. We had such special weekends together and were in constant contact. We particularly loved strolling around St Stephen's Green and Grafton Street.

On Saturday afternoons, we often found ourselves in the Dandelion Market. This was the cool place for students in the seventies. Opened in 1973, it was a busy, noisy place, jammed with a hotch-potch of people browsing stalls with vintage clothing, records and furniture, whilst inhaling incense and listening to buskers. For two young people in love, ambling around hand in hand, it was pure magic.

Then there were our favourite restaurants, to be visited on the odd occasion when funds would allow it. In those days, Captain Americas was the place to be. With edgy music blaring out and a packed crowd, it was a treat to eat there late at night. It is hard now to imagine that Chris de Burgh began his career around this time, performing gigs there. I remember one particular evening we were waiting in the queue at the bottom of the stairs when someone in the group ahead of us became weak and fainted. There was an initial panic in the crowd, and I moved in to assist, explaining that I was a medical student. Thankfully, all's well that ends well and the person recovered. To our delight, we were subsequently whisked to the top of the queue and given a special table and a glass of wine on the house.

There were a few other restaurants that we frequented. My personal favourite was Thunderbird, situated upstairs on the Bewley's side of Grafton Street. The second was The Universal, a Chinese restaurant off Suffolk Street. To this day, we still laugh at the precision of how each portion of mushrooms and onions was placed on the plate in exactly the same manner each visit. But it was cheap and cheerful. Then there was Bewley's café itself, with its lovely sticky buns, another beacon of light that's still in operation to this day. What memories!

Then there were those weekend walks together. Those special trips. Our favourite place to visit was Howth, often on a Sunday. We would take a bus out to the village and ramble onto the head, then wind our way to the summit with its stunning views, throwing ourselves onto the bracken to rest en route. Then we would take the bus back down to the village and, if feeling naughty, stop for a bite to eat in the hotel at the bottom of the hill, now sadly boarded up. I can still remember the steak sandwich they served.

On other occasions we would make our way out to Dún Laoghaire and walk along the pier, hand in hand. As long as we were close to the sea, we were both happy. Then there was Greystones. I have such memories of lying on the beach, listening to the sound of the sea lapping over the pebbles. Occasionally too we would bus out to Glendalough and ramble along its hallowed trails, or to Laragh for some hill-walking. I treasured these times of peace amidst the frantic rush to finish my medical studies.

It was following a visit to Greystones in 1976 that I wrote 'The Waifs' for Brenda. I often read it and marvel at how the sentiments expressed came to pass:

*The Waifs*

Snuggled in their little cave,
Peeped at by an impish wave,
Floating on a sea of pebbles,
Lay our wild and windswept rebels.

Intruders in a land of dreams,
Where nothing is as it seems,
Enchanted by Love's magic spell,
As their lives, she did foretell.

How hearts alive and spirits free,
Linked in love, their lives would be,
How together, they would roam,
To distant lands, far from home.

All the suffering, they would find,
All the joys, they'd leave behind,
How the seeds of love, they'd sow,
Into flowers of peace would grow.

> How their music through the years,
> Would conquer many doubts and fears,
> How they'd banish dark despair,
> With their soft and haunting airs.
>
> The precious gift she would send,
> When their lives were at their end,
> The loving spell that she would cast –
> 'May love so true forever last.'

•

But finally, the day arrived and it was over. All the years of hard work were at an end. The main exams were in medicine and surgery. I can distinctly recall sitting the final written papers in the Aula Max. Like every other student in my class, I was anxious, as so much was riding on them. But it was the clinical exams that filled us most with trepidation. You never knew what type of case you would be presented with and there was a lot of thinking on your feet involved. But I had put in hours examining patients clinically, so I felt that I was well prepared.

There were two remaining hurdles to negotiate. The first related to the exam results themselves. The second depended on the first, namely whether I had gained a place in the hospital of my choice and, more importantly, which consultant would choose me as their intern.

The first hurdle is indelibly printed on my mind. All of us who began in 1970 found ourselves crammed into a lecture theatre in Earlsfort Terrace as a stern-faced registrar read out our results, name by name, subject by subject. In some cases, there was deadly silence, when a candidate would hear the awful words 'Medicine: Reject' or 'Surgery: Reject'. This meant that they had failed those subjects and were required to repeat their medicine or surgery exams. This would of course exclude them from beginning their intern year.

Thankfully, I heard the magic words 'Medicine: Honours, Surgery: Honours'. I had passed the final hurdle. The relief was simply enormous. The burden was lifted. I was finally on the road to becoming a doctor. Most of my friends and colleagues, especially my three closest ones, Jimmy, Ignatius and Paddy, all survived this ordeal. I remember the excitement of letting Brenda, my family and Kitty know, and the sheer joy of the moment.

A wild night of celebrations was held in a restaurant in Howth for the whole class. It would be the last time we would all be together, unaware in some cases that we might never see each other again.

The last link in the chain related to which intern post each one of us would get. Those who had spent their time in St Vincent's would seek posts there, while others, like myself, who had spent time in the Mater sought a post there. It was nerve-racking, waiting to discover which consultant we would be appointed to.

I was shocked – and deeply honoured – when the professor of surgery in the Mater, Professor Eoin O'Malley, chose me to be one of his interns, starting on 1 July 1976. For someone with no family medical background, an outsider who had always struggled – but worked as hard as he could – it came as such a surprise. I am eternally grateful to him for putting his faith in me. It gave me the start I needed. Sometimes it only takes one person to believe in us, to give us the encouragement and confidence in ourselves to make a difference.

I have always believed that if you want something and are prepared to work hard, you will get there. I have relayed this message to so many young people throughout the decades. It is often not brains, or good luck, or charm, or to whom you are related, that matters. It is the fire within you, the work you are prepared to put in, the acceptance that discomfort and toil will be regular companions on the journey. These are what will sustain you to last the course and reach your destination. Some might call this emotional resilience.

# PART THREE

# *The Apprentice*

## CHAPTER 10

## *The Fledgling*

Empathy: the ability to sense where another person is at from an emotional point of view. I have always considered this to be one of the greatest of all human resilience skills. I now believe that I had developed some empathetic traits in my youth. While the seeds may have been laid down then, it was during my hospital years as an apprentice that they began to flourish and grow. In the beginning, it was emotional empathy which I found myself engaged in, where I could feel what others were feeling. It was much later that I added cognitive empathy to my skill-set, where I could truly understand others' thoughts, feelings and experiences. Empathy allowed me to reach into the hearts and minds of the patients and their families whom I cared for over the course of my early hospital years. It also allowed me to bond with fellow colleagues; I could understand what they were going through – their thoughts, feelings and anxieties – as I was experiencing them too. I even began to develop some empathy for myself, as I struggled emotionally to survive this period. I discovered that self-compassion, and treating yourself with kindness, is critical in order to survive and thrive in a highly charged environment like the Mater.

A fledgling describes a young bird that is not quite ready to leave the nest and take flight. How unprepared all of us as raw and inexperienced interns were at the beginning of our medical careers! We resembled the fledgling. We had spent six years soaking up theoretical information relating to illness and how to manage it. Now as interns we had to translate this information into clinical practice. I was twenty-three, in July 1976, when my internship year began. It was a momentous year, personally and professionally.

I bid a tearful goodbye to Kitty and the inmates of Thirty-Six, including my college friend and roommate Murdoch. Then, with guitar in hand and a few worldly possessions, I moved into the residency in the Mater. I used to strum an acoustic guitar and sing some ballads as a way of de-stressing. In those days, you spent your intern year onsite in the hospital.

At first it seemed so exciting. On went the white coats with our name tags. Into the pockets went the *MIMS* (*Monthly Index of Medical Specialities*) – the drugs bible for the doctor. It contains the names, doses, side-effects and interactions of all of the common drugs being used in practice. Also to be found in our deep pockets were writing materials, auroscopes, tendon hammers, and casually draped around our necks were our stethoscopes. We had arrived as doctors! But had we?

If you were chosen to intern with the professor of surgery, you would be working with the cardiothoracic team, which included Mr Maurice Neligan and Professor Eoin O'Malley, both of whom specialised in open-heart surgery, and the up-and-coming cerebrovascular surgeon Mr Tom Corrigan. Four of us had been chosen as interns, and we were rotated around to cover the three specialists.

Our day-to-day job was to admit new patients, usually for open-heart surgery the following day, and to discharge them when leaving. Even writing a simple prescription at the beginning was fraught with difficulty as we were unused to the task. A lot of my work took place on St Cecelia's ward in the Mater, where patients were admitted prior to heart surgery. Most of the nurses on the wards were more experienced than the interns, who were supposedly meant to know more.

This period of 1976–7 was an exciting time to be working in the field of open-heart surgery. Apart from our day-to-day tasks as interns – admitting and discharging patients, doing ward rounds with the consultant and being on call – an important function was to assist with some of these operations. One such routine operation was to replace diseased heart valves, such as the mitral or aortic valves, which had been damaged by illness. The most common illness at the time creating such damage was rheumatic fever, which was caused by a simple bacterial infection such as a strep throat. It was truly heartbreaking to have to admit seriously ill women, many of whom had young children, with cyanosis and shortness of breath. For them, surgery was risky, yet potentially life-saving. We saw both men and women, but the women were often young mothers and so it seemed to be especially sad to see them struggle so much. We would never know which patients on admission would survive and which ones would not.

Open-heart surgery was a major operation at the time. It was truly humbling to see great surgeons such as Maurice

Neligan, Eoin O'Malley and Freddy Woods in action. Firstly, the sternum was split and the chest wall splayed open. Then the heart and lung functions were transferred to a heart-lung machine, called a cardiopulmonary bypass pump (CPB). This would ensure that there would be a bloodless field for the surgeons. It would allow them to begin operating on the patient in earnest. The diseased valve would have to be identified and removed. A new metal valve was then sewn in.

When this surgery was completed, the riskiest part of the whole procedure involved switching the CPB pump off and kick-starting the patient's own heart into action. This whole process took hours and the surgeons, nurses and anaesthetists must have been exhausted. It was a privilege to observe these wonderful professionals in action.

Sometimes, the patient didn't make it. There seemed to be a special silence when, as an intern, someone you admitted the day before was no longer with you the next day. Even those who made it through the operation were not out of the woods. They had to survive their post-op time in ICU. They had to be placed on anti-coagulants and were constantly at risk of the new valve becoming infected. This was a very serious and indeed life-threatening condition. Some of the cases we dealt with were those who had previous surgery and whose valves were now infected. In serious cases, the diseased valve itself would have to be replaced, which was a procedure fraught with difficulty.

Apart from heart valve operations, I witnessed some of the early coronary bypass surgery operations. This procedure was slowly becoming mainstream, but was still relatively new in Ireland at the time. Coronary heart disease was a major killer in the 1970s due to a combination of poor diet and smoking, which was rampant at the time. There was little emphasis on how to prevent the illness. The disease occurred when some of the main arteries of the heart were severely blocked. It only took a small clot occurring on top of one of these blockages to trigger a major heart attack, and often death.

This new procedure would allow the surgeon to remove a section of a large vein in the leg and, following similar procedures as outlined above for open-heart surgery, to operate on the diseased coronary arteries, replacing them with a bypass of the blockage and using the person's own vein to form a new channel. It was a tricky and delicate surgery. I was fortunate on occasion to witness Maurice Neligan in action. What a professional.

It was a procedure fraught with danger. It was not uncommon for the patient to go into cardiac arrest, where the heart would stop. On a number of occasions I witnessed such arrests occur either on the operating table or sometimes in ICU. Surgeons would sometimes tear open the chest wall following surgery to massage the heart, trying to kick-start it. It was also common to inject adrenaline straight into the heart to get it beating again.

Nowadays, we are accustomed to simple stents being inserted in the majority of cases to bypass coronary artery blockages, and it is difficult to imagine such a period where major open-heart surgery was the norm. But these surgeons were pioneers and there are many patients who proceeded to live normal lives due to their bravery, dedication and skill.

As well as assisting in major surgeries, one of the most important tasks of being an intern involved preparing for consultant ward rounds. The specialist was like the Pied Piper, with a long retinue of medical staff and students following him from patient to patient. There was a clear hierarchy. At the top was the specialist, then the senior registrars. Then came the senior house officers, junior house officers and interns. Then there was the ward sister and relevant nurses and finally, trooping along behind, the medical students.

At the bedside, the consultant would look expectantly at the intern, awaiting an update on the condition of the patient in the bed. Woe betide anyone who did not have the relevant information to hand. He would then fire off a list of instructions for the intern to carry out. With a cheerful smile at the patient, he would then progress to the next bed. The whole process often took up half a morning and it was usually a relieved intern when it was over.

Professor Eoin O' Malley always seemed to be ahead of me, no matter how much I tried to keep abreast of his patients. I had such respect for the man that I would be especially well-versed in each patient before ward rounds. But he would still manage to discover something I had not thought of. Eventually the ward sister put me out of my misery. She explained that the eminent man had a habit of coming in much earlier and doing a quick round with her. He would innocently present himself as knowing nothing about the patients and then interrogate this unfortunate fledgling. Maybe I was not as poor an intern as I thought!

Being on call would especially challenge us interns. We would be on call when the specialists had gone home, leaving the hospital in the hands of a few senior registrars and senior house officers, all of whom passed the initial responsibility of taking care of patients to us untrained interns.

This reality came home to me forcefully when my colleague Martin and myself, on our first day on call, found ourselves in ICU beside a poor man who'd had major seven-hour open-heart surgery performed by Mr Neligan that day. Mr Freddy Woods, a senior registrar at the time, popped in to let us know that he was on his way home now that the patient was stabilised, and we were only to call him if something major occurred. Looking at this poor man with wires and drips coming out of every orifice, I can distinctly recall my sense of panic. How would we cope with this new situation into which we had been thrust? In the event, thankfully, both the patient and the interns survived.

It is impossible to appreciate how exhausting the on-call marathons were at that time. These days, interns and junior doctors have much more protection. The European Directive on Working Hours recommends a maximum of sixty-five hours per week for junior doctors. This is understandable. In our time, apart from our normal working days, we were expected to spend that much time just on call. It was routine, if on call for the weekend, to begin work on a Friday morning and to continue day and night, including on call, until Monday evening, and then to begin normal duties on Tuesday, as if nothing had happened.

Each intern had a bedroom in the hospital's residency for the year. They were small spartan rooms, but we brought in our belongings to make them slightly more homely. If you were on call, you could easily be called at night and have to leave the comfort of your bed in the residency to attend a patient in the hospital. I found night-time calls particularly distressing. I have always been someone who can go to bed late, but I struggled to handle interruption after interruption, night after night. I became exhausted and demotivated. But that was the way it was then – all of us interns were going through the same experience. There was, however, wonderful camaraderie between us all. We tried to encourage each other and had great fun in the residency sitting rooms, set aside for relaxing whilst on call. We would also hold each other's bleep when on call if someone wanted to slip out to do something. But we quickly came to dread that bleep. It meant trouble was brewing, either in one of the wards, in casualty or in the ICU.

Etched firmly into my memory is one such time where I had to deal with a tragic situation while holding someone else's bleep. It involved a close friend and colleague. He had been chosen to work with the famous F.X. O'Connell, a renowned gastrointestinal tract surgeon in the Mater. My friend was a gentleman and a total rogue. His father, a busy GP, began experiencing a restriction in his swallowing. He was diagnosed with early oesophageal cancer, and arrangements were made for him to have surgery performed in the Mater by F.X. O'Connell. Little did my friend think that he would be working as an intern for the very same surgeon while his dad underwent major surgery. His father at the time was only sixty. At first everything went well. The surgery was a major success and it was only a question of recovering from the operation itself. But then he began to develop complications. On the afternoon in question, my friend approached me to hold his bleep, as he had a chore to do. I was happy to do so, because we tried to help each other out during those busy months. Shortly after he departed, his father suddenly passed away. Inevitably, it was me who had to pronounce him dead, which was surreal and deeply upsetting. My friend was completely grief-stricken on his return. I never thought that it would be me who would have to write out his father's death cert. I shared a real emotional empathy bond with him, as he struggled to come to terms with such a devastating loss.

We were constantly told that working long hours would benefit us – that it hardened us up, made us more resilient, better able to cope with difficulties as they arose, and accelerated us faster on the learning curve of becoming fully trained doctors. In retrospect, it did achieve some of these goals, but at what cost to our physical and mental health? To this day, I cannot pass the Mater without experiencing feelings of nausea at the thought of spending one more hour of being on call within its walls, even though I have always loved the hospital and I hold a special place for it in my heart.

CHAPTER 11

*Love*

Meanwhile on the home front, Gerald was due to get married in the summer of 1976 in Nenagh. There was great rejoicing in both houses when he and his girlfriend Patricia got engaged. They had been going out for a few years before Gerald got down on one knee. Patricia was a legal secretary in her father's practice in Nenagh. Both she and Gerald were heavily involved in the local tennis club, so you could say it was a match made in heaven. The two sets of parents met to mark the occasion. That night, Patricia's father was chatting to my mother. He reminisced about a time during the war years when he was ensconced in a room in a sanatorium with a young doctor. Both of them were extremely ill with TB and their chances of survival looked bleak. He noted sadly how his roommate was heartbroken as he was unable to be with his fiancée due to his illness.

A new drug called streptomycin had become available and was touted as a possible cure for the illness, but it was extremely expensive. If the two men in question could find the money, it could be procured. Both men did find the money and the streptomycin injections were administered. Sadly, the doctor died, while Patricia's dad survived, despite having to spend three years in the sanatorium.

My mother was stunned. It was her long-deceased former fiancé that Patricia's father was talking about. How difficult it must have been to absorb this new information. How cruel could life be? How fickle. How one man died while another survived. How the twists and turns of fate could unfold in such a manner. Patricia's dad told his daughter that evening what he had learned. My mother never revealed this information to the rest of us, and it was only years later that I discovered the truth from my grandmother.

As a footnote to Gerald and Patricia's large joyous wedding day, Brenda, who had found herself increasingly attracted to the idea of becoming a primary school teacher, was informed that very day that she had been accepted onto a one-year course in Sion Hill to train as a Froebel teacher.

Had Gerald's wedding inspired me to propose to Brenda? Perhaps, but an engagement was already firmly on my mind by then. Brenda and I had been a couple for two years and we spent all of our time with one another, and we were already planning our lives together. I was totally committed to this woman, who I loved deeply. I had found my soulmate. I proposed to Brenda in Clifden, and I vividly remember the day she and I went shopping for her engagement ring. On the afternoon in question we met up in a small German-run jewellery store off Grafton Street. Brenda decided on a beautiful Claddagh ring, as she loved the sentiment behind it, which stemmed from over three hundred years ago in the then poor fishing village of the Claddagh. There are three elements to the design of the ring. The first is a heart, symbolising love. The second is a crown, representing loyalty. The third is that of two hands, which stand for friendship. In earlier times, when you got married the Claddagh was worn on the left hand with the heart turned in. As Brenda hailed from Galway, her heritage was steeped in the tradition of the Claddagh. For us, that ring still symbolises so much. Love, loyalty and friendship have tied us together in an unbreakable bond.

Nowadays, an engagement would lead to the mother of all parties, with drink flowing freely and friends and family gathered. Ours was a slightly lower-key affair. After choosing the ring, we headed instead for the Tea Time Express on Dawson Street. There, amidst tea and sticky buns, we began to plan our future together. We were both so excited.

Then it was back to real life. Brenda to continue her Froebel course, me to continue my intern saga. But something had changed. We were now a unit. All decisions from then on would be made together. That day and that beautiful Claddagh ring remain an abiding memory.

One of our first considerations after our engagement was: who should we ask to marry us? It was then that I thought of Fr Martin Brennan, my botany lecturer back in Belfield. He still lived in the house in Leeson Street, together with a number of other Jesuit priests, where later they would discover a Caravaggio casually hung on one of the walls. I contacted him and asked him if he would marry us. He was delighted, and he and Brenda immediately clicked. With his white hair, gentle sense of humour and obsession with theatre and the Irish language, he was the perfect person to conduct the ceremony. Thus began a long friendship.

My most vivid memories of this lovely gentleman priest were trips to the Wicklow and Dublin mountains in his little Renault 4 car. He also loved to go with Brenda (and sometimes myself) to the Abbey Theatre. He would always have a box of chocolates in hand.

Fr Martin was a true eccentric. He made his own wine, which he would always bring with him when he visited us, although sometimes I wished he didn't as it was terrible. He went to Las Palmas in Gran Canaria for three weeks every January, where he would stay with his order. I found it easy to talk to him about the 'big bang' theory, and evolution, and where he felt God entered the equation. He was such a breath of fresh air. There was no religious cant; he simply spoke the honest truth as he saw it. Brenda and myself were lucky to have found this wonderful man who would later bless our marriage.

•

I have always been prepared to go out on a limb, to take a calculated risk. One of my mottos is: *They can only say no*. Another is: *Assess the risks, then go for it*. Maybe this is one of the advantages of being an outsider: I'm more prepared to take chances and to speak my mind, even if it's not deemed the 'done thing' in the circumstances. If you feel that there is nothing to lose, but everything to gain, then you should go for it. Too often, we fail to speak out at a critical juncture and later regret our silence.

Acquiring a new placement is still a huge bugbear for young doctors nowadays, but back in the seventies it was a major headache. Every six months, as your time spent with your current team neared its end, you would have to rely on references and luck to acquire another six-month placement.

Much as I had enjoyed my six months with the professor of surgery, I knew that soon I would have to switch to medicine for the next six months. For those colleagues with parents who were specialists, or well-known GPs, their future was secure. For this poor intern, life would not be so easy, and I knew I would have to pull out all the stops to secure my next placement.

I had always admired and liked Professor Timmy Counihan who, at that time, was professor of medicine in the Mater. Originally from Kerry, he was a dapper, softly spoken man, and seemed to have a constant twinkle in his eye.

The great day arrived and I knew I had to seize the moment. The man himself, followed by his usual retinue, came striding down the corridor. I stopped him, mid-stride, and explained that I was working with the professor of surgery at the time but would be honoured if he would consider me as a potential intern for the following six months. I am sure the man was flabbergasted at the cheek of this young upstart but, gentleman that he was, he smiled and told me he would keep me in mind, before sweeping away.

Luckily, Professor Counihan did choose me as one of his interns. I was safe for another six months! Fortune had favoured the brave.

After a high-octane six months working with the cardiac surgery team, my memory of the following six months with Professor Counihan was of a calmer, more peaceful period. He was the main heart specialist in the Mater but he also looked after a wide variety of other medical illnesses, so it was a most interesting time.

It didn't make the onerous on-call regimen any easier, however. I can still remember regularly annoying the registrars, at all hours of the night, seeking advice as to what to do in certain situations. Professor Counihan was fiercely protective of those who worked for him. He was a quiet, well-mannered gentleman, but one always sensed steel behind the outer demeanour.

I had one memorable experience of this when, in the middle of a busy ward round with a retinue as long as the train of a royal wedding, he said, 'Harry, would you pop down and get me the scans for this patient from the professor?' I trotted down to the office of the consultant in question. The door was open, but said person was not in residence. I waited patiently for a few minutes until he returned. He glared at me as I explained the purpose of my visit, and then growled, 'F**k off out of my office,' and slammed the door. This was an era when specialists could get away with treating interns like dirt on their shoes.

I returned to Professor Counihan and his retinue without the scans. 'Professor told me to f**k off out of his office,' I said. There was a pause. His face turned puce. The eyes narrowed. 'I will have words with him later,' he growled, before sweeping away to the next patient. I never heard the outcome, but would love to have been a fly on the wall at that meeting.

In the real world, matters were getting increasingly hectic. Brenda was working flat out to complete her course, which would finish in the summer of 1977. I would be finishing my internship around the same time. Then there were the minor details of organising a wedding, which had been set for 13 August. No sweat.

During my time in the Mater and Brenda's time in Sion Hill, we had reverted in the main to using bikes to get around. But finally, in May 1977, I acquired a Yamaha 50 motorbike. We both grew to love this noisy, diesel-smelling, snarling machine, even if it struggled to reach any great speed.

From the moment I climbed on the back of it, I felt the most amazing sense of freedom. I learned how to cajole it along and how to change spark plugs. Brenda was my pillion passenger as we chased from one place to the next. With helmets on and biker gear protecting us, the easy riders had come to town.

Sometimes, it seemed as if it would never happen. But by the summer of 1977 our joint ordeal was coming to a close. Brenda passed her final Froebel exams and I had survived the marathon course which the intern year in medicine and surgery was. Suffice to say, the relief we both experienced was huge. Brenda could now apply for a teaching post and I could look forward to my next exciting journey into the world of paediatrics.

With the assistance of references from Professor Eoin O'Malley and Professor Counihan, I was appointed for the next six months as casualty officer at the biggest children's hospital in the country, Crumlin. A new chapter was about to begin.

## CHAPTER 12

## *A Magical Year*

Nowadays, organising a wedding seems more like planning a military campaign. Back in 1977, things were different. We were penniless students. The church part was easy: it had to be the Jesuit church in Galway, as Fr Brennan was going to marry us. This beautiful old church, on the Sea Road in the city, was close to the Claddagh. My brother David was best man; it was customary at the time to have the brother who was next in line perform the best man duties. Brenda's youngest sister, Joan, was her bridesmaid. Her eldest sister, Mary, did most of the arrangements.

We picked 13 August for our special day, the day on which Brenda's parents had also got married. We had a small wedding party of around thirty people and it was a beautiful ceremony. Brenda wore a white gypsy-style off-the-shoulder broderie anglaise dress with a simple white veil. I, for once, looked half put together in a grey suit. Fr Martin knew both of us so well and made the whole ceremony special. The wedding ring was a simple Claddagh band, made by the same jeweller in Dublin who had made Brenda's engagement ring. Our two hearts were now forever entwined. To have this happen in a beautiful old church beside the Claddagh itself made this moment even more special.

Then off the entourage went to the reception, held in the Cloonabinnia Hotel outside Moycullen with picturesque lake views. It was a glorious day with the sun shining on the water. We had a delicious meal and there was love, conversation and a special atmosphere. Having spent the evening with our friends, families and loved ones, we changed into our 'going away' clothes and Brenda's brother-in-law Pádraic drove us back into Ceannt Station in Galway city to take the night train to Dublin.

When we arrived at Heuston Station, our trusty Yamaha 50 motorbike was waiting for us. Laughing, we hopped on and took off, roaring back to our flat in Donnybrook. There we each had a glass of Blue Nun and some Mikado biscuits. A wedding day with a difference!

Brenda and I decided that we would spend our honeymoon in the Scottish Highlands. There was one difficulty: neither of us could drive a car. Our only option was to rely on the Yamaha 50 to get us around and so, undaunted, on the day after our wedding we hopped on again and headed off to Dún Laoghaire to catch the ferry. Relying on me as navigator was not the wisest decision. On arrival, we discovered that the ferry was actually departing from Dublin Port. So we hurriedly remounted, and another mad dash ensued. We made the ferry just in time; it was not the most auspicious start to the honeymoon.

If any of you are considering a honeymoon in Scotland, remember a Yamaha 50 is not the ideal form of transport.

Chugging up those hills put strain on the poor bike, never mind its passengers. But there were many highlights. The scenery was truly magnificent. I remember the beautiful town of Oban and a lone Scottish piper playing his mournful tunes out on the heath. I also recall lying on a beach, suddenly realising that we were on the flight path of RAF jets coming in to land on the airstrip behind us. By the end of our honeymoon we were eager to get home and begin our new life together.

Our first real home, if only for a two-year period, was the upper part of a house in Eglinton Park in Donnybrook, Dublin. Brenda and I were happy there, and it became a real centre of comings and goings. A number of Brenda's friends and family were regular visitors, as was Fr Martin. For me it became a place of refuge following those long periods of being on call. I always associated Eglinton Park with music, as it regularly filled the house. We loved John Denver and Gordon Lightfoot, and it was the music of John Denver which resonated with us the most. He captured hope, love, sadness and care for the environment. Many of his messages are still relevant today.

It was also from here that Brenda would set forth on her new adventure, taking up a teaching position in St Mary Help of Christians School on the Navan Road.

It was clear at this stage that we needed a car, and I applied for my first provisional driving licence. I was paying off my student loan at the time but managed to get a car loan, and at the end of 1977 the great day arrived. Daffy the Datsun was procured, and life was forever changed.

The scarlet-red second-hand car was our pride and joy. Brenda was especially pleased, as she could now take over riding the Yamaha 50. Attired in a long coat, with helmet and gloves, she was to become a terrifying sight for Dublin motorists. She even took my youngest brother, Kevin, for a spin on it when he visited us in Eglinton Park – an experience he never repeated! But the sight of Brenda on the Yamaha was not as terrifying as the arrival of Daffy the Datsun.

Gerard, Brenda's brother, who was studying veterinary medicine in Dublin, was already a familiar sight. His own car, Betsy, was seen regularly around the streets of the capital, usually stranded with Gerard's head under the bonnet. He agreed to the onerous task of teaching me how to drive.

We began in the Phoenix Park with its open roads, ideal for a relaxed driving experience. Round and round we went. Suddenly, a string of expletives came out of Gerard's mouth. I looked in the mirror and groaned. How could this be happening again? Behind us was a garda car. Round and round we continued, and round and round it tailed us. One of the tasks of the gardaí was to provide security for the president and his residence in the Phoenix Park. The Troubles were particularly intense in Northern Ireland at the time, and the guards were on high alert for any sign of suspicious activity. I think they must have thought we were terrorists, but finally realised what we were doing and decided to pass us by. The tell-tale signs of a learner driver were evident: my driving style was jerky and uncoordinated. Gerard just couldn't understand why I was not responding to his instructions. Then he twigged it, and another stream of invective poured forth. He had noticed that I was holding my left foot up in the air, hovering over the clutch pedal. 'What the f\*\*k are you doing that for?' he managed to splutter. I tried to explain that that was what I thought you had to do. We got the technique sorted, and I began to drive more smoothly.

•

Thankfully, in the real world, my foray into Crumlin Children's Hospital was advancing more smoothly too. From the second I stepped within the hallowed walls, I felt at home. The doctors and nurses who ran the place were the most wonderful people to work with. There was a great sense of love. Empathy abounded. At the time, Crumlin was considered the leading children's hospital in the country. It was seen as a leader in a number of areas, including cardiac care, childhood cancer, cystic fibrosis, genetic conditions and burns. Although only in existence since 1956, it already seemed well worn by 1978, but that was never apparent when you were there all the time. Casualty in Crumlin could best be described as mayhem, especially during the summer months when children were off school. Mick, the casualty consultant, was an institution and taught me everything I needed to know about treating the children who swarmed the hospital on a daily basis.

In those days children had a lot of freedom. We saw a constant stream of fractures, lacerations, burns and so on. With Mick's assistance I became a dab hand at suturing lacerations and putting on plasters for greenstick fractures, where the upper limb was bowed rather than broken. Children who break a bone in their arm have more of a greenstick bend than a clean break, but are treated the same. I was astonished at how quickly they would heal, often within six weeks or so. It was an insight I would carry into my professional career: children can get sick quickly, but can recover just as speedily.

Casualty was also where sick children from around the country would arrive as first port of call, and we would have to rapidly assess and have them admitted under the appropriate team. It was a responsible position. Just as in the intern year, we had to go on call, but the duration of such periods was not as prolonged nor as tiring. I came to love Crumlin's corridors and wards and the people who manned them. I was blown away by the children themselves, many of whom were extremely ill, and how stoical they were. It was a privilege to serve them and their parents. Crumlin Hospital was an inspirational place.

Following six months as casualty officer, and yet another interview, I was appointed to work the following six months with paediatric consultant Dr Deasy, who was an expert at the time in renal disease in children. Once again, I fell on my feet, as he was a gentleman and so kind to those of us who worked with him. I was happy for these six months. There was something about working with children and their families that made me glad that I had decided to become a doctor.

There was only one pitfall. Now that Brenda had joined the ranks of easy riders, it was up to Daffy the Datsun to drive slowly up and down the canal each day, usually during rush-hour traffic. In January 1978, with the sweat rolling off me, I would trundle down the canal, dreading those moments when traffic would stop on one of the bridges for a red light. I found holding the car difficult. I was determined, however, and kept at it, day by day, week by week, month by month, until eventually I got the hang of it. There was one final hurdle to cross, however – my driving test.

Gerard, who had taught me the basics of how to drive, also played a critical role in helping me pass the test, my success in which, to this day, still mystifies him. Money for driving lessons was in short supply, so he agreed to take me once again under his wing to help me prepare. We drove the test route repeatedly and, in particular, practised hill starts on Milltown Hill, a favourite spot of the driving testers. He despaired of me ever getting it right. For days and nights before the test we practised reversing around corners, something I am poor at even to this day. He explained in his best Galway accent that I would never be able to distinguish left from right and that his task was impossible.

Undaunted, I set out on the day of the test. It was a typical snowy, icy January morning, which did little to settle my nerves. With my heart pounding I arrived at the test centre. Gerard had repeatedly warned me that not making forward progress was a recipe for failure, and so the tester found himself ferried swiftly from place to place. We reached Milltown Hill and, as I had prepared for, we took off from a stationary position halfway up the incline. The wheels began to spin and beads of sweat formed on my forehead. But nothing ventured, I thought, and, turning to the tester, said, 'Icy morning, isn't it?' before continuing as if all was well. To my shock, when we returned to the centre he passed me.

I returned to Eglinton Park, chuffed that I had finally obtained my full licence. Gerard, arriving presumably to commiserate, was stunned that I had passed. He proceeded to describe the testing procedure in the most colourful language, especially the dangers of allowing his brother-in-law onto the roads. To this day he is trying to come to terms with the fact that I passed, even if he was secretly pleased that his pupil had done so well.

For all of the challenges involved in travelling back and forth to Crumlin, I truly loved my year working with children and was sad to leave. In later years I discovered that much of what I'd learned in Crumlin Children's Hospital, both in casualty and on the medical wards, was invaluable. I especially appreciated how you were given responsibility and were expected to learn quickly how to do things. This was so refreshing. At last we were being treated like capable doctors. It was also so easy and natural to create an empathetic bond with both the children and their parents. All of us wanted the best for the sick children we were caring for. In addition, I sat my Diploma in Child Health (DCH) while in Crumlin, which was essential for entering general practice.

From the beginning of our relationship, Brenda and I had regular discussions about what we wanted to do with our lives. My decision to work in Crumlin and her decision to become a primary school teacher had their origins in some of those discussions. Did these conversations come from some fundamental desire on both our parts to care for people, to show compassion and empathy to others who needed help and reassurance? Perhaps they did. We knew we both shared a similar dream of helping those less fortunate than ourselves, either in Africa or South America.

Our career decisions were based on making those dreams a reality. This clashed somewhat with my parents' wish for me to become a consultant. A specialist in the family would fit the bill nicely. I never shared this dream, however; I had always wanted to become a GP. This decision was strengthened while working in the various hospitals. I simply did not like the strict hierarchical atmosphere, and I saw my future more in the community. I do feel that this tension with my parents in relation to my career was always there, even before I met Brenda. Somewhere down the line, however, both of us decided that we had a duty of service to those who experienced hardship and poverty. We were both young and idealistic, and we wanted to share our good fortune with others. This was always embedded deep within us, without really knowing or understanding why.

Initially we thought of going to Peru, but this idea was quickly squashed when I discovered that I would have to repeat my medical exams in Spanish. We then approached APSO (Agency for Personal Service Overseas). This wonderful state-funded organisation helped place Irish professionals such as doctors, nurses and teachers overseas in different parts of the world. One of the countries where they organised placements was Tanzania in East Africa, then one of the poorest countries on that continent. They put us in contact with the Medical Missionaries of Mary (MMMs), who were running a number of hospitals in Tanzania during this period. The MMMs were a missionary group of sisters who were dedicated to providing healthcare to underdeveloped parts of the world, especially in Africa. They were founded in 1937 by Mother Mary Martin. The motherhouse was in Drogheda. What attracted us was their absolute pragmatism and their total commitment to the provision of modern healthcare to those less well-off in countries such as Tanzania, Nigeria and Uganda, to name but a few. Once we came in contact with these wonderful women, we were hooked. Tanzania it would be.

## CHAPTER 13

## *Expect the Unexpected*

While we were busy hatching plans for our future, my years of training continued. The year from July 1978 didn't start out so well. As detailed already, young doctors had to keep lurching from hospital job to hospital job. I had already spent my undergraduate time in obstetrics at the National Maternity Hospital in Holles Street in Dublin, under the watchful eye of Professor Kieran O'Driscoll. He was widely regarded as the father of a new approach to labour, called active management. He was an affable man who took his task of teaching us very seriously indeed.

I was confident that my previous posts and academic results would earn me a six-month placement in obstetrics, and I prepared well for the interview to work once again in Holles Street. It turned out to be a disaster. The master of the hospital, Dr Dermot MacDonald, seemed extremely cynical as I outlined my plans to work in Africa. The more I tried to justify the decision, the deeper the hole I seemed to dig. It was the interview from hell. I left feeling completely dejected and rang

Brenda to explain that I would not be working in Holles Street. I would have to explore other possibilities, and apply to the Coombe or the Rotunda, or even other maternity units around the country. To my great surprise, I was later contacted by Holles Street to inform me that I had been accepted for the six-month post. The mystery was solved by the master himself, who later explained that he too had spent time in Africa and had given me a hard time at the interview to ensure that my intentions were genuine. He then offered to afford me every opportunity to learn what I would need to know when I did go, including standing in at caesarean sections. He was as good as his word, and even later he continued to support me by sending out much-needed supplies. I never forgot his kindness.

I believe, in retrospect, that following this interview and his subsequent explanations, we created a powerful bond. He, more than most, was incredibly empathetic to my situation and understood and supported my decision. Given that he had made a similar decision himself and had spent time among those less fortunate than ourselves, he took it upon himself to give me guidance. By sharing with me his expertise and knowledge, he was trying to prepare me for the realities of Africa.

Holles Street, however, was such a change from the free-flowing atmosphere at Crumlin. In Crumlin we were encouraged to take responsibility, sign up for meds as required and to think and behave like doctors. Holles Street was rigidly controlled. Junior doctors like myself were not allowed even to prescribe paracetamol without checking first with the assistant master, who was God's overseer. I was fortunate to be placed with Dr Comerford, a kindly gentleman who took wonderful care of his patients and those who worked for him. He made the six months easier than they might otherwise have been.

Holles Street was unique, however, in the quality of the meals provided to staff. Unlike the hospital canteens at my previous two posts, here we experienced the luxury of a sit-down meal with an excellent menu. I can still remember those meals and the camaraderie between us all. Friends made during this period remained so for life.

The labour ward was more like a factory assembly line. Thousands of women gave birth there each year. Active management was the name of the game, where every step of the labour journey was plotted, and if it was not progressing quickly enough, the woman's waters were broken. We spent a lot of time in the ward, where the sisters in charge were seen as more relevant than the consultants. We often felt like we were interlopers on the scene. However, I did become adept at breaking waters, monitoring labours, delivering babies, dealing with retained placentas and performing episiotomy suturing.

I learned much from my first six months in Holles Street, but I cannot say I enjoyed the experience. It was too tightly controlled, too mechanical. We were losing sight of the mother during this whole process and there seemed to be an overall lack of emotional empathy.

Little did I realise at that moment in time the surprise that awaited Brenda and me.

•

County Clare is, and always will be, in our bones. It is our spiritual home. North Clare is a special place, where the slate-grey rock of the Burren sweeps down to meet the foam-tipped waves of the Atlantic. It's a place of magic, where the colours constantly change, especially when the sun is shining. Wildflowers peep out of every crack in the limestone, and we are faced with the reality that, compared to Mother Nature, we are small players indeed.

From Kinvara and the Flaggy Shore, along towards Ballyvaughan, out along majestic Black Head and down to the golden sands of Fanore beach – Brenda's childhood was spent along this stretch of coastline. I too had fallen in love with the entire area, stretching down to Lahinch and Miltown Malbay. Then there was Doolin, where the majestic wild waves of the Atlantic crash into the rocks and where sometimes on a stormy day mighty waves thunder over the massive cliffs facing out into the ocean.

It was inevitable, therefore, that Fanore would be where we would first get an inkling of the surprise in store for us. We were camping locally, on a beautiful August day. We decided to climb the rocks behind Fanore to reach what seemed from the road to be a series of caves. Halfway up, Brenda began to struggle. She is normally as agile as a mountain goat and I find it difficult to keep up with her. On this occasion she was feeling short of breath and very tired. I was immediately concerned so we climbed back down.

When she also admitted that she was feeling a little nauseated, the penny suddenly dropped for both of us. Maybe she was pregnant? In those days, there were no simple over-the-counter pregnancy tests available. The moment we returned to Dublin, I brought a sample into Holles Street, to discover that Brenda was indeed pregnant.

We were overjoyed, if initially overwhelmed. What would this mean for our planned trip to Tanzania? But on the grounds that there is never a right time to have a baby, we decided to plough on with our plans regardless. She began to attend Dr Comerford, who was so kind to both of us.

These days couples can find out in advance whether they are expecting a boy or a girl. Back then, it was customary for this to be a big surprise. Once Brenda had survived the danger period for most pregnancies, the first fourteen weeks or so, we began to discuss a name for the baby, whether a boy or a girl. It was in Glendalough, down by the lake, where the momentous decision was made. We had just seen the film *Dr Zhivago*, one of the great epics of that time, and both of us had been deeply affected by it and had been in tears during its showing. The heroine of that movie was called Lara, short for Larissa. It just seemed right that if the baby was a girl, she was going to be called Lara.

•

I completed my six months of obstetrics in December 1978 and managed to obtain my Diploma in Obstetrics. The master, true to his word, showed me how to perform caesarean sections and many other procedures. I also managed to secure my final six-month hospital placement in Holles Street, this time in neonatal paediatrics.

This was like entering a new world – one filled with incubators, dedicated nurses and tiny babies who were struggling to survive, having come into the world at anywhere from twenty-six to thirty-six weeks, the normal gestation period being forty weeks. I loved being with the little tots, even if I sometimes felt overwhelmed by the enormous responsibility.

I became a dab hand at breaking off an orange needle from its source and taking blood from a premature baby, literally drop by drop. We also learned how to intubate babies if they were born flat. This happens when a baby is born and is unable to take a breath and so they are at risk of hypoxia, or lack of oxygen in their bloodstream. To counter this, we would insert a tube through their larynx so that air could be pumped into their lungs. This would often prompt the baby to breathe by themselves. I remember working with families whose babies were born premature and were put on ventilators in the ICU to help them breathe until they became more mature. In other cases, we would have to try to insert IV drips into small blood vessels on their heads, often using plaster of Paris to cement them into place. Other babies were born with rhesus disease, where a mother with a rhesus positive blood type has a rhesus negative baby. Due to a mixing of their blood in the womb, antibodies form which can attack the baby's blood cells and lead to anaemia. We tackled this by doing exchange transfusions.

It was a wonderful learning experience, and one that would be crucial later in Africa. But the hours worked were simply inhumane. It was almost as bad as working as an intern in the Mater. On one occasion I fell asleep from exhaustion in the middle of an exchange transfusion at three o'clock in the morning. I tried to remonstrate with the professor in charge. He told me to toughen up, and that they all had to work the same hours at my stage, so to get on with it. I was learning resilience, but not how it should be taught or developed. There was clearly a lack of emotional empathy at the time, as demonstrated by the consultant in question. How many young doctors are unable to give their best, even nowadays, through extreme exhaustion?

It continues to be a matter of concern for all of us in the medical profession. We now understand the importance of self-empathy, and of taking care of and being kind to oneself. Hopefully this will lead to a generation of doctors who will fully understand just how crucial this is.

Brenda's pregnancy was all going well, or so we thought. She had been attending Dr Comerford regularly and was set to deliver her first baby in Holles Street. By this stage, I had acquired a good knowledge of both obstetrics and neonatal paediatrics, so was happy that the baby would be born in Holles Street, despite my own more negative experiences of working there.

At thirty-seven weeks' gestation, Brenda and I decided to pay a final visit to see my parents. But Mother Nature, and my soon-to-arrive child, had other ideas. In the early hours of 8 April, Brenda went into labour. I was considering driving her back to Holles Street, when the decision was wisely taken out of my hands by the local GP and my parents. It was too long a journey and one fraught with risks. The local district hospital would look after her labour and delivery. Instead of the bustling, busy wards of Holles Street, it was down to a single midwife, myself and the local GP!

Thankfully, all went well, and by morning Brenda had given birth to a slightly premature but healthy baby girl. Lara had come into our life and has enriched it so much ever since.

How often does a small baby enter the world just as someone else at the end of their life departs? A window opens just as the front door shuts. The endless eternal cycle. On 14 May 1979, a month after Lara's arrival, Granny Murray died. She had been the great matriarch of our family, the one constant in our lives. Despite many changes during my childhood and young adult life, she was always there for me.

Nellie was eighty-nine. What a life she had lived. Sadly, towards the end, she developed dementia. My uncle Paddy had married, and my mother brought her down to a nursing home in Thurles to be closer to her. She had 'died' so many times during our earlier years that it seemed impossible that this time she had truly left us. She was interred in Glasnevin Cemetery, with her husband and eldest daughter, Mary. An era had come to an end.

It doesn't matter how well prepared one is for the arrival of a small baby, it's still a shock when it actually happens. We had attended the usual courses and read the parenting books. It made little difference. It was especially tough for Brenda. Our emotional resilience was tested to the full in those early days. Neither of us had any real support at the time. Our families were living far away. We did get some assistance from friends and from the public health nurse, but much of the burden fell on Brenda. There was no recognition of the importance of family leave and I was still attached to Holles Street until the end of June 1979, so I was gone for long periods on call. I tried to be there for her as much as possible, but it was a difficult time. I felt terrible, leaving her alone with our little daughter for hours on end. But that was the way it was. This is the loneliest of times for a new mother, when everyone is getting on with their own busy lives, as they are left to care for and bond with the new baby.

We were also battling with the reality that it would soon be time to begin our African journey, and it was hard to prepare for this when adjusting to life with a small baby. Eventually things began to settle down and we adapted to our new life as a family of three. My one abiding memory was of carrying Lara in a baby sling. It felt so lovely to feel this little bundle snuggled in front of me as I perused books in the bookshop or went for a walk with Brenda. In Africa, as we would discover later, mothers prefer to carry their babies wrapped around their backs. There is no better way to bond with a new baby.

Lara's arrival impacted our lives in countless unexpected and joyful ways, and it made us all the more determined to undertake our trip to Africa in summer 1979. We had done extensive research before travelling to Tanzania as to what we would need for the two years we had committed to work there. We decided, on consultation, that the most efficient way to transport our provisions was to ship them in six tea chests to the port in Dar es Salaam, and then onwards to where we would be living. Brenda and I spent many months putting together this list of vital supplies. Clothes for the new baby, all the way up to the age of two. Clothes for the both of us. Medical books, electrical equipment, books to read. A sewing machine. The list went on and on. In retrospect, we were so innocent. We did not have the insight to realise that such supplies should only be sent by air or in heavily sealed containers that could not be opened. Anything else was fair game to be ransacked and stolen along the way.

We had other last-minute preparations to complete. From final vaccinations (which included smallpox, cholera and yellow fever for Brenda and me), to completing an induction course with APSO, to selling Daffy the Datsun and our beloved Yamaha 50 – it was all go. We took a few days' break before leaving and headed for Lahinch in County Clare where we stayed in the Atlantic Hotel. I have fond memories of those last few days. It would be the memories of the Burren, the pounding waves and the beautiful scenery that would keep us going in the years to follow.

Then it was time to say goodbye to our families. In my case, this did not go as planned. My father strongly disapproved of our decision to go to Africa, concerned that it might impede my chances of becoming a specialist. I could understand why he was upset: he came from a merchant and banking background, so he struggled to understand the medical world. He clearly had great hopes for his son to make something of himself. This did not make it any easier, however, to accept the disapproval. We left Ireland under a cloud, wondering if we were mad to be taking a small child into the heart of East Africa. But the die had been cast and we would have to see where the winds of fate would take us.

The final stages of my training, and working with babies, children and their families, really allowed me to develop empathy. I learnt that having an emotional understanding and showing compassion and care can go a long way in helping someone through hard times. I also found the empathy bonds created during the hospital years to be extremely nourishing and fulfilling for me as a person. But I was about to discover that it would be much harder to set up such bonds where we were going.

# PART FOUR

*Africa*

## CHAPTER 14

## *Tanzania*

Service. In a world of individualism, the concept of service seems outdated. To be there for other people. To make personal sacrifices to ensure that others might have a better quality of life. To owe a duty of care to those less fortunate than ourselves. That whatever talents you have should be directed towards those in need.

Back in the mid-seventies, the idea of service was somehow engrained in our consciousness. Was it imparted to us at school? Was it down to past generations living through famine and war, which imbued this sense of helping others when they were most in need?

In our case it was not rooted in any religious belief but in a simple acceptance that it was the right thing to do, to help those who most needed it. To give something back before moving on with the rest of our lives. It was this desire to donate our skills, expertise and time that brought us to Africa. There I would learn that service was multi-faceted in nature. It would involve sacrifice and hard work. Resilience and grit. Joy and pain. It would teach us much about life and ourselves as human beings. It would reinforce the importance of teamwork in its delivery. We learnt so much about self-reliance and making lifelong friends. Our time there prepared us for life. We left with the understanding that service rewards those who take part with multiple unexpected gifts. We would gain so much more than we would give.

For me personally, I arrived in Africa as an idealistic young adult and left as a fully mature man, rooted in pragmatism, resilience and a deeper understanding of what service, and life, was all about.

Little did we realise, however, on arriving in Tanzania, that our decision to serve others would have such an impact on the rest of our lives. For it was here in Africa that so much would happen and would shape us. Our love was to be tempered in a furnace, the likes of which we had never experienced before and never have since. If we survived this period, we knew we could cope with whatever life could throw at us in the future. We were so naïve as to what was to come, and maybe that was for the best. Perhaps it is better that our futures lie shrouded in mystery. Otherwise, we might give up before we even start. Maybe that 'veil' is crucial for our survival.

Lara was around four months old when the three of us set off on our adventure in the summer of 1979. Our final destination was Kabanga Missionary Hospital, situated in north-west Tanzania. Before progressing to detail our African experiences, I feel it is necessary to describe the country as it was then.

Following independence in 1961, Tanganyika (as it was called then) united with the neighbouring island of Zanzibar in 1964 to become Tanzania. It was ruled by its president Julius Nyerere from 1963 to 1985. He encouraged strongly socialist and self-reliant policies in his time in office and also placed a strong emphasis on agriculture as a means of improving the lot of his people. He also identified literacy and healthcare as key priorities for the future progression of the country. It was a one-party state. His socialist policies, however, led to a rapid deterioration in Tanzania's economic circumstances. It struggled to attract foreign investment, for political reasons. Tanzania in 1979 was an extremely poor country by any reckoning. Most of the population lived in rural areas, where they eked out a very basic existence. There was hardly any infrastructure; the road network was primitive, with only a small percentage of roads actually paved. It made the transport of goods and people extremely challenging.

In October 1978, almost a year before our arrival, Uganda, under dictator Idi Amin, had invaded north-west Tanzania, where we were heading. This led to war, with Tanzanian troops eventually invading Uganda and taking control of the capital, Kampala. Idi Amin fled the city, ending the conflict in April 1979. The war placed a major burden on the already struggling Tanzanian economy. Inflation was rampant, which led to major shortages of food and critical medical supplies in particular. Fuel was also in short supply, which was hampering the cold chain of vaccinations nationally. The result was that many local and district hospitals, especially in remote rural areas of the country, such as where we were headed, struggled to care for their patients. Only for the assistance of outside medical agencies such as the Medical Missionaries of Mary (MMMs), the situation would have been dire beyond description. At least with foreign aid there was some access to medical supplies and vaccinations.

During the two years that followed, Tanzania would encounter a post-war economic recession, rampant inflation, a cholera epidemic, a crop failure ending in famine, a gross shortage of everything from food to fuel (petrol, gas and kerosene) to medicines, constant breakdowns in the rail and bus systems, and a disastrous road network – to mention but a few challenges. All of these difficulties were amplified in rural areas.

And yet, despite everything, the people of Tanzania always seemed to be happy and joyful. A smile was never far from their faces. They took pleasure in the simplest of things and were, without fail, grateful for any assistance which was given to them.

•

Unless you have visited Africa, it is hard to describe the visceral shock to your system on disembarking the plane. Nothing prepared us for the reality of Dar es Salaam. This was an ancient city which, together with Zanzibar, had been for hundreds of years the centre of the slave trade on the east coast of Africa.

There was the intense sunlight that was blinding in nature. Then the barrage of heat, ferocious in its intensity. The cacophony of noise was deafening, allied to the chorus of different languages mingling with the sounds of the airport itself. Finally, there was the mad scrum of passengers, each one trying to reach their luggage before it disappeared in front of their eyes. It was a long way from Dublin Airport.

Amidst the noise and chaos, we were met at the airport by an MMM nun. Following an overnight stay in a hotel in Dar, we flew west in a small propeller plane across the vast terrain of Tanzania to reach our destination, Kigoma. It was a hair-raising, turbulent flight. One had to experience those internal flights back in the seventies to truly understand the terror they instilled in the passengers on board. It was a journey we would not repeat.

Kigoma is a large town in the north-west of Tanzania. The main centre for the region, it is situated on the shores of Lake Tanganyika, the second largest lake in Africa. It was up the road from Ujiji, where Stanley met Livingstone, which gives an idea of how remote the region was.

We were met in Kigoma by, once more, the MMM nuns, who drove us by Land Rover to the closest village of Kasulu. From there, we made the final seven-kilometre journey to the hospital complex in Kabanga. It was not a road, rather a track. We often joked that it was not the road that ran out before reaching the hospital, it was the track! The ground was baked hard and the soil was brick red in colour. The heat was overwhelming, but there was little humidity, which was the bane of other African countries such as Nigeria. Finally, we arrived at our destination, Kabanga Missionary Hospital, where we would spend the next couple of years of our lives.

The complex was composed of the main hospital, the convent where the nuns lived, some individual houses for hospital staff, an area for patients' families to cook food, outpatient buildings and a nursing school. While all of this might seem quite normal, the reality was that the hospital buildings were basic in construction, and just about able to cope with the patient influx encountered on a daily basis.

The hospital itself was divided into a number of key sections. There was an adult male ward and an adult female ward. There was an obstetric ward, where so much drama would ensue. Then there was the children's ward, where at least two children filled every bed and where the turnover was constant. Most family members would sleep beside their relatives on the floor of the hospital.

There was a TB isolation building and a separate leprosy isolation building. These would house more long-stay, highly infectious patients. It also had a small but effective lab, a pharmacy, an X-ray machine and outpatient clinics where so much work was performed every day. In addition there was a busy mother and child outpatient clinic, where hundreds of mothers would attend daily for vaccinations, nutritional advice and antenatal care. At the heart of the hospital lay the operating theatre, where so many emergencies would end, thankfully with high survival rates for the patients.

It is important to grasp the significance of this busy little hospital. Theoretically, it had a bed capacity of around 120, but it was permanently over-filled. There was a local government hospital in Kasulu and a district hospital in Kigoma. The main regional hospital was near Mwanza on the shores of Lake Victoria. All of these were chronically understaffed, underfunded and short of medical, diagnostic and surgical materials. As a result, we were the main hospital for a catchment area of at least one million people. Nowadays, it serves over three million. Outpatient clinics were overflowing and the hospital was always under siege. Though we considered ourselves constantly short of medical supplies, in comparison to the rest, we were functioning well.

Brenda, Lara and I were the lucky ones. We lived in a two-bed house with a garden area replete with banana and paw-paw trees. The floors were concrete and the roof was galvanised. Over the beds, and over the cot for Lara, were mosquito nets, about which I was neurotic from the beginning. The back door had a netted area to allow air in and to keep insects out. We had running water. We were told on arrival that our tea chests would almost certainly be ransacked, which is what transpired. This was only the beginning. There was no functioning fridge as there was no paraffin available to run it. There was a shortage of batteries, petrol, even soap. Welcome to rural Tanzania.

Electricity was provided by a generator during the daytime, but at night, light was provided by bush lamp. The only exception was a night-time emergency in the hospital, where the generator would come on, providing extra light. The cooker was run on gas, but this too was often unavailable. Cold drinking water was earned. You first had to filter the water, to get rid of sediment. Then you had to boil it to eliminate infections. Later, when paraffin became available in early 1980, the water would be stored in the fridge to keep it cool.

Supplies of food were scarce and unpredictable. Ugali, a kind of porridge, was the local food. We quickly moved to black tea. Fish and meat were either unavailable or inedible. Flour was frequently in short supply. It had to be sieved first for stones, sediment and foreign bodies. Rice was also frequently unavailable and had to be treated similarly. Cheese, when it was available, was a staple, as was fruit. We were to rely heavily on the weekly trips to the market in Kasulu to buy potatoes and vegetables. The main source of basic foodstuffs such as flour, cheese and tinned foods was the White Fathers, a missionary order of priests and brothers who had first arrived in Lake Tanganyika back in 1879. They got their name from the distinctive white habit they wore. They were involved in pastoral care, education and assisting orders such as the MMMs in accessing food and vital supplies. They also catered for the spiritual needs of the MMMs. They were really kind and helpful to us during our stay in Kabanga, as were the Van Deuns, a Belgian family who also lived in the compound, who kept us going when food and fuel were in short supply. Dr Van Deun was the leprosy/tuberculosis doctor for the region and would travel vast distances to ensure that patients were being looked after medically in their communities.

Then, there were the insects. Flies were endemic. You learned quickly to simply drink your tea regardless. Mosquitoes were a constant night-time hazard. Each night when the lights went out and you went to bed, the cockroaches would emerge in their hundreds, swarming over every part of the kitchen, scuttling rapidly away if a light came on. During the rainy season, hordes of insects would batter against the wire door. On one occasion towards the end of our stay, an invasion of red ants threatened to swarm the house and everyone in it. Only kerosene sprinkled around the house saved the day. We were lucky that we were not living in a tsetse fly area. The tsetse fly carried the parasite *Trypanosoma brucei* that causes sleeping sickness. If you were bitten by the tsetse fly, this organism was injected into your bloodstream, causing you to fall into a coma. People frequently died unless they received medical assistance. The other constant menace was rodents such as mice and, more seriously, snakes. Brenda's first introduction to these reptiles was to meet a black mamba, one of the deadliest of snakes, at the back door. We learnt to carry at all times a snake stone – a flat black stone that is placed quickly on a snake bite to draw the venom out. Thankfully, the hospital did have supplies of antivenom shots.

It was the isolation that we found most difficult to come to terms with. There were no phones, no newspapers, TV or radio, and of course no internet. The only real form of communication with home was by letter, which was painfully slow. There was also a once-weekly radio link for the MMMs to other MMM groups and to Nairobi, where the flying doctors were based. It was only to be used in an emergency. Otherwise, we were on our own. We relied on visits to and from friends made during this time to keep us going, along with occasional visits from Irish or Tanzanian officials. Our social circle was small, so we really valued the friendships we formed. On one occasion, we had a visit from the junior minister for health in Tanzania, who was very interested in some of our projects. Over the two years, it would be the constant letters and parcels from our families and from good friends like Fr Martin, who had married us, which kept us going. Brenda, for some time after our arrival, was also able to assist in teaching English to many of the nurses who were in training.

A few months after our arrival, the six tea chests eventually arrived, and our hearts sank. They had been completely ransacked at the docks in Dar es Salaam. Gone were all the clothes put aside for Lara for the duration, clothes for ourselves, raincoats, shoes, nappies, toiletries, text books, novels, batteries, materials, thread, buttons, tape cassettes and recorder – the list went on and on. We did salvage a sewing machine, an oil lamp, a storm lamp, a baby chair and car seat, a frying pan and a pressure cooker. All the rest had been pilfered.

This really was an emergency, as we had no clothes for Lara, and few indeed for ourselves. The day was saved by an Australian couple – part of an Anglican missionary group in Kasulu – who were departing and gifted us clothes, nappies and toys for Lara. Frantic messages were sent by letter to our families, who to their eternal credit all sent out supplies. We were so grateful for the support.

What an introduction to life in Africa!

Because we were seven kilometres from the nearest village of Kasulu, transport was essential from the beginning. Hence our introduction to a vehicle that would become crucial to our survival over the following couple of years, namely a white Volkswagen Beetle. How I loved this tough little car, which we bought from the local White Fathers. In retrospect, we were never owners of this machine; we were more its caretakers who looked after it, used it and re-sold it on departure back to the White Fathers.

It was like no other car I have known. The engine was at the back rather than the front, which felt strange, but it always ran sweetly, even if it sounded high-pitched. What was really unique was the metal plating that protected the undercarriage of the car. This helped to shield the vehicle from the hostile terrain over which it had to travel. The wheels were tough and had to be, as the roads were at best rutted tracks, suitable only for large four-wheel drive vehicles like Land Rovers.

We used the car to travel into the market on Saturdays to locate that most precious of vegetable so beloved of the Irish – potatoes – along with whatever edibles we could find. At this stage, Brenda had not learned to drive a car, so I was the chauffeur. At the market we made acquaintance with a lovely Tanzanian woman who was usually there with her child.

She would have potatoes and other vegetables for sale. We managed to converse with this lady in our pidgin Swahili and built up a special relationship. Swahili was the main language spoken in Tanzania at the time, with the usual mixture of local dialects. Very few, apart from medical personnel or those working in the hospital, spoke English. We never really learnt to speak the language, which made our stay more difficult.

There were important rules of the road when driving in Tanzania. The first was to get out of the way – sometimes off the track itself – when you saw another vehicle approaching. This greatly increased your chance of survival, as such vehicles had a habit of driving as if you were not there. The second was that, regularly, you had to drive with two wheels perched on the mound in the middle of the track. It felt so strange at the beginning to be driving while constantly tilted to the side, but after a while you got used to it.

Indeed a lot of things seemed strange when we arrived first, but they soon became routine, and even normal.

## CHAPTER 15

## *No Hiding Place*

There is simply no way to prepare for what one faced on a daily basis while running a hospital in Africa in the late seventies. You had to suspend the normal rules and protocols of how you perceived medicine, paediatrics, obstetrics and surgery should be carried out. You found yourself thrust into a world of survival – both your own and, more importantly, the countless stream of really ill people whom you would encounter on a daily basis. It was a baptism of fire, and you either succumbed or quickly adapted to the new reality. Two examples relate to the twin worlds of sick children and of mothers giving birth. I had a good grounding in both disciplines from my hospital years in Dublin, yet it was still an overwhelming experience.

There was no hiding place on my first ward round in Kabanga. A wonderful Tanzanian doctor called Dr Swai was holding the fort until myself and Sr Petria, who would be the doctor in charge, took over. There was only one problem: Sr Petria was not due for a further six weeks and Dr Swai was all set to depart that very week.

To say that I panicked during that first ward round would be an understatement. I still come out in a sweat as I recall what, to those used to working in the hospital, seemed like a routine day at the office. It began with the easy part, the male and female wards. On the medical front, I was confronted in these wards with every known tropical disease, alongside the usual pneumonias, TB, sickle cell anaemia, heart failure, diabetes, among many others. On the surgical side of these wards lay the orthopaedic cases, those awaiting hernia and hydrocoele or other operations, trauma cases, burns victims and women awaiting major gynae surgery. The list went on and on.

The children's ward was a battleground, with every known tropical condition present. Then there were the maternity and labour wards. There we would encounter multiple difficult pregnancies and births. Next up was a trip to the isolation buildings, where those with open TB and leprosy were admitted, and decisions needed to be made regarding treatment of more complex cases.

There was a clear hierarchy present in the hospital. We, the doctors in charge, would be seen as the point of reference for the rest. Below us were the medical assistants who would vet every case, both in the outpatients and in those admitted. They were wonderful medical personnel, similar to junior house doctors at home. They were very experienced, and they managed the day-to-day routine, allowing us doctors to focus on more serious cases. The Medical Missionaries themselves were essential for the daily running of the hospital. They ran the wards, lab, pharmacy, X-ray unit and theatre.

I needed time to find my feet, so I spoke up honestly about my misgivings. Dr Swai agreed to stay on for a few more weeks, until shortly before Sr Petria arrived, and to show me the ropes in the meantime. True to his word, he did just that, and I embarked on a sharp learning curve as to how best to run a busy rural hospital in Tanzania.

Child mortality rates there were very high. Infant mortality was over 10 per cent, while some children struggled to reach the age of five. But there was nothing like seeing the consequences of malnutrition, infection and malaria in practice to reduce the most hardened doctor to tears.

Every evening, the children's ward would fill to capacity, with at least two children per bed, sometimes three. These children were the sickest. Others had been vetted in the daily outpatients and placed on appropriate treatments. It was like a scene from *M\*A\*S\*H*. You would move from child to child, trying with the help of the medical assistants, nurses and interpreters to decide in each case what was going on with the patient and how to treat them. The parents or family of these children would sleep on the ground beside their beds and would provide food during the day.

The commonest problem was malnutrition. There were two types. The first was marasmus, a severe form of protein-energy malnutrition that occurs when a child is not receiving enough protein and calories. We would often see this where the child was being breastfed, but lacked sufficient supplementation. It usually occurred in situations where there was poverty and extreme scarcity of food, and the child would present with stunted growth, extreme weakness, excessive folds of skin, visible bones, dry skin and brittle hair. Often they were under one and gravely ill or dying. This was a nutritional emergency, which would, if left untreated, lead to the death of the child.

The second and commonest form of malnutrition was called kwashiorkor. I often describe this as the illness a child develops when it is replaced at the breast by a subsequent child. This is traditionally around the age of two. It is a type of malnutrition characterised by severe protein deficiency, which in turn leads to extreme fluid retention, often with a swollen, distended abdomen. It is associated with brittle dry hair, a plaintive cry and stunted growth. In Kubanga this was often the result of children being fed ugali only, a form of maize that had little protein present. One of our achievements in Kabanga was to persuade local mothers to simply add nuts to their ugali to reduce the incidence of this condition.

Then there was infection. Sometimes the child would have severe bronchopneumonia which could only be managed with intravenous antibiotics. Others were struggling with TB. Then there were the children with meningitis. I can recall in the middle of ward rounds regularly performing a lumbar puncture. If I saw the tell-tale pus, a sample would be sent to the lab and the child placed on immediate IV antibiotics. Then it was on to the next child.

In other cases, the child would be dying from severe gastroenteritis. Sometimes we would struggle to get intravenous fluids into the child as, due to extreme dehydration, they would have no veins palpable. I learnt the technique of putting an intravenous drip into their abdomen, where the fluids could be absorbed through their peritoneum to resuscitate the child, restore their veins and allow normal intravenous infusion.

At home we often hear that a child is dehydrated from gastroenteritis. But when you see a child who is unresponsive, with large folds of skin and eyes sunken in their heads, you realise what severe dehydration means in practice. A tragic scenario, often witnessed in outpatients, would involve a mother, who might have walked kilometres to get assistance for her child, opening up her kitenge, which was a colourful garment worn around the body, to reveal a child who had already died from gastroenteritis. It was truly heartbreaking.

We also had a major problem with malaria, endemic in the area. Malaria is an infection carried by mosquitoes, which usually attack at night, passing over the infection into the bloodstream. Some of these children were extremely ill with cerebral malaria. This required rapid intervention. Other children had a further difficulty, having inherited the gene for sickle cell anaemia from their parents. These children would break down, or sickle, their red blood cells when they were attacked by malaria and would be admitted extremely ill, dying of heart failure as a consequence of severe anaemia. We would attempt to locate some relative to give blood, while trying to manage their heart failure. It was often a race against time to save them.

Many of these children were also infected with roundworms, often picked up through their bare feet. One of the many horrifying sights I witnessed was these long worms coming out of the nasal and oral orifices of dying children. Others were infected with schistosomiasis, also known as bilharzia, with symptoms of abdominal pain, bleeding into the stools, stunted growth and even kidney damage. This was caused by infection from parasitic worms, often picked up by swimming in infected water. This was another common cause of chronic illness within this group.

If all of this was not enough, these poor children were also exposed to illnesses like measles, which was devastating, polio, which was still prevalent at the time, and of course TB. HIV AIDS had not yet materialised, but sadly it would add further to their misery on its arrival shortly after my stint was completed.

These conditions would regularly appear together. One of the worst procedures I had to perform was on a child with severe kwashiorkor who was completely bloated, so much so that we struggled to find a vein. This poor child was dying from heart failure, due to sickle cell anaemia caused by malaria. I had to cut through the oedema in his neck to reach a vein, to get blood into his failing system. He survived. You did what you had to do. Being an interested spectator was not an option.

Every morning, I would discharge as many children as possible if I felt they were improving. By evening, the ward would once again be packed, and the cycle would begin all over again. It is important to acknowledge the wonderful work that everyone looking after those children did. These are the unsung heroes. One such person was Sr Kieran Saunders MMM. She was to teach me much about life, death and the world of self-acceptance. On reflection, this is where I felt most at home, when in Kabanga, fighting for the lives of these little children. Each one that survived was a victory. Maybe that is all that really mattered.

Nothing in my previous experience could have prepared me for obstetrics in Tanzania. If the children's ward was full of drama, the maternity unit was a war zone. Most Tanzanian women at the time never gave birth in a hospital. They gave birth in their huts in their villages, often under the care of the local midwife. This is where the problems began.

There was a tradition of the native midwife giving the woman in labour a local medicine, or 'dawa', which was supposed to assist her in the delivery. Sadly, it could have the opposite effect: it frequently paralysed the muscles in the womb. This meant that labour, instead of taking eight to ten hours, was often extended to over thirty hours. This put significant pressure on the woman and the baby she was trying to deliver. Many cases would involve trying to save their lives, despite the best efforts of the native midwife.

If the mother did eventually deliver her baby, this was unfortunately not the end of the affair. The native midwife would only get paid if she delivered the placenta or after-birth. It was common for her to do anything to ensure this occurred. This would often include twisting pieces of sticks or wood around the umbilicus to try and unsuccessfully wrench it out. The after-effects of this practice was not an uncommon sight in the labour ward.

With this information as a backdrop, the maternity ward was a tough place to be. In general, a woman would only attend the hospital if she'd had a history of recurrent stillbirths, if she was unable to deliver the baby herself for reasons already discussed, if the placenta was retained or due to other complications such as twins, breech delivery or heavy bleeding from the placenta. All of which spelt trouble for those of us tasked with helping her to have a normal labour and healthy child. Sometimes the baby was already dead, even necrotic, by the time the woman would arrive, or on occasion half in and half out of the womb, the dead body disintegrating if you applied any pressure. In those cases, infection of the mother was the primary concern. It was a sight that still haunts me.

We would try to avoid performing a caesarean section, but at least once or twice a week we would have to operate, often at night-time. The concern was that if the woman did end up with a scar on her womb from a section, and subsequently got pregnant and was dispensed native medicine by a local midwife, she might rupture her uterus and die. But regularly we were unable to save the life of the child or, on occasion, the mother. One of our major achievements in Kabanga was a reduction in the section rate – which was around 10 per cent on my arrival and a mere 4 per cent by my departure – by introducing the concept of active management of labour.

When I arrived I was immediately concerned by a situation in which mothers were frequently in labour for over eighteen hours. Through the introduction of active management of labour, we succeeded, with the assistance of the nurse-midwives, in reducing this to less than twelve hours. It also helped to reduce the section rate.

The most difficult problem was the absence of a blood bank. Mothers were dying as they arrived at the hospital due to the amount of blood they had lost. By the time we had procured blood from a relative, they had often passed away. A second challenge was how to save the lives of those babies who were most at risk of being stillborn.

There was one baby delivered by section who left an indelible mark on my emotional memory. It was an emergency section, as usual, and the baby was completely flat and unresponsive when he was delivered. I briefly left the mother's side to intubate the baby, and then returned to finish the procedure. I then returned to the baby, who was still struggling. We infused a special intravenous solution and continued to assist him in breathing through the tube. Normally if a child was not responding, we would cease. In this case, I had an intuitive feeling that this baby was going to make it. Long after the surgery was over, we continued to work on the baby. Sr Kieran came in to assist me, and we called the infant Baby John.

Eventually, the newborn baby started to breathe on his own. I asked the nurses to cut a hole in the net above his cot, to allow the tube to stay in place overnight, and to then remove the tube the following morning. If the child died, then let him go. If he survived, then our efforts would have paid off.

Baby John survived when the tube was removed and was reunited with his mother. It was one of the great moments of my time in Tanzania. A year later, Sr Kieran informed me that Baby John was back in the hospital with a routine malaria infection, but otherwise toddling normally around the ward. If I was only there for that one child, it was all worthwhile.

CHAPTER 16

## Team Effort

It quickly became apparent to me how much of a team effort was involved in running the hospital. I had such admiration for the MMM sisters who had dedicated their whole lives to the service of others. Some of them had experience from other African countries, such as Nigeria, and some from even further afield. It was an honour to work alongside them.

Over my time in Kabanga, I was fortunate to encounter so many special MMMs. The different matrons, such as Sr Geraldine and Sr Mary; Sr Moninna and Sr Pascal the pharmacists; Sr Carmel and Sr Breda who ran the administration; Sr Noeleen who ran the lab; Sr Áine who looked after X-rays; and of course the indomitable Sr Damien who ran the mother and child clinics. Then there was Sr Kieran who seemed quietly to be everywhere there was a need and whose skill was nursing care, and Sr Assumpta who was in charge of training new nurses. Last of all but by no means least was my colleague Sr Petria. These wonderful women took this African novice under their wing. I was simply a cog in the wheel. I was determined not to let them down.

Apart from the sisters themselves, there were some wonderful Tanzanian medical assistants, nurses, lab assistants, theatre nurses and drivers, all of whom were deeply committed to assisting those who sought medical care. They too formed part of the team, which kept the whole operation going.

Another core member of the team was Tommy Mullen. With a name like that, he could only be Irish! We were delighted when he arrived in the autumn of 1979 to upgrade the generator and electrical wiring in the hospital, which was so vital for our work.

Tommy came from Galway and was like a breath of fresh air. We rapidly became great friends and remain so. He was a regular visitor to our house, where we would swap stories of the day.

He never lost his west of Ireland accent, which became especially prominent when seeking out one particular member of his team who tended to 'disappear' for a siesta on a regular basis. It was better than a scene from *Tom and Jerry*.

It was with an overwhelming sense of relief that I welcomed Sr Petria to her post in Kabanga. I finally had someone to share the load of command with. Dr Swai had given me a good introduction to the hospital routines and what was expected of me, but it was a great comfort to have a doctor of her experience on board. Sr Petria was Irish and had spent much of her life in the global south. Her expertise was surgery, especially gynae surgery, at which she excelled. She had, however, been suffering for some time from chronic hepatitis, with resultant constant fatigue. She relied on me to manage many of the non-surgical and paediatric cases in the hospital.

I learnt quickly from her and we worked well together. We were scheduled to work a week on, week off rota system. This meant that we both performed our usual daytime work, but one of us would also cover the night and weekend shifts. This was gruelling beyond description. If you were on duty, you were up most nights trying to deal with some emergency. It became a regular occurrence for the emergency generator to come on as one or other of us headed for the operating theatre.

Slowly but surely, I fell into the rhythms of the hospital and built up a relationship with the medical assistants, nurses and sisters themselves. The outpatient clinics were long and gruelling, with an endless line of patients – on one occasion there were two hundred lined up to see us – with every type of ailment. At least once a day, the pharmacist, usually Sr Moninna, renowned for her sense of humour, would put her head in the door to inform me which drugs were now in short supply and which ones we could use.

Sr Petria and I would swap the male and female wards every month. This allowed one or the other to cast a fresh eye on difficult cases. On one occasion we had been treating a young teenage boy, who was unconscious, as a case of sleeping sickness and we were using the usual heavy metal drugs prescribed for this condition, but he was not responding. I queried the diagnosis, and asked Sr Áine the radiographer to do a chest X-ray, which showed a classical pattern of miliary TB. We switched his treatment to strong TB drugs. He responded and survived.

I found after some months that I was increasingly comfortable in managing any obstetric emergency and in performing whatever caesarean sections were necessary. Sr Petria came into her own when there was a difficult surgical procedure to be performed, especially for infertility. Such was her interest in fertility that she set up a fertility clinic. For a young woman in Tanzania at that time, infertility was considered a disaster. There were many reasons for this condition. In some cases, it was primary: where the woman had never been able to have children. In other cases, it was secondary and this was often due to venereal disease (VD).

VD was a common problem. It was caused in the main by one of two sexually transmitted infections, namely syphilis or gonorrhoea. The men would frequently travel for work, pick up venereal disease on the journey and pass it on to their wives on their return, who would then develop adhesions and infertility. In other cases, the cause might be endometriosis with secondary adhesions. Women would travel long distances to get assistance, and Sr Petria was simply a genius in this area. She was also superb at operating on women with fistulas between the bladder and the womb, where they would pass urine through their vaginas. These occurred as a consequence of childbirth and were extremely distressing for the woman involved. As the months progressed, I became increasingly comfortable with many different forms of surgery, but would always bow to her expertise in these areas. We were a good team.

Another force of nature was Mama Damien. Larger than life, Sr Damien was in charge of the mother and child outpatient programme for the surrounding areas. On a regular basis this wonderful lady and her team would pack up medical and vaccination supplies into a Land Rover and, with their driver, embark on their next journey to some far-flung rural village. I had the privilege of joining her on a few of these outings and they were truly awe-inspiring. The villages were often only accessible by Land Rover. I found the journeys to be tiring but very rewarding. The people were so friendly. With their colourful kitenges, broad smiles and children at the ready, they were a pleasure to assist. Sr Damien ran the vaccination programme like a military operation, where everyone knew their role. Within a short time of arrival, the locals were lined up to have their children vaccinated and for any other issues to be resolved. She was known affectionately by the locals as Mama Damien and it was easy to see why. She simply loved children. Everywhere she would go, the queues would gather. Mothers had come to realise how important these vaccines were in preventing illnesses such as polio, diphtheria and tetanus. She was also able to bring medical care into more remote areas. The fact that we were now seeing fewer cases of active polio in the hospital was down to the sterling work of sisters like her. There were sadly no vaccines available at the time to prevent malaria, which was killing so many of these children, especially those with sickle cell anaemia.

When I was with her I would assist with the more complex medical cases, but this was not as important as the work she was doing. To gain the respect of the local populations and persuade them to vaccinate their children was the most significant task of all. Sr Damien was most at home in the dust, heat and poverty of Tanzania, amongst the people she loved and who loved her.

I found myself regularly working alongside Sr Kieran Saunders, and as the days and weeks went on we formed a close bond. Sr Kieran was a legend in the MMM community. It was she who had co-founded the first medical missionary clinic in Tanzania – in Makiungu in the centre of the country – in 1954, which over the following fifty years would grow to be a major hospital. She then progressed, in her fifties, to learn Mandarin and opened up a similar clinic in Taiwan, where she spent many years, before returning to Tanzania to continue sharing her nursing skills.

If either of us had a difficulty, the other would seek to find a solution. We were struggling with severely infected wounds, some proving impossible to heal. She suggested a therapy as old as time itself, namely the introduction of maggots into the wound. In a modern world obsessed with the latest antibiotic or treatment, this might seem an archaic proposal, but Sr Kieran had seen it work in practice. We began to insert maggots under the bandages. Amazingly, it worked; the necrotic tissue was quickly gobbled up by the maggots, and healing began. It was miraculous.

Sr Kieran was always there for me professionally and personally during my time in Kabanga. On one occasion, a woman who was due to undergo a caesarean section grasped my hands and beseeched me to do a tubal ligation. She had a history of six previous sections and a flock of children at home. I announced before the operation that I was going to do so and was met, understandably, with resistance from some of those present, on moral grounds. We went ahead and performed the section and tubal ligation. Sr Kieran knew that I would be upset and arrived immediately to support me and backed the decision. For her, love and the care of mothers and children lay at the heart of any true spirituality. She was pure love in action. 'Those children need their mother,' she exclaimed. I didn't want to be the cause of any distress to those present, but the care of that mother and her children was paramount to me. Sr Kieran understood that. It was then I knew that this lady was different.

I have met many wonderful and amazing people in my life, but only one genuine saint, and that was Sr Kieran. She was often late for a service, as she was helping the women or children in the hospital. When everyone else had left, she was still there. She lived and breathed her spirituality in practice.

One particular life-changing experience for me personally occurred late one night when I was checking in on a sick patient in the hospital. There I found Sr Kieran on her own with an old man, who had been left to die by his family and community and was simply in the most dreadful state. He was clearly not going to see the morning. She was busy taking the maggots out of his body and dropping them into a bucket, all of this done with her bare hands.

'Kieran,' I pleaded, 'why are you doing this? This poor man is dying and is not long for this world.' Her answer haunted me for the rest of my life. With that beautiful smile, she explained, 'Harry, I will not let this man go before his Maker looking like this,' and continued removing the maggots. It was then I realised that I was in the presence of a genuine saint. Humbled and in awe, I quietly retreated and left her to her work. There was nothing more to be said.

Sr Kieran had a profound effect on me personally. Her calm, her quiet service, her smile, her love for each person who came under her care, her acceptance of me as a person and not simply as a medical colleague, her words of wisdom. Little did I realise at the time just how much she helped to shape me into the person that I am today.

CHAPTER 17

*The Fragility of Life*

Approximately every three months we would receive a visit from the flying doctors. These were warmly welcomed by those of us working in the hospital. They came across the border from Nairobi in neighbouring Kenya and would include specialist surgeons who would perform complex procedures such as prostatectomies, thyroid surgery and major eye surgery. We would gather together our patients and have them ready for their arrival. They would come in a small plane, ideally suited to land in bush areas.

My introduction to the flying doctors was not such a happy event. It was within the first few months of our arrival. The plane, as per usual, buzzed around the hospital three times before landing on the airstrip in the neighbouring village of Kasulu. From there the surgeons would travel overland to Kabanga. The pilot, however, was unhappy with something mechanical in the plane, and having repaired it, took it up on a test flight to check that all was well. Some local dignitaries accompanied him on the flight. Shortly after taking off, the plane crashed, bursting into flames in the process. The survivors were brought to the hospital, having being pulled out of the inferno.

The burns they received were truly horrific and it was immediately obvious that many of them, due to the large surface area covered by burns, were going to die. We did our best to make them comfortable, but there was little we could do to assist them. Nobody survived.

One of the men who died in the crash had looked after the garden for us, and so we found this event particularly upsetting. It brought home the bravery of these pilots and surgeons, who risked life and limb to help others less fortunate than themselves. It was a wake-up call as to just how fine a line there was in Africa between life and death.

The plane crash was an unexpected tragedy. But there was also a larger-scale tragedy happening right in front of our eyes. Even as far back as 1979, it came as an enormous shock to see the ravages of polio. This terrible virus had been tamed in Ireland by a mass vaccination programme, which was extremely successful. But in Kabanga we could see the after-effects of polio all around us. This virus mainly attacks children under five, often leading to long-term paralysis of limbs in those who survive the infection.

My most vivid memory of this in practice was one lady, a polio survivor, who lived in the local village crawling in on her elbows and knees, with her small child on her back, to attend a clinic. It was a heartbreaking sight, but she was always so positive, despite the enormous efforts it must have taken to get through every day. I loved to see her coming. I was in awe of her resilience.

We would see teenage children with contractures so severe that their legs would be bent at almost 180 degrees and who consequently would struggle to stand or walk. In other cases it would be their arms that were paralysed. It was sad to see these lovely young people with their whole lives in front of them facing such challenges, especially those who would never walk normally again. I became determined to do something. There had to be a way to deal with their permanent handicaps.

All of this was due to the difficulties involved in creating a functioning vaccination programme, which would have prevented it from happening. We have already outlined many of the reasons, in particular difficulties with the cold chain so vital for vaccination programmes. Thankfully, Sr Damien was having great success in filling this void.

But polio was by no means the only illness affecting the local population. Meningitis strikes fear into the hearts and minds of medical personnel and laypeople alike. At that stage, there were no vaccinations available to prevent this illness. It was caused primarily by the bacteria meningitis B and was often life-threatening. You can imagine the panic when word came in from one of the villages that an epidemic was sweeping through.

As they started to carry these really ill patients into the hospital for treatment, I became anxious that Brenda or Lara would come down with the same infection. Some people were dying in the village, some in the hospital and many others were extremely ill, so my concern was justified. It was a terrifying time, as the death toll was high. I took the unusual step of pouring antibiotics into all three of us. I am not sure if it was the right thing to do, but we survived. The epidemic began to wane and life slowly began to return to normal.

Apart from polio and meningitis, cholera had also managed to creep into Tanzania by the late 1970s. This was another serious illness, extremely contagious and hard to treat. It was caused by the cholera virus, which led to fulminating, bloody diarrhoea and profound dehydration. There have been many serious epidemics in Tanzania since, even up to recently. Many of the cases we dealt with were really ill. There was a great fear at the time that it would turn into a full-blown epidemic, but thankfully in our area this did not occur. It still created major problems for those of us in the hospital, who had to manage so many conditions where intravenous drip sets were vital. I can recall on occasion having to decide which children were sickest and preserving the intravenous sets for them. What a terrible choice to have to make.

I wrote to the master of Holles Street at the end of 1979, detailing our great shortage of intravenous drip sets and the difficulties we were experiencing as a result. He sent me a lovely letter in response. He had shared my correspondence with other staff members in the hospital and they set about sending us out drip sets. There is little doubt that his assistance saved many lives.

Apart from these more acute infections, which caused so much distress to the local population, there was leprosy. From biblical times there has been a stigma associated with this chronic illness. Also called Hansen's disease, leprosy is caused by a slow-growing bacterium that comes from the same family as TB. It causes long-term damage to the skin, eyes and especially the nerves. It can be an extremely disfiguring illness and those who experience it, described as lepers, are often shunned by their communities, terrified that the illness will be passed on to them. It is, like its cousin TB, an illness where poverty and close contact are risk factors for developing the condition.

It was for this reason that those with leprosy were confined to an isolation unit in the hospital. I often reflect on how they must have felt. Even though the chances of developing this illness through routine contact were low, those patients were still deemed abnormal.

They were lovely people, often struggling with chronic foot, bone and skin infections, as the nerve supply to these areas was badly compromised. I would perform surgery on the more severe cases where bone infection was present, sometimes removing areas of necrotic bone. Those in the unit were usually on long-term multi-drug therapy, to try to clear their underlying leprosy. It was our task to assist them with whatever medical or surgical problems they were experiencing as a consequence of their illness and then send them back into their families and communities to continue their treatment there.

It was becoming apparent that life in Africa was fragile. That service was often reactive in nature, with a special emphasis on the world of acute care. Whether it was medical, surgical, obstetric or paediatric in nature, we seemed to be constantly reacting to whatever emergency arrived next. Trying to cope with this onslaught was exhausting, if rewarding. Often it was regularly tinged with sadness when, despite our best efforts as a team, someone would die.

CHAPTER 18

## *The Home Front*

If it was challenging for me on the hospital front, it was even more so for Brenda on the home front. Initially she had taught English to the Tanzanian trainee nurses, but as Lara got older, Brenda had to put all her energies into keeping our little unit functioning. Staying alive was very labour-intensive! Sourcing food, bread-making, cooking, filtering and boiling water, and looking after the needs of a small infant were not easy tasks. All meals were prepared from scratch and took time. Snakes, mosquitoes, cockroaches and insects of every description were a daily hazard. She found the intense heat suffocating, especially at midday.

Brenda greatly missed her family and friends back home and struggled with isolation and lack of stimulation. But we had the back-up of the MMMs and the White Fathers, and we really enjoyed the visits of Tommy, and later of Peter, who was involved in a chicken project in Kasulu, both of whom became lifelong friends. Brenda became close to the Van Deun family, especially Reinhilde and her three children.

What saved the day was her beloved sewing machine, salvaged from the ransacked crates. She loved to make clothes, both for herself and for Lara, from materials sent out in parcels from family and friends back in Ireland. This was a life-saver for both. We also ran an open house. If anyone appeared on our doorstep from other regions or from Ireland, we would offer them a bed for the night and some hospitality. In Africa, this was the norm.

When Lara became mobile, she loved to toddle down to the mother and child unit, and would also sit on the doorstep of our house, chatting with women and babies passing by. She was a novelty with her blonde hair. She was a happy child.

For me, home was my refuge. Somewhere I could rest, read and listen to music when the generator was on. Despite any privations, we were fortunate in comparison to those we looked after. We had a house, access to food, clean water and a car. What else could we need?

In many ways our first Christmas in Kabanga was the nadir of our trip to Africa. Christmas is normally such a happy family event to be shared together. In Kabanga in 1979 it was different. We were on our own in a foreign land that was in many ways alien to us. We had little contact with family or friends back home. We were devastated by the loss of our belongings, packed into those looted tea chests. We had only a small number of friends. On that particular Christmas I was also on duty. As any doctor will know, sickness and illness do not cease just because it is a holiday feast.

Brenda and Lara became extremely ill with gastroenteritis. Lara lost a lot of weight and Sr Petria wanted to admit her into the hospital. I was afraid she would pick up further illnesses there, so we decided to manage the situation at home. My abiding memory of the day was sitting down to a Christmas dinner of bananas and feeling sorry for myself, but even more so for Brenda and Lara. Had we bitten off more than we could chew?

But as we all know, life is tough and we have to battle our way through such periods. It is not about how we cope when everything is going well that matters, but how we cope when things get rough. Brenda and Lara made a full recovery and from that moment on, life began to improve. The following Christmas, in contrast, would turn out to be the complete antithesis, and one that was truly memorable for a host of other reasons.

But there were some highlights too from our time in Africa, and one of them was our visit to Kigoma Hotel!

You can imagine our reaction, years later, when watching TV and we saw seasoned traveller Michael Palin in Kigoma Hotel laughing hysterically as the lights went out. There was nothing else he could do. We knew just how he felt.

To us, Kigoma seemed an exotic destination. This regional centre was situated on the shores of Lake Tanganyika, an enormous lake spanning several countries. We were nine months into our placement and had never left the compound other than for some local visits. We needed a few days' break; some rest and a change of scenery would do us good. Life on the compound was not only a drain on our energy, but also extremely monotonous. So, in high spirits we departed for Kigoma.

The journey there was itself an adventure. Driving along the route, we reached a dried-up river bed. To continue the journey, we would have to risk travelling over it. To do so, one had to descend a sandy bank, cross over three wooden planks laid over the river bed, then climb up a 70-degree tilted sand bank. Undaunted, and clutching the steering wheel of our trusty armoured Beetle, we closed our eyes, hoped for the best and gunned the engine. We made it across with an appreciative audience of little boys and continued our action-packed journey.

We booked into the main hotel in the town, Kigoma Hotel. That was when the fun began. When one thinks of a hotel in Ireland, even the most basic of rooms will have a nod to some décor, floor covering, bed and toilet facilities. We arrived in our 'room' and couldn't decide whether to laugh or cry. We chose the former. If you can visualise a prison cell with cement floors and walls, a lumpy bed with a mosquito net perched on top of it and a hole in the ground as the only toilet facilities (where snakes might make an appearance), then you get the picture. We were at this stage used to 'basic' but this was meant to be a break! No wonder poor Michael Palin found himself swathed in a mosquito net in such a room, laughing himself to sleep. It was that or cry! Welcome to Tanzania, Michael.

One nice memory of this visit to Kigoma was that of eating at a local restaurant and being served the most delicious meaty fish, straight from the lake itself. After months of basic rations, it tasted like heaven. Needless to say, however, we did not return again during our stay to sample the joys of Kigoma Hotel. Maybe life on the compound was not so bad after all!

Despite the brief respite of our trip to Kigoma, I was slowly but surely becoming burnt out. I was disheartened by the constant tsunami of children pouring into the hospital, many of whom were extremely ill. What was wearing me out was a feeling that the world out there didn't care whether these children lived or died. I was railing against the injustice of it all. Why should so many women and children have to suffer so much? Why was life so stacked against them, often from the beginning? Why did God, if he existed, allow such suffering to continue unabated?

It was Sr Kieran, of course, who came to my rescue, as always. She sat me down and with those eyes of love gave me some advice, and her wise words still resonate with me to this day. From that moment on, I would be a changed person.

'Harry,' she said gently, 'there will always be suffering, poverty, unfairness and inequality. You did not cause this problem, which is bigger than either of us. Neither can you solve these issues. They are simply too vast and too complex and neither you nor I can ever hope to change them. You will have to come to an acceptance that this is, and will always be, the case, otherwise you will no longer be of use to yourself, your family or those you want to help.'

Things began to make sense to me then. Sr Kieran continued: 'Your task is to focus completely on the person in front of you at that moment in time. You cannot change the world, but you can listen to this person, empathise with their problem and do your best to help them manage it. That is your role, and will always be so. It is in that one-to-one interaction that you will find peace. To be there for another human being who is in crisis and who needs your assistance, in whatever form that takes, that is your task.'

Oh Kieran, how I loved you, and how I miss you and your wonderful words.

CHAPTER 19

*A Journey of a Lifetime*

It was sheer, unadulterated madness. Nobody in their right mind would dream of crossing from one side of Tanzania to the other, traversing the Serengeti National Park in a VW Beetle. This vast terrain was only meant to be crossed with a large, fully equipped Land Rover and a team of guides. Anything else was a recipe for disaster. When you are young, however, you foolishly believe you are invincible and can overcome any obstacles. It turned out to be a long, hair-raising journey, sometimes terrifying, sometimes exhilarating, but one we will remember for the rest of our days. The stuff of dreams and nightmares combined. A time when you discover what you are truly made of.

The decision to embark on this trip was made long before it began. We had to take a break from the crushing workload in the hospital. Kabanga was out in the bush so we only had two options. One was to fly to Dar es Salaam and on to some other destination. We had already experienced the hair-raising flight from the capital to Kigoma and were in no rush to repeat the exercise. The second option was to drive up to Mwanza on Lake Victoria, turn into and navigate the vast Serengeti Plains towards Arusha and then on into Dar es Salaam. This latter seemed an exotic, exciting option. This would be our chance to see the teeming wildlife for which Tanzania was so famous. To experience Africa in the raw.

We researched the trip as best we could. We consulted maps and sought advice from the White Fathers and the MMMs. Tommy gave us mechanical advice. Bit by bit, we put together the relevant items we would need for the journey. The key was to traverse the Serengeti before the rainy season arrived. When this happened, the tracks and trails across this wild terrain became a mudbath and might be completely unpassable for months on end. We decided that September 1980 was the best month and planned accordingly.

The White Fathers and Tommy advised us on the equipment we would need. Spare tyres, extra fuel cans and many other accessories were the minimum requirements. The route was planned. We would head up towards Lake Victoria, cross over the lake on a ferry into Mwanza and eventually turn into the Serengeti National Park itself. Then we would drive to the Serengeti Game Lodge and spend a night there. We would continue through the park, emerging close to the Olduvai Gorge, before travelling up the Ngorongoro Crater, heading for Lake Manyara and on into Arusha. From there the plan was to head for the capital Dar es Salaam. On the map it looked straightforward, a walk in the park. Nothing could have prepared us for the reality.

In the middle of these preparations, we received another unexpected surprise. In June 1980, when Lara was fourteen months old, Brenda discovered that she was once again pregnant. We had no idea of specifics, but as best we could worked out the expected date of delivery. Mother Nature works on her own time schedule, and these dates would quickly go out the window. Did this news scupper plans for our upcoming trip? Not at all. We decided that as Brenda would be heading into the second three months, this was the safest time to travel. The only change was the addition of a spare obstetric kit in case of an emergency en route. Madness!

As we were busy planning for our expedition, life once again intervened. In June, our good friend Tommy, by then an institution in the hospital, had a serious accident. He had fallen from a height and broken his back. I arrived at the scene to find absolute hysteria. The room was full of wailing, distraught – if well-meaning – staff. Serious back injuries require a definite response. It certainly did not include being carried along by workmates into the hospital. If it had been an unstable fracture, he could have been paralysed for life. Fortunately, it was a stable fracture.

I am at my best in a serious crisis and at my absolute worst when dealing with some minor drama. I ordered everyone out of the room and calmly proceeded to examine my good friend. He clearly was in agony and very shocked. Following immediate analgesia and some X-rays, we diagnosed a serious fracture. It was clear that he would have to be airlifted out. He went back to Ireland for further treatment. This was a big blow to Brenda and me, as Tommy was by this stage a close friend. The priority was to ensure that he would make a full recovery. Despite the setback, we decided to go ahead with our plans and in the final days of August 1980 began our safari.

It was a portent of what was to come. On the map, it looked so simple. We would drive from Kabanga up to Mwanza, a key regional centre, on the lower edge of Lake Victoria. There our journey would begin. The area we were driving through, however, was home to the tsetse fly, which carries the parasite which causes sleeping sickness. If we wanted to relieve ourselves, we had to do so in a hurry, to prevent a bite from these insects. This first day was also our introduction to the surfaces over which we would be travelling for the rest of the journey. The tracks encountered consisted of potholes, ridges, boulders and sharp-pointed stones whose main reason for existence was to rip out your tyres. There were also sand drifts, diabolical unmarked curves and bridges, to mention but a few road blocks. Another menace were those occasional thundering lorries that one would meet. All this before we encountered the wildlife!

We were rattled and thrown around as we tried to navigate, with the assistance of our little Beetle, these Tanzanian tracks, always tilted at a 45-degree angle. I felt sorry for Brenda, in particular, who was carrying our second child. Lara in the back was a trooper, and coping better than the rest of us. It didn't take long for the first casualty to occur. The oil gasket punctured and oil spilled out. This was accompanied by a steering problem, the result of the terrain we were travelling through. What a start to the trip! Thankfully, this occurred close to a garage, a miracle in itself. We managed to get these minor difficulties fixed up and continued our journey. We took a rickety ferry across the lake, the stuff of nightmares, and finally entered Mwanza. There, we were able to make contact with Sr Consolata, the regional MMM superior. We stayed a night with her, then continued on our journey before finally turning right and entering into the Serengeti National Park. We had arrived.

When we crossed that remote border post into the national park, time stood still, and we knew that we had entered somewhere special. A number of important challenges faced us on that second day. Scattered along the side of the road, clearly comfortable with their surroundings and oblivious to us visitors, were the lions. To see a lion up close is a scary and humbling experience. Their presence did not encourage any loitering. The next challenge was to reach the centre-point of the park, the Serengeti Game Lodge, by evening, before the sun went down. On the roads we were travelling, this would prove to be a daunting task.

There were no GPS systems in those days. You were relying on simple maps. I still retain the map we used for the journey and look at it in awe. Were we stark raving mad? When you are in the middle of nowhere, with the sun baking down and with a toddler and pregnant wife, you feel under a certain amount of pressure to reach safety. A night under the stars with the wildlife was not a viable option.

How do I describe, however, the wondrous sights which revealed themselves in their natural glory? What a beautiful place the Serengeti was. Every exotic species was there in abundance. Huge herds of gazelles, giraffes – my favourites, who seemed to float majestically across the landscape – wildebeest, buffalo, lions, warthogs, monkeys and so much more. One amazing sight was that of an ostrich in full flight, running alongside, keeping pace with the Beetle. They were all coexisting naturally in this vast landscape. It was a reminder of how small and insignificant we human beings are in the overall scheme of things.

We took photos for posterity, but the real memories lie buried for all time within our emotional memory banks. The sight of these animals in the wild, as they should be, has stayed with me. Inevitably, within range of the lodge itself, we sustained yet another puncture, this time a slow one. We limped into the hotel, completely exhausted after our day of travelling, but greatly relieved knowing we were safe for the night. The lodge was a mainstay for tourists who would come on their safaris, usually with their Land Rovers, sometimes with guides. It was an exotic place to stay, with exorbitant prices to match, but a haven. We were just happy to have made it.

The evening meal was memorable. We were hysterically exhausted, but determined to make the most of our stay. We ordered food and then queried if there was any wine available. As was usual in Tanzania at the time, there were shortages of just about everything, especially away from the big cities, so the answer was in the negative. Was there any type of alcohol available? They did have one bottle of vintage champagne, but at a price. We both burst out laughing and decided, 'Let's go for it.' Between exhaustion and the ingestion of a few glasses of bubbles, we fell into bed that night and slept like logs.

The following morning, we came down for breakfast. Having feasted on papaya, which was growing outside our house in Kabanga and available everywhere, we waited expectantly for the next course, to realise that nothing else was forthcoming. Just the coffee. They still charged us an extortionate price for the overnight stay.

Having mended the puncture, we set off refreshed to take on the next stage of the journey. Once again, we were mesmerised by the sights of the Serengeti, but thankful to traverse it safely, without any further mishaps.

On the eastern side of the park, on our way to the Ngorongoro Crater, we passed through the Olduvai Gorge, a hot, deserted area. There was something quite haunting about this forlorn place, among the most important archaeological sites in the world. It was here that one of the oldest human fossils was discovered, a 175-million-year-old skull. It is believed that human beings originated from this area and migrated to the rest of the known world. We definitely felt that we were passing through hallowed ground.

Our next challenge was to traverse the Ngorongoro Crater conservation area. The crater was the site of an extinct volcano, situated in Tanzania's Rift Valley. The crater itself was home to one of the highest densities of wild animals in the world. It was a veritable natural zoo, where tourists could see up close every wild animal species present in Tanzania at the time.

This was of little interest to these poor travellers, however, who arrived at the bottom of the track that led from the base of the old volcano to the summit. It was blisteringly hot at the base and, as we would discover to our surprise, cold, damp and miserable at the summit. The journey was a nightmare. There were massive rifts in the track, where a slip would be fatal. The surface was awful. There were huge boulders. The poor Beetle really struggled, as did its occupants, who spent the time with hearts in mouths. Would we ever arrive safely at the summit?

The closer we got to the top, the darker and colder it became. The sun and blistering heat faded into the distance. Finally, we limped our way to the summit, to find a completely different world to anything we had experienced in Tanzania. Everything was clammy and chilly; even the bedclothes in the lodge we rented on the summit were damp. There was a bustling tourist influx, all excited about travelling down into the core of the crater to see the 'big five' (lion, leopard, rhino, elephant and buffalo).

By the time we reached the summit, we were so relieved to be alive and in one piece that seeing more wildlife was well down our list of priorities. Food and sleep were higher. I particularly remember the wildebeest steak. After so many months with little meat, it was one of the most delicious steaks I have ever eaten.

The following morning, we began to descend the crater, the mists swirling in a ghost-like manner around the car. Then out of the mists, slap bang in the middle of the track, emerged a lioness and her cubs. Since one never argues with a lioness who is guarding her young, we came to a full stop. She glanced at us and then one by one grabbed each of the young cubs by the neck and simply fired them off to one side, a most extraordinary sight, never to be forgotten. Having made the point that this was her terrain, she sauntered off, leaving some scared but relieved bodies to continue on their madcap journey.

I can remember our relief, as we descended, on seeing the sun and warmth reappear. There was something unpleasant about the summit of the Ngorongoro Crater, and we were glad to be on our way.

We were now heading towards the Lake Manyara Game Reserve. I would love to say the terrain got easier, but it was more of the same. We were excited, however, about reaching

Lake Manyara as we had heard so much about the pink flamingos that made the reserve so famous. The area was renowned for its vast hordes of elephants and tree-climbing lions, but for us it was all about the lake itself. This was the one stop on the journey that we really loved. The lodge was a nature's paradise. The monkeys owned the place, screeching and hopping from tree to tree near the room in which we were staying.

I cannot describe how beautiful the pink flamingos were as they flew majestically across the lake. They have to be seen in their natural habitat to be fully appreciated. We simply loved the place and were sad when it was time to move on.

It is the little things in life that trip us up the most. It should have been a simple journey. We had traversed the mighty Serengeti, clambered up and down the Ngorongoro Crater and made our way to Lake Manyara. The final part of the trip was, on paper, a simple run to the major regional capital of Arusha. But then disaster struck. We had been lucky up to that point. We always carried a spare wheel, so when a puncture occurred, which was often, we could replace the wheel and move on to the next staging post to get the puncture mended. I did carry a puncture mending kit, but had not required it to date.

We developed the inevitable puncture and, as usual, changed the wheel and continued onwards. This time, however, we suffered a subsequent puncture in the tyre of the replacement wheel. Now we had a real problem. Off came the wheel and then the fun began. VW Beetle tyres are tough, and needed to be. Out came the tyre lever, but no matter how hard I tried, I was unable to remove the tyre from the wheel. I couldn't mend the tyre if I couldn't remove it. We were stuck, literally.

This was not good. It was boiling hot. We were kilometres from Arusha, with no hope of assistance. There wasn't a single vehicle in sight. All we could see was vast emptiness. We were in real trouble. I toiled away unsuccessfully to remove the tyre, my efforts becoming more and more frantic. Thankfully, somebody up there was looking out for us. Out of the swirling heat came a Good Samaritan. His name was Verle and he was driving a Land Rover. Verle was an American architect who was in Tanzania assisting the MMMs in designing new buildings, and currently living in Arusha. What were the chances?

Together Verle and I tried to lever the stubborn tyre off its wheel, but without success. He then came up with the bright idea of driving the Land Rover over the tyre, in an effort to pop the stubborn rubber off the metal. Incredibly, this worked, and we mended the puncture. Verle offered to follow us on our journey into Arusha. It was as well that he did, as we managed to get yet another puncture on the way.

When Brenda and I reached Arusha, we decided that driving to Dar es Salaam was simply one leg too far. We decided to park in Arusha for the week, and what a great decision that was. In the parable of the Good Samaritan, the latter brings the victim to a safe lodging and agrees to pay for his keep until he recovers. In our case, Verle played the role. Not only did he rescue us from a risky situation, but he offered to put us up in his home for the week. He was going to be travelling some of the time, so we would have the place mainly to ourselves. We will never forget his kindness. Such an offer was like manna from heaven. To take in a young doctor, his pregnant wife and small toddler was a Christian gesture at its purest.

What can I say about Arusha itself? We loved the place. It was like dropping into a different existence. It was colourful, exotic and filled with the goods and services that we had craved back in Kabanga. It was a vibrant, bustling city, and the entry point for most of the safari tours heading into the various national parks through which we had just traversed. Nowadays it is also the entry point for those who want to climb Mount Kilimanjaro, the fourth most prominent summit in the world.

More importantly, it was also home to a postulant centre for the MMMs. To our delight, they were happy to mind Lara every day for a few hours, to allow us some space and time to explore the city. We managed to get some decent meals, some with Verle. Brenda even managed to get her hair cut. We picked up some small presents for those at home. We were also able to ensure that the Beetle was fit for the return journey.

I have such fond memories of this lovely city. It helped us to recover and recuperate, not only from the arduous journey, but from the toll created by the heavy workload back in Kabanga.

Have you ever noticed how a return journey seems to flit by more quickly and, for some strange reason, with less fuss than the original journey? Whereas I have such vivid memories of every step of the trip from Kabanga to Arusha, my memories of the return trip are vague. We said our goodbyes to Verle, leaving him a present for all his kindness, and set out on our return journey. There was some apprehension as we knew already how tough a trip it could be.

We retraced our steps back to Lake Manyara and I do remember our sojourn there. It was such a beautiful place. I have little recollection of clambering up and down the Ngorongoro

Crater again. Maybe that's because the brain tries to protect us from nightmare memories! I do remember coming back through the Serengeti and drinking in the sights and sounds of all of the wildlife. My most vivid memory, however, relates to the Serengeti Game Lodge.

As we arrived, a Land Rover powered in and out popped a group of Americans. They looked ashen-faced. One of them, brushing by me, turned and asked, 'Does this place have a bar?' before chasing into the lodge itself. We subsequently heard their story. They had arrived in Arusha and hired a Land Rover. They'd decided against a guide and on their journey through the Serengeti took a shortcut. They found themselves totally lost in the wilderness; all they could see and hear were the sights and sounds of wild animals. One of them then hit on the bright idea of using the sun as a guide to get them back on track. All this explains their agitated behaviour on reaching the lodge. We, however, had our own tales to tell.

Following more adventures, we made our way from there to Mwanza and back along the dirt tracks to reach Kabanga. I have never lost my admiration for that plucky little Beetle. We had, amongst many mechanical difficulties on the journey, at least eight punctures, a ruptured oil gasket, damaged steering and the back fender fell off, but it still got us there and back in one piece. What a car. What a trip.

## CHAPTER 20

## *A Seasoned Veteran*

After six to nine months, I had become adept at coping with whatever situation was thrown at me. I was now a seasoned veteran, increasingly useful working in these challenging circumstances. I felt comfortable being left on my own to run the hospital when Sr Petria was away on holidays, unwell or on retreat.

It was time to make some improvements in services and in particular to pass on skills to the local medical staff. These would continue to be used long after I left. Chinese philosopher Lao Tzu once said, 'Give a man a fish and you feed him for a day. Teach him how to fish and you feed him for a lifetime.' We need to rely less on the experts and more on our innate human resources and skills.

I began with teaching staff the skill of intubation.

Imagine what it would feel like if you were being constantly woken up out of a deep sleep at least several times a week. You are drowsy, irritable and struggle to become rapidly functional. It is a horrible sensation. This was a constant during my stay in Kabanga, and contributed greatly to my feelings of exhaustion.

First there would come the rustle. Then the footsteps, the tap, tap, tapping on the bedroom window, and finally the voice, 'Doctor, doctor!' This usually occurred in the middle of the night when I was on call, which roughly translated into every second week. The voice would, more often than not, belong to one of the nurses on duty for the night. This cameo usually played out with me rushing down to the hospital and deciding by torchlight on how best to manage whatever trauma had presented. This would often lead to the emergency generator coming on, as we prepared for an urgent section or life-saving surgical procedure.

For the first nine months, there was one constant emergency. This was where a baby would be born flat, with no clinical evidence of a heartbeat or normal breathing. Sadly, by the time the midwives would have attempted to manage this themselves, eventually coming to get me, the baby in question would be dead. I found this heartbreaking.

My family and work colleagues would agree that I am a master of the art of delegation. Its origins lie in my experiences in Kabanga. If I wanted to change the status quo, I had to be brave enough to train others in the skills required, then pass responsibility onto them. This would be service in action. It required a major change in my thinking. I gathered together those who played any role in the delivery of a baby. They spent hours learning how to intubate, and we didn't stop until each person was competent in the skill. I also drew up a special intravenous solution that all midwifes or nurses would use following the intubation of a baby who had been born flat.

Several days later, as dawn approached, I could hear the usual pitter-patter of steps and the tap on the window. It was this lovely Tanzanian nurse who struggled with a severe limp from old polio, the butt of many comments. She had come to share her good news with me.

In the middle of the night, a high-risk mother had gone into labour. She had lost both of her previous babies who had been born flat at birth in the bush, and she had come into the hospital to deliver her next child. As before, the baby was born flat and unresponsive. My nurse friend intubated the baby, as I had shown her, and injected the solution, as I had suggested. The baby, miraculously, began to breathe on its own. This midwife, once dismissed, was now seen as a miracle-worker, a cause célèbre, a hero. She had successfully intubated and saved a baby's life.

Never again during my stay in Kabanga was I called to intubate a baby born flat. The nurse-midwives developed and perfected the skill. As a result, many babies were saved. More importantly, the nurses were empowered with a skill for life.

The next improvement involved setting up a blood bank, something previously considered impossible.

There is nothing harder for a doctor than to see a young mother die due to the unavailability of blood. This was the situation facing us in Kabanga. It was tragic and I was often in tears. Mothers would arrive in to the hospital bleeding heavily, for a variety of obstetric reasons. Some were already dying, with the baby itself distressed or dead. We would attempt to resuscitate them, putting up drips and setting up for emergency surgery. But what they needed most was simply blood. By the time a donor could be found within the family members or community, it would be too late, and despite our best efforts, these women would die. It seemed like a pointless waste of precious lives, not to mention the hardships that now faced the children left behind.

A similar situation was also developing when dealing with small children admitted with advanced heart failure from a sickle cell crisis following a bout of malaria. In some situations, by the time a suitable donor appeared it would be too late.

I constantly suggested the setting up of a blood bank, to have blood immediately on hand, but the idea was always discounted for one major reason. The local villagers and many of those who attended us refused point blank to give blood. They believed that it weakened, and in some way diminished, them. This barrier seemed insurmountable. But this young Irish doctor was extremely stubborn. So often in life, we only see black and white, while the solution so often lies in the grey. I knew I had an ally in Sr Noeleen, who ran the lab and who would support any attempts I would make in this area.

Nervous but undaunted, I went down to the local village and held a public meeting, with the help of an interpreter. I explained what was happening and that our plan was to set up a new blood bank. I then introduced the idea of the carrot and the stick. From now on, anyone who came to the hospital seeking surgery on a hernia or hydrocoele, or any other form of surgery, would have to first provide the hospital with a pint of O negative blood. This was a canny move. The men, in particular, were streaming in seeking surgery for hernias and hydrocoeles. Now, if they wanted this procedure performed, there would be a price. The secret here, of course, is that O negative blood could be given to any person who required blood. This would then go into the blood bank, once it was cleared by Sr Noeleen. We now had instant access to blood for use in emergencies.

We also set up a new system. If blood was given from our new stocks to someone requiring it, the family or community involved would have to replace it. If someone came from a distance and needed surgery, we would try to encourage them to provide a unit of suitable blood. Slowly, but surely, we had a steady supply of blood.

In time, the blood bank would come into its own. One day, two very similar emergencies arrived in. If ever a veteran was needed, this was the time. Sr Petria was away on a break, so I was on my own. It began with a classical obstetric emergency. A woman presented, bleeding heavily from a placenta praevia. This is where the placenta is situated below the baby, rather than to the side. As the pregnancy proceeds, the risk of a heavy placental bleed increases dramatically. This is what happened to this unfortunate lady. She was in shock by the time she reached us, and at serious risk of dying. I could still get a faint foetal heartbeat, so there was a possibility of both mother and baby surviving. Before we had created the blood bank, this lady and her baby would have died. Now, with instant access to blood, we could attempt to resuscitate her. We then made arrangements for an emergency section.

Just as we were organising this, another obstetric emergency arrived. A second woman was brought in with the exact same diagnosis. She too was extremely ill and bleeding heavily. We had to quickly divert our energies to save her life. Once again, with the assistance of our new blood bank, we were able to stabilise this lady. Sadly, in her case, there was no foetal heart audible. Her baby was already dead.

We performed an emergency section on the first lady, who was now stabilised. We delivered the baby, dealt with the placenta, intubated the baby, who was born flat, and completed the operation, allowing her and her baby back to the ward to recuperate. Both survived.

There was no rest for the wicked. The second lady was still in danger, from persistent bleeding from her placenta. We performed an emergency section on this lady, removed the placenta, sadly delivered the dead baby and completed the operation. She made a full recovery.

It took over eight hours, but by the end we had two live mothers and one live baby. It was one of those times when all the hard work paid off. It took a team to achieve this: those who made the blood bank work, the nurses and medical assistants, the theatre staff who assisted in performing the operations and the midwives who had by now been taught the necessary skill to intubate the baby who survived. Finally, all of those who had taught me how to recognise and manage placenta praevia back in Holles Street and, more importantly, in Kabanga.

I had never been prouder of us all than when those women and that baby left the hospital alive. Life is about teamwork.

The blood bank was a great success. No longer were mothers dying before we could help them; they were surviving and thriving. Every time this happened, I rejoiced. I may not have been the most popular figure, especially among the men who resented this change, but that was of little consequence. It was about saving lives. It was also wonderful to see children survive who might otherwise have died from severe anaemia.

My next task was to try and improve the lot of those who were struggling with the consequences of old polio. It was such an upsetting sight from the beginning. All of those beautiful boys and girls attacked by polio at a young age and, now in adolescence, with fixed contractures in one or both legs. To paint a picture, grab your leg and bend it at complete right angles so that your foot is now behind your thigh. Now try to walk. The best these children could do was either hop or use a stick as a crutch, and somehow make their way along the rutted tracks around their homes.

An idea began to form when I heard that an American orthopaedic surgeon was going to be available for a short time to perform any operations beyond our capability. Slowly the pieces began to come together. I had a chat with one of the MMM sisters who could lay out the relevant physio exercises. The main issue was going to be providing the callipers and other necessary equipment. I thought of our good friend Peter Mumford, an English volunteer staying with the Anglican community in the neighbouring village of Kasulu and who had originally been recruited to set up a chicken farm. He was amazingly talented with his hands and could make whatever we needed.

Dates were organised, and the children were brought in. With the most incredible surgery, the American doctor loosened the terrible contractures that had crippled these children, allowing their limbs to be straightened. These limbs were then placed in callipers made by Peter. Using crutches also designed by him, these children began to stand on two legs for the first time in their lives. The physiotherapist would in time teach them how to walk.

It was truly a modern miracle. Bit by bit, the lame began to walk, beginning with faltering steps. They would never look back. All it took was the hard work of caring, dedicated people to make it happen. What a joy to see these young people upright and looking forward not to a life of constant limitation, but one where they would in time be able to achieve their potential.

Another area of need centred around those children who struggled with facial scars. It was Sr Kieran who first approached me about them, the terrible facial scarring and disfigurement the result of falling into an open fire after an epileptic seizure. The deep burns suffered led to deformities of the facial skin. Only Sr Kieran would care enough to either notice or want to do something to help them.

I was not an expert in how to manage such scarring. We came up with a plan. Once we had removed the worst of the scar tissue, I would surgically, with the assistance of some fine equipment, remove skin from other parts of the child's body and graft it onto their face. Sr Kieran would then take on the task of dressing the grafted areas involved. This was the most delicate part of the whole operation, and the most important. Sr Kieran was simply a magician, so I knew these children were in safe hands. We began to perform these 'minor' procedures on some of the children and, buoyed by positive results, we continued.

It was lovely to see the changes in children who would otherwise have had to face a lifetime of disfigurement and probable emotional consequences as a result. More and more,

Sr Kieran and myself were bonding and becoming a really effective unit, especially when it came to care.

But as was frequently the case, situations regularly presented themselves where events would be out of my control. This would often involve some lateral thinking, as proved in the case of the Black & Decker.

It was like a scene from a horror movie. A local man, who was a diabetic, had gone into a coma due to a head injury. He was clearly dying. On examining the back of his eyes, there was evidence that his brain was under severe pressure from oedema (fluid swelling). We had no scanning facility to clarify the situation, so such assessments were clinically based.

By sheer chance, the flying doctor surgeons had flown in that day. I asked one of them to take a look at the man to see if there was anything we could do. Following a detailed examination, he shook his head. 'We could probably make an opening into the skull, to relieve the oedema causing this pressure, but we lack the relevant surgical instruments.'

I asked him what he would need. He explained that at the very least, he would require a drill.

I thought of my good friend Tommy, the electrician, and wondered whether we could use his Black & Decker drill. On consultation, the surgeon agreed that this might work, but that it would have to be completely sterilised. We went ahead and began the process. We agreed that the surgery would take place the following morning.

I was very uneasy about this upcoming procedure. Together with the nurse on duty that night, we decided that we would pour in large amounts of steroids intravenously, in the hope of shrinking the oedema, which was slowly killing this man.

Somebody up there was looking out for him, because this last-ditch therapy worked. Towards morning, he slowly began to come around. Whether it was the steroids or not, I will never know. Thankfully, neither will I ever know what would have happened if we'd had to use the Black & Decker drill.

The man made a full recovery and Tommy got his drill back.

Another memory that haunts me, but does not have such a miraculous ending, involves treating a boy with rabies. I had handled crashes, epidemics, obstetric and surgical emergencies, amputations, panga (machete) injuries to head and abdomen, spears in the chest, men and women dying following being 'bewitched' by witch doctors, every type of tropical illness, severe trauma and 90 per cent burns, to name but a few, but this particular death was truly horrendous.

Rabies is a virus that attacks the brain. It is caused by a bite from an infected animal which passes an RNA virus, of the rhabdovirus group, into the person bitten. The rabies virus is carried by wild animals, foxes and especially wild dogs. It is occasionally found across the plains of northern Europe and more commonly in Africa, South-East Asia and Latin America. In Tanzania, it was not an illness one encountered regularly. If a person was bitten by an infected wild animal or rabid dog, we had the capacity to vaccinate them in time. The virus has a long incubation period that could take from one to three months, usually dependent on how close the bite is to the brain. We would on occasion vaccinate someone over a four-week period if they were bitten by a suspect animal. This vaccination would prevent the disease from infecting their brain. It is an illness that few doctors will ever see. I knew the theoretical physical symptoms, but never thought that I would see them.

This adolescent boy had been bitten by a rabid dog, but he was not vaccinated in time. He was already in the final throes of the illness and it was clear that there was nothing we could do but make him as comfortable as possible.

I will never forget his screams or his death. He began to develop muscle spasms so severe that we had to strap him down for his own safety. His face began to take on the shape of a wild animal, something I had only read about in textbooks. He was foaming at the mouth and trying to bite anyone who came close to him. But it was his screams that still haunt me. He survived for several days, and no matter where you were on the compound, they could be heard.

We injected large amounts of tranquillisers and other drugs to try and ease his passing, but nothing made any difference. Finally, the poor boy went into a coma and died. I have never felt so helpless. For all of the developments in medicine, we are still vulnerable to these terrible viruses, as we experienced with Covid-19.

What made this death so tragic, apart from the boy's age, was that it was entirely preventable. That was one of the lessons of this harsh environment. So many of the illnesses that kill are preventable. Heeding Sr Kieran's advice helped me cope with this situation. My task was to be there for this boy and his family, and to help them as much as I could. The rest was outside of my control.

CHAPTER 21

## *The Final Months*

Imagine if you bought a few packets of sausages and rashers and began to divide them into small sections, storing them carefully in the freezer, to be taken out only on special occasions. Your family and friends would become worried about your sanity. But this is what happened in practice when living in rural Tanzania.

Every three months, the flying doctors would come to see us. They were a lovely group of specialists, whom we came to rely on. But their medical skill was not the sole reason we looked forward to their arrival. Joe, the pilot, was a fellow countryman and would always make a beeline to see us, and we became great friends. He was especially welcome as he would bring with him some badly needed supplies from Nairobi, where food was readily available. Rashers, sausages and all kinds of treats were gratefully received; we stashed them away, like squirrels with nuts, to savour over the following three months.

We also could not have survived without the kindness of so many people back home.

Following the tea-chest debacle, and a series of frantic letters, the parcels began to arrive. My father, so against our coming, was overwhelmed by the outpouring of goodwill from groups such as the Lions in Thurles. They took an active interest in what we were doing and forwarded food and much-needed supplies on a regular basis. Brenda's family and my own began to send clothes, food and other supplies. What was particularly helpful was clothes for Lara, who was growing rapidly by the day.

The local doctors in Thurles put together parcels with vital drugs and medicines for the hospital. We began to distribute what we could to other local hospitals, who were also short of supplies. All of these parcels had to be sewn into special packets to prevent them from being pilfered on the long journey from Ireland. Without this steady stream of support, we would have been unable to last the pace. 'No man is an island' is an oft-used expression. Never was this as true as in Kabanga.

The same expression could be used in a different context when describing our interactions with Fr Chevalier.

There is something about the game of chess. I am not a fan of board games, even less so of card games, such as bridge. There is, however, much you can learn about a person by playing a game of chess with them. It can tell you a lot about how they think and operate.

One great lesson from chess is the importance of being strategic in your thinking. You have to learn to accept the loss of a key piece if, in the long run, it puts you in a better position to win the game. In Kabanga, there were few who were interested in chess. But every now and then, there would be a knock at the door, usually in the late evening. Standing there, chess board nestled under his armpit, would be the padre.

French in origin, Fr Chevalier was a priest whose flock was out in the wilderness. He was tall, lean and gentle. He revealed to me, on one occasion, that he was the only survivor of a chaplain group accompanying the troops who landed on the beaches of Normandy on D-day. This amazing priest would carry a sick member of his flock down from the hills for medical treatment in the hospital. A few games of chess could be had after his patient was safely deposited. It didn't matter who won or lost. It was about the company. He must have been incredibly lonely out there on his own. The chess was an opportunity for human connection.

Loneliness is all around us. Chess was his way of breaching the gap. It was an honour and a privilege to be in the presence of this genuinely spiritual man. I hope he found another fellow chess traveller after my departure.

It was sometimes easy to forget, while safely ensconced in the compound in Kabanga and having a genteel game of chess with a friendly priest, that we were in an area where danger lurked in every shadow and around every corner. You could never let your guard down, and woe betide if you did. This stark reality was laid bare the night I met the leopard.

The leopard is one of the big-five wild animals in Tanzania, a fearsome predator who could rip open the head of a baboon with a single swipe of a powerful paw. A puny human like myself would never have stood a chance. It was late October 1980, not long after our trip through the Serengeti. I was on duty that night. It was my custom when performing night rounds, or returning from an emergency, to take a shortcut through the garden. I could, of course, have taken my trusty Beetle and driven over and back. But we were in a secure compound, so danger was the furthest thing from my mind. On this fateful night, I was returning from a late visit to the hospital. It was dark, so I was carrying my torch and case.

It was my amygdala that saved me. Buried in my emotional limbic system on both sides of my brain lies this ancient, but vital, organ. It has the job of scanning the environment, seeking out danger and acting at lightning speed to prepare my body to face it. The amygdala is in charge of our inner stress system and has a huge say in our lives, even if we are oblivious to its actions.

We are all familiar with 'fight or flight' and understand that they represent the human response to danger. Few of us get it fully right. It should be 'freeze, fight or flight'. Boy, does this minor adjustment make a difference. It certainly did for me that night, and I am grateful to this day that my amygdala understood the nuance. Contrary to general opinion, the first response of both animals and humans to what is perceived as a major threat is to freeze. It is now seen as the most basic of all physical responses to danger and is triggered by the amygdala.

The idea is to give the body and brain the time to assess danger. As we freeze, the amygdala rapidly sends information to our adrenal stress glands (one over each kidney) to pump out one of two hormones. The first is called adrenaline. This is the so-called flight response, where the decision is to run, and quickly. The second is called noradrenaline. This is where you are forced to face the threat head-on. It is the fight response. Over the aeons, the amygdala has very sensibly come to regard the former as the safer option. Would you seriously consider tackling a leopard?!

Before I fully registered that there was a leopard right there, I froze and turned my torch towards the ground. Then I was hit with this wave of physical symptoms: shaking, sweating, dry mouth, tensed muscles, stomach in knots, a pounding heart rate and rapid breathing, all combined with a sense of total dread. Only then, to my horror, did I see the leopard pacing slowly across the garden, straight in front of me.

It was only later that I would understand what was happening. The fast heart rate and rapid breathing were preparing me to run. As was the blood being taken out of my gut and mouth and sent to my muscles. Even though I was primed to run – and boy was I primed – the amygdala refused to let me move, but continued the freeze response until the leopard had advanced twenty or more paces, slinking along, silent and deadly. Finally, it released me to run for the door of the house. Crashing inside, I tried to explain to Brenda that I had encountered a leopard. She thought I was hallucinating. Ten minutes later, the physical symptoms had ceased as the danger was gone.

The leopard was shot the following morning in the local village. He was old, no longer physically capable of taking down game, and had come into the compound seeking easier prey, domestic or human. Only for my amygdala, it could have turned out differently. My amygdala and I have been the best of friends ever since!

Decades later, when explaining to people who are struggling with panic attacks and phobias what is happening to them physically, I use this leopard example to demonstrate how our amygdala works in practice. These conditions are caused by the amygdala firing incorrectly, as it 'thinks' there is a danger, leading to adrenaline rushes. It is amazing how a full explanation, and teaching people how to manage these symptoms using a technique called flooding, has transformed the lives of so many. Flooding is where we learn to go with the physical symptoms, allowing them to wash over us like water from a shower. Most people fight them, which triggers the amygdala to fire more, which in turn worsens the attack. Learning to go with the symptoms teaches the amygdala to switch off quickly and to down-regulate future responses.

From that night onwards, I also made a pragmatic decision to take the Beetle whenever there was a night-time emergency. Once almost bitten, twice shy.

This became the norm while living in Africa. We seemed to lurch from one crisis to the next. Learning to deal with the unexpected became second nature, as we were about to experience.

•

Babies have a timeline of their own. And so it was with the birth of our second child. We had discovered in June that Brenda was pregnant, but without scans to confirm dates, we had clinically estimated that the baby would be born sometime in February 1981. But on 23 December 1980, Brenda went into premature labour. As we were heading into the night-time, I asked one of the nurse-midwives to be on hand to deliver the baby in the labour ward.

Then another emergency occurred and the midwife had to depart suddenly to deal with it, leaving Brenda and me alone, with only a bush lamp for light and the fireflies around us. No sooner had the midwife gone than Brenda began to get heavy contractions, and I found myself delivering by bush lamp our second child, Daniel. It was a classic case of 'life happening when we are busy planning for it'. His arrival into the world was an amazing bonding experience for all of us.

It was immediately apparent that he was premature, probably thirty-two weeks at the most. Back in the early eighties that was considered significantly premature. The first concern was that he might develop respiratory distress syndrome, where a premature baby struggles to breathe as the lungs are too immature. This would have been managed back home by placing him in a ventilator in a special neonatal unit. Fortunately, this was not the case for Daniel.

There were other challenges facing us. It is routine to keep a premature baby warm in an incubator in a neonatal unit. Then, there was the inability of a premature baby to ingest the normal amount of milk, breast or formula. Daniel needed tube feeding.

As always, Sr Kieran came to the rescue. We decided that the baby would be comfortably swaddled in his cot with hot-water bottles. We started three-hourly feeds through a nasogastric tube. Brenda came home that day. Sr Kieran and Brenda continued the three-hourly feeds for the next number of weeks, until gradually the baby grew strong enough to change him onto normal feeds.

I remember that Christmas fondly, in stark contrast to the one which had preceded it. Peter, who by then had become a good friend, had made Lara a really beautiful wooden toy car, painted yellow and brown, and which captured all of our hearts. We now had the best present of all, a new brother for Lara. Peter also brought a chicken for dinner and we had managed to lay our hands on new supplies of food. It turned out to be a Christmas of joy and excitement, one never to be forgotten.

After a number of weeks Daniel was baptised in our house, with Sr Kieran acting in lieu of his godmother and Tommy in lieu of his godfather. Daniel was Sr Kieran's special project. To this day, I believe she is still watching over him.

Sadly, soon it was time to leave Kabanga. It was the summer of 1981. Before we left, I helped out with the establishment of a nutrition clinic. One more tragedy was to befall us before our departure, which was very sad and happened towards the end of our stay. A young woman was brought in to the hospital, extremely ill. It was the lady who had been our source of potatoes at the local market. She was dying from advanced open TB. Despite our best efforts, this lovely lady died, leaving behind a young family.

Our time in Tanzania was fast drawing to a close. We had made so many friends, amongst the hospital staff, the MMM community, the White Fathers and the Anglican community in Kasulu. We found it hard to say our goodbyes. Our beloved Beetle went back to the White Fathers. We said farewell to Tommy, who had returned with an assistant following his accident, and also to the Van Deuns. The most difficult goodbye of all was to my dear friend Sr Kieran. Little did I realise that our paths would again cross in the future.

I do remember her taking me aside before our departure and once again sharing some words of wisdom. She counselled that I had 'done my bit for the global south' and that it was 'time to take my family home and look after them'. What she was saying indirectly was that our time in Africa was now over and that a new chapter would begin.

We had left for Tanzania with a small baby, only a few months old. Little did we think then we would be returning with another, who by this stage was six months old. It was time to go.

But Africa was not yet finished with us. We decided to travel via neighbouring Burundi with the Van Deuns to board a flight from the capital. We got as far as the border. There we encountered the usual African story – your papers are not in order. Stalemate ensued. We were unsure as to whether this was simply normal bureaucracy or a veiled attempt at bribery. You were always afraid to presume the latter in case it worsened the situation. Some hours later, for no obvious reason, the block was lifted and we arrived in Burundi.

After a few days, we boarded a plane headed for Belgium. My most vivid memory of the flight was landing for refuelling in Entebbe, Uganda, with the army in full gear escorting us into the airport. When we finally did take off it seemed as if the plane was travelling so low across the water that we would ditch. The nose began to slowly rise. The bush family were heading back to Ireland, their African adventure coming to a close.

Tanzania has progressed enormously since 1979, both economically and socially. Life expectancy levels have increased greatly. It remains one of the most peaceful countries in Africa, and now has a multi-party political system and experiences steady annual growth. Access to water, education and health services has improved substantially over the last few decades. It has been especially successful in introducing universal primary education for all. There has been a decline in both infant and child mortality rates under five. One exciting statistic for me was that 50 per cent of Tanzanian women now give birth in a public health clinic. What a change, even if maternal mortality figures are still problematic.

A third of the country, however, still lives in poverty, and there are gaps in the medical, energy and educational fields, especially in rural areas where three-quarters of the ever-increasing population (3 per cent growth per year) live. Kasulu alone is now populated by over 250,000 people. Although transport links have greatly improved, only a small percentage of the road system is properly paved. Over the last few decades, the MMMs have handed over hospitals and clinics under their care. The health system has greatly improved, but there are still many challenges including staffing, resources and supply lines. Tanzania, like the rest of Africa, is also struggling with the impact of climate change, with a reduction in rainfall affecting electricity supplies and agricultural yields. This, allied to a rapidly expanding population, may be the greatest threat to its onward growth.

Some of the largest zinc deposits in the world have been discovered and are now being mined in an area a few hundred kilometres from Kabanga. There have also been major gas and potential oil reserves discovered offshore. The country is also rich in other minerals. These discoveries will lead to greater prosperity, but it will take some time to come to fruition. The tourist sector is also growing rapidly, now accounting for 18 per cent of GDP.

Kabanga Hospital is still there, having been passed over to the diocese by the MMMs. It has grown and developed. Alongside the other district and regional hospitals, it now has a treatment catchment area of over 3.5 million people. It is mainly run by Tanzanian specialists and is contributing greatly to the lives of the local people.

I remember my time in Kabanga with great fondness. It was there that I truly learnt the skills of emotional resilience and how to adapt to whatever life would throw at me. How to cope when life was tough. I discovered the importance of empathy, compassion, teamwork and delegation. Most of all, I realised the importance of unconditional self-acceptance, wisdom and meaning. The lessons learnt there were to form the bedrock for my future and continue to do so to this day. Kabanga changed me more than I changed Kabanga.

PART FIVE

*Donegal*

# CHAPTER 22

## *A New Beginning*

For all of the gifts that my time in Africa brought into my life, there was one thing missing. I struggled for the whole period to stay in touch with my feminine side. To survive in such a harsh environment required me to show tenacity and stoicism. I found it difficult to master Swahili, the language of the country and region. All consultations were carried out in Swahili through an interpreter, and this linguistic divide hindered the development of a genuine empathetic bond with those I cared for. I even found it more difficult to read their body language, given the different cultural and social norms.

I have always believed that each of us has a masculine and feminine side, which varies enormously from person to person. In my case, I am more comfortable in tapping into the feminine. To me, the feminine means to be intuitive, nurturing, patient and sympathetic, although I understand that it means different things to different people. It was only when I returned to Ireland and embarked on a new career as a GP that I realised just how important these traits were in my chosen role in the community. They allowed me to be a better listener, more empathetic, compassionate and caring, and emotionally more nuanced. I have often wondered if it was this side to me that encouraged Sr Kieran to advise that my stay in Africa was over and it was time to begin anew at home? Did she sense that my real strengths might lie here in Ireland? We had toyed with the idea of extending our stay in Africa, but had come to the conclusion that our time in Africa was now done. Sr Kieran felt the same.

Our arrival home in June 1981 was joyful; there was much to catch up on with loved ones. But we also felt strange and a little adrift. We were not the same people who had departed two years previously. We had lived many lives in the meantime. Even physically I had changed; I had lost over two stone in weight and I had also sadly lost my mad mop of hair following two years of anti-malaria prevention treatment.

It felt overwhelming to enter a shop and actually experience choice. In Tanzania, it was about survival; choice was not an option. Brenda and I found ourselves on our return struggling to make the smallest of decisions. Ireland seemed like a magical place where you could get anything. Something else, however, was also subtly occurring. Our experience was unique to us, there was no one to share it with and nobody could understand what we had been through, what we had witnessed.

If you chat to a soldier returning from conflict or an aid worker back from a war-torn or disaster-struck country, they will all agree. You are coming from a different world, one that people simply cannot relate to, despite best efforts. We found ourselves shutting down and ceasing to discuss what we had seen or done.

# BENEATH THE SURFACE

We had no home. Brenda's parents Nicholas and Ciss took us in to their home in Eyrecourt in County Galway. And what a challenge for them, four extra bodies. My parents were glad to see us home safely and were proud of the work we had done. Brenda's brother Gerard, still despairing of my driving techniques, had managed to locate a second-hand car for us. We had little money and few prospects. But this was about to change.

The Ireland we returned to in the early eighties was a bleak place. It was a period of unemployment and prolonged recession, with many people emigrating for work. There were few houses being built and many businesses went bust. Vacant shop fronts and boarded-up windows dominated towns around the country. It was also a time of intense political turmoil, when the Troubles up north were dominating the news headlines. There was a general mood of pessimism and despair throughout the land. It was especially difficult to find a job as a young doctor embarking on a new career. My heart was set on becoming a GP, but there were few opportunities available, especially for someone without GP experience. I had been in contact with Jimmy and Ignatius, but apart from offering a locum position, they were unable to help. The other option was to move to Canada, where they were always seeking doctors.

I was becoming increasingly concerned as the weeks went by. I had written a number of articles about my experience of working in a rural African hospital for the late Dr John O'Connell, founder of the *Irish Medical Times* or *IMT*, a weekly newspaper for doctors. He had been very good to me when I was in Tanzania. I wrote to him now for assistance in securing a GP position and he placed a massive free ad at the back of the paper for several weeks running, which would be extremely unusual at the time. From this came a number of job offers from around the country. I am grateful for his assistance as it gave me the start I required.

One of the calls I received was from a senior GP called Brendan, based in Ardara, County Donegal. I can remember excitedly talking to him on the phone in the small alcove in Eyrecourt about a potential job opportunity. I drove to Ardara and met him in the local hotel to interview for the post. He was offering me the opportunity to become an assistant GP. We immediately clicked and I accepted the offer, and so Brenda and I set about moving our little family to rural Donegal. Brenda was delighted that we would not have to emigrate to Canada. Although it would be a distance from her family, she was really happy with the prospect of the move. It was to be a most important five years. It allowed us space and time to recover and heal, and to begin our journey into the world of general practice.

•

Nicholas Lahart despaired of his son-in-law when it came to packing a car. With his assistance, however, we eventually loaded up our paltry worldly possessions and began the long trek to Donegal. I can still remember driving over the winding mountain road from Donegal Town, stopping at a spectacular viewing point where we could see the village of Ardara below. I can clearly recall the flocks of sheep that wandered across this road. Ardara was a small town with a population of around eight hundred people. It was nestled into the lee of the mountains on one side and the sea on the other. In winter, only the locals remained, but when the summer months rolled around the population swelled massively thanks to an influx of tourists from all over Ireland and the UK, and it became a bustling place with lots of entertainment and activity. It was full of tourist shops selling knitwear, in particular. The main industries at the time were weaving and knitwear. There was one hotel, and the usual supermarket, post office, bank and of course the church. There were also a number of pubs and restaurants.

We descended into our new town with much excitement, arriving at the house where we would spend the next few years. It belonged to a local shopkeeper, Jim, a native of the town. His wife, Peg, ran a bed and breakfast across the road from the shop. Jim was a well-known character in the town with fixed views on just about everything. He was also a chain-smoker. He was very kind to our little family unit and took us under his wing. The house was situated in a very old building facing the square, or the Diamond as it was known locally. On one side of the building, Jim ran his shop, selling just about everything. On the other side, connected to the shop, was our new home, which we rented.

I was a product of Thirty-Six and both Brenda and I were veterans of Tanzania, so we had good survival skills. The kitchen had the all-original big black solid-fuel range. This provided heating and a place to cook. Every morning, Brenda would coax the turf-fuelled range back to life. There was a small front room on the other side, where I would see patients on call. Upstairs were some bedrooms, one of which became a large workroom/playroom for Brenda and the kids. At the back of the house was a yard. We were in the heart of everything, post office on one side, shop on the other, pharmacy across the road, surgery around the corner.

Jim's family became our family, especially to Lara and Daniel. He began every day smoking like a trooper, combing the daily newspaper. Geoffrey, who ran the pharmacy across the road, became a close confidante over the years. Beside the pharmacy was the hairdresser's.

The building beside us was the local post office and telephone exchange, a place where Daniel would very happily spend much of his day as he grew older. One of the girls in the post office took a real shine to him, so had goodies for him on the many occasions he pottered in to see them. The telephone exchange played a vital role in the town. It is hard in an era of mobile phones and instant connection to visualise a time when you would have to go through a local exchange to make a call to anywhere in the country. Sometimes you would even have to book a call. Up the road from the house was the local hotel, and we became great friends with the owners. This was Lara's go-to, as she became good friends with the owners' daughter.

It was so safe. We never locked the front door or the car. It would have been unheard of for anyone to break in to either. Although we were, and would always be considered, outsiders, we were quickly absorbed into the life of the community.

# CHAPTER 23

## *The Surgery*

I will never forget my first day in the surgery in Ardara. I was initially struck by the opening times. While the rest of the world might be up and busy by eight in the morning, this sleepy village was much slower to come to life. The clinic opened at 10.30 a.m. We would pop in to morning mass and then begin the day. As a result of the late start, the clinics would extend further into the evenings.

The initial premises we worked from was situated around the corner from Jim's house, so we didn't have to travel far. I recall with fondness the open fireplace in the surgery room. One of the tasks of Kathleen, the secretary/receptionist, when the weather became colder, was to light a fire before the clinic started. It was so cosy and intimate in the wintertime.

It was all very low-key and relaxed. After the frantic, life-challenging conditions in Tanzania, it seemed tame in comparison. In retrospect, maybe that was for the best. One could not keep working at that rate. The majority of patients had medical cards and came from all over the district.

It was a sharp learning curve. I had to gear back my expectations of what would be possible in general practice. This took some time. Most conditions we were dealing with were routine. Suturing wounds, sick children, high blood pressure, diabetes, heart conditions, arthritis, URTIs (upper respiratory tract infections), UTIs (urinary tract infections), back pain, pregnancy checks, vaccination, phlebotomy – these were the norm. There was no such thing as a practice nurse, so the GP did it all. For emergencies or more complex cases, there was the regional hospital in Letterkenny, a number of kilometres away. Because of the distance, we dealt with most issues ourselves. Brendan, the senior GP, was excellent at chiropractic techniques and injections, in particular. He was a wonderful teacher and I learnt much from him.

As the junior in the practice, it fell to me to perform most of the routine monthly calls. This was where I fell in love with Donegal. Ardara itself was like the hub at the centre of a wheel where the spokes connect. One spoke went out to Portnoo and Rosbeg, two lovely seaside areas. Another went out to Loughros Point, and what a beautiful drive it was along the stunning estuary; it was one of my favourite places.

Another spoke brought you out to the amazing white sands and caves of Maghera, where an early-morning walk is as close to paradise as you can get. Along this road was a cascading waterfall, and when you got to Maghera, a winding narrow road called Granny's Pass led up into the mountains, to where more of our patients lived.

Finally, there was a road that brought you down into the enormous valleys at the foothills of the mountains towering over the area. Then it was up the Glengesh Pass, a steep, winding, terrifying route, similar to Corkscrew Hill in County Clare, only more dramatic. When snow and ice arrived each winter, it was a nightmare. One-third of our patients resided on the other side of the pass, up in the mountains.

I felt such a great sense of freedom when I was out in my car and visiting patients, most of whom were extremely old. Eighty or ninety years old was the average age and I loved them all. They were such fascinating people – always grateful for your visits and keen to impart their wisdom. The purpose of these calls was to check on the person, perform some physical examinations and ensure that they were on the right medication. In retrospect, the calls were as much social as medical, as most people were extremely isolated, and many were lonely. It was so important to them that someone cared, and was happy to listen to their issues and was just there for them. It taught me that being a family doctor was more than simply being a physical healer. It would involve taking care of the whole person. In the winter, I learned to leave them prophylactic supplies of antibiotics for times when it would be impossible to reach them.

There was a lady in her late eighties who lived in a cottage on Loughros Point. I would come to the open door and a cloud of smoke from the turf fire would greet me. Situated beside the fire, in the midst of swirling smoke, I would find herself. It was like a scene from another era. With the big kettle on the stove and metal utensils hanging over the fire, this lady would be happily rocking away in her chair, so content. She loved to have a chat.

These regular house calls connected me with the most vulnerable elderly folk in this vast area, who did need someone to keep an eye on them. They are one of my most cherished recollections from my Donegal years. I found that it was easy to create a nurturing, empathetic bond with these people. I loved to listen to their stories and many became friends.

A classic example of this in practice was my visit to two older men, brothers, who lived in the most idyllic rural setting. It was to be the scene of some of the happiest moments experienced in Ardara, and some of the saddest. The brothers were of a good age, both healthy and reasonably fit. I had to clamber over stiles and a gate to reach them. They lived surrounded by geese, chickens and donkeys, and a beautiful apple orchard. They survived, as many did at the time, by doing some home weaving. This was a widespread occupation right across the district. You could hear the constant clackety-clack of the machines as you approached the house.

It was one of my favourite calls and I became friends with both men; it was a pleasure to look after them. Many times when I visited, if apples were in season, I would be brought down to the orchard and given a large bag to bring home with me. Then one day, a call came in from the guards to inform me that they had found both of them dead. I was asked to visit the house to confirm their deaths. There was no sign of foul play. We worked out what had most likely occurred. One brother had taken a massive stroke and died. The second brother found him and dropped dead of a heart attack from the shock. It was so sad and yet so beautiful. They had been so close together in life. In some senses, it was appropriate that even in death they would also be together.

Some of the more light-hearted moments in Ardara related to my dealings with the local parish priest, Fr Mac. We would often bump into each other while both of us were out on routine calls. A tall, stern man with thick black glasses, a deadpan face and a dark sense of humour, he was an institution in the area. He was there before I came, and was still active on my departure.

He would have done well as an undertaker; his morbid humour would have carried him far. His masses and sermons were pumped out in the local church with the graveyard beside it. I grew accustomed to his 'positivity' after a while.

He was especially positive and animated each spring. I would meet him emerging from the home of an elderly person, while visiting them on call. He would shake his head sadly. 'It has been a long, hard winter. It is nearly time for the springtime clearance,' he would whisper, and head off.

An abiding Donegal memory was in the company of the great man. One of my favourite patients, an elderly woman who lived on the top of a mountain best accessed via the notorious Granny's Pass, was dying, and her family had reached out for help. She was a sweet lady, whom I had brought Brenda and the children to see at her request. Her time had come and I would not let her down.

Fr Mac contacted me and asked for a lift if I was going to visit her. There was only one problem: it was wintertime and the snow had fallen. Granny's Pass is a narrow, twisty, steep, climbing road, tricky to navigate at the best of times. With snow on the ground, it was a terrifying prospect. If the car slid on the ice, it would be a long way down to the valley below.

The padre was as sanguine as ever. He was strapped into the front seat, with the host resting on his lap. Seeing me gripping the steering wheel for dear life, anxiety written on my face, he tapped me on the shoulder and hit me with one of the great one-liners of my career. 'Don't worry, Harry,' he exclaimed, holding up the host in front of him. 'If we go, we will be in good company!' What more was there to say?

We did make it to see the lady in time, who subsequently passed away peacefully, and we did manage to make it back down Granny's Pass unscathed. Maybe we really were in good company that day.

The people of Ardara were so kind and showed their appreciation of the work we put in. They were especially good to us each Christmas. The door would open and in came the gifts. From whole fish to sides of meat and bottles of alcohol of every description. Even doing rounds at Christmas, there was offer after offer of some 'hard stuff' to thank you for your service.

There is one gift that stands out. There were three well-known characters — two brothers and a sister — renowned for 'minding their money'. If one or other was unwell, there was a slew of cars outside the house, filled with relations who hoped someday to be remembered in their will. They were now of advanced age, but still busy doing the home weaving. They were most afraid of the tax man calling, so every knock on the door was greeted with suspicion.

One day, the sister became unwell and a call came for me to visit. I remember coming to the front door and knocking. After a frantic few minutes, with low voices and much rustling, the door was finally opened and a face peered out. 'It's you, Doc?' asked the voice, and on verification of my identity I was quickly whisked in to see the sick lady. I made the relevant diagnosis, laid out a course of treatment and arranged to see her a week later.

The day of the check-up visit arrived and I was once again admitted to the inner lair. The sister was now making a good recovery. There was a huddle in the corner. The eldest brother, clearly the boss, approached me. 'Doctor, because of your great kindness to our sister, we have something for you.' He then asked me to follow him to a large shed out the back. At this stage, I was intrigued, but well aware of just how momentous an occasion this was turning out to be. A gift from this trio was indeed a rare phenomenon.

There followed a couple of minutes of rustling, with his back to me, and then he turned around with a beaming smile. 'We would like you to have these.'

He then presented me with a small paper bag of potatoes. I almost collapsed with the shock, but managed to control myself until I returned to the car, where I proceeded to laugh uncontrollably for five minutes. It is possible that I was the only person in the previous fifty years who had received such a gift. The potatoes were lovely, but just about covered a meal.

Such gifts, however, did not make being on urgent call any easier. One of the most challenging aspects of rural general practice in Donegal was the amount of time spent on such calls. I was well used, both from hospital medicine and Tanzania, to hard work and being regularly on call. However, I found the on-call rota in Donegal especially tiring.

I was on call every second week and, when Brendan was away on holidays, continuously for some weeks. This was exhausting. For twenty-four hours, day and night, and including weekends, you were fielding a constant flow of calls coming into the practice, seeking assistance. These could relate to any medical condition, but especially to sick children.

Then there was the terrain. It was such a vast area. The roads were narrow, twisty and difficult to traverse, especially at night. One-third of the practice was over the Glengesh Pass and this was of particular concern in the winter months. My car was no match for the terrain we had to cover. There was also no GPS then, so locating patients was a nightmare, especially in the dark.

The next difficulty lay with communications. There were no mobile phones. You could have gone out at three in the morning to see a sick patient, along one of the peninsulas or over the pass, and on returning home be told that there was another call back in the same vicinity. This was frustrating and exhausting in equal measure. It meant that hours were spent on the road, often unnecessarily.

But it was the weather that broke my spirit and really accelerated our eventual departure from this lovely, idyllic spot. If it was raining in Dublin during the winter, it would usually be snowing in Ardara. From November right through to the spring, snow and ice were constant companions. It meant that being on call was often a nightmarish ordeal; you'd be in fear of your life on some of the higher passes. Then there were the massive storms that would hit the area, with winds taking the slates off roofs and rain thundering down. On one occasion in the middle of the night, I had to literally float the car across a flooded area to get to a sick person.

Finally, there was the exhaustion. It is difficult to imagine the levels of fatigue that accompanied being constantly on call, having to face into busy clinics the following day. I grew to hate being on call, but it was part of the learning curve if I wanted to become a fully fledged GP.

## BENEATH THE SURFACE

There was one on-call memory that stands out. It was a Sunday afternoon and Ardara was taking on a neighbouring village in a GAA match. It was like being back in Africa. One after another, the victims were brought in. Lacerations, head injuries, limb sprains and fractures. Clearly, it was a grudge match. As always, we patched up and referred on as required. Just a routine afternoon on call.

# CHAPTER 24

# *Donegal Life*

There are moments in life that remain with you forever, like the time I found Sr Kieran with the dying man. Such a moment in Donegal occurred when all four of us were on an evening stroll along one of our favourite looped walks above the town. On another of these regular strolls, Lara had raced ahead and unfortunately run into the back of a scythe being carried by a local man. I remember the hysteria and having to suture her lip myself, not trusting anyone else to do it at the time.

But this particular sunny summer evening was to have a happier ending. Part of the stroll took us by some idyllic fields lit by a slanting evening sun. It was there we encountered a most extraordinary sight. The field was full of sheep, grazing. But what was truly amazing was that there was a rabbit perched on the back of each sheep. If only mobile phones had been around and we could capture the image to prove that it had really happened! It was Mother Nature at its best. It was almost more extraordinary than all of the wildlife we had seen in Africa!

There were other wonderful, memorable moments. One of those related to a special guest who joined us for Christmas dinner every year. When I was out on my routine calls, I visited a man called John, who lived in a mobile home in complete rural isolation. He was an elderly man, with no family or relatives. I came to know him well. It must have been very lonely for him, living in such a remote area with little or no human connection, but he never complained.

At the time, we had a tradition of always inviting someone to share our Christmas dinner. I was really delighted when this lovely man agreed to join us for the festive meal. I would go out and collect him and he always presented himself in his best suit. With lovely twinkling eyes and full of stories, he was a pleasure to have as a guest. He loved spending the day with us, especially with the two children. He enriched the day so much and it was a lesson I never forgot. How opening your house and heart to someone who is lonely, especially at times such as Christmas, brings such happiness to yourself, not to mention being a lifeline for the person who is so isolated.

In time, John too would become unwell and leave us for a better place. But he left behind such beautiful memories. When we eventually moved to a different part of the country, it would be somebody equally special who would fill the empty seat at the table during Christmas.

As much as we loved Ardara, its beautiful scenery and wonderful people, we were becoming increasingly doubtful as to whether it was going to be our long-term home. If I was to consider a move to another area or wanted to become a principal GP in my own right, the Membership of the Royal College of General Practitioners (MRCGP) was a must. It is hard nowadays, accustomed as we are to the presence of the Irish College of GPs (ICGP), to remember a time when there was no such college in existence. In the early eighties, the only option was to become a member of the Royal College of General Practitioners (RCGP) in London.

In 1983, midway through our stint in Donegal, we realised that this was a post-doctorate qualification that I had to acquire in order to progress any further along the general practice route. Most interviews for major posts were decided on whether you had this qualification or not, combined with your years of experience.

To attain the MRCGP was a daunting challenge. You had to first study how the British medical system worked, and then anticipate the myriad of potential exam questions that could be asked. There was a written test, which included a severe multiple-choice exam and some essays. These exams were held in Dublin. If you were successful, then you had to travel to London to face two gruelling face-to-face orals. The failure rate at the time was incredibly high, with many candidates repeating the exam a number of times before being successful.

I was at such a disadvantage, isolated in Donegal, doing a one in two on-call rota while helping to rear two small children. I was also not part of a GP training scheme; such schemes assisted trainees in doing the exam.

I was fortunate, however, in having the support and help of a fellow assistant GP, Dr John Flaherty, who had gone through such a scheme and had successfully passed the exam. He and his wife Margaret were at the time living in Killybegs, and Brenda and I became close friends with them. John would later become a principal GP in Loughrea. I spent at least 50 per cent of my time studying what they were seeking in the exam and the rest researching the topics. I then applied my usual five-step skeleton approach. With heart in mouth, I went to Dublin to sit the exam.

Fortunately, I performed well enough in the written exam to be called to London, with Brenda accompanying me. I remember those few days and how stressed I was. The first question in the initial interview was a no-brainer: 'Is an ECG machine an essential instrument for a modern practice?' The answer, of course, was no, as up to 50 per cent of those with angina have a normal resting ECG.

They then tried to throw me a curveball. The question seemed to be a hypothetical one, about how to manage an acute pneumothorax, which occurs when a hole appears in the lining of the lungs; air pours into the space, collapsing the lung and pushing the heart to one side. In Tanzania, I had encountered this where the cause of the pneumothorax was a spear in the chest, the procedure of which I began to explain. There was a deadly silence, and I was unsure if I had blown it or not. But at the time I simply answered without thinking it through. Was it not obvious that this is what you would do?

The second interview was even more trying. At one point, one of the interviewers asked innocently about the role of the doctor in healing. It was a trick question. Luckily, Brendan and myself had discussed the work of the famous Dr Michael Balint, who believed that the GP was himself part of the cure. I had read some of his work so I was able to discuss this concept: when there is a good interpersonal relationship between the family doctor and the patient, the latter will often open up as to what is going on in their wider world. This might, in some cases, explain the physical symptoms the person is presenting with. It is all about the power of connection and empathy. Even if the doctor has to convey bad news, there is that implicit understanding that the doctor will assist the patient in dealing with the issue. However, the interviewer did not appear happy with my answer, so I thought I had blown this oral as well.

That evening, in our anonymous hotel room in London, I was very down. I woke up drenched in sweat in the middle of the night and told Brenda that I believed I'd blown it with my story about the spear in the chest. To my great surprise and delight, I was subsequently informed that I had passed the exams and orals and was now a Member of the Royal College of General Practitioners. In 2023, I was made an honorary life member.

•

So often in life we reach a crossroads where the route chosen can have a significant bearing on what is to follow. This was where we found ourselves in Donegal after I attained my membership. Should we stay or go? What a momentous decision it was to be. But before that juncture, there would be many twists and turns.

We were overjoyed in 1984 to discover that Brenda was once again pregnant. She attended an obstetrician in Sligo Hospital. All was progressing well, until at twenty-eight weeks her waters broke and she nearly lost the pregnancy. There was only one course open to us. She would have to stay in hospital for several weeks. Brenda's mum, Ciss, arrived on the doorstep to hold the fort until we could come up with a plan. Eventually, the mother of our secretary, Maggie, agreed to look after the children and

Ciss retreated back to Eyrecourt. In time, Brenda was allowed to return home for a short period. None of our children seemed to understand the concept of a normal pregnancy lasting forty weeks and finishing with a full-term baby. They always seemed to be in a hurry. Maybe it was genetic. It also seemed as if their births would inevitably herald the advent of some major change in our lives. The arrival of our third child proved to be no exception. Luckily, Brenda returned to Sligo Hospital in time, where she delivered a baby boy five weeks prematurely in June 1985.

I was present at the birth and witnessed the panic that ensued on his arrival. He was born with the umbilical cord wrapped around his neck, which made his entry into the world a dangerous one. Luckily, he survived his turbulent introduction. We named him Joseph, but he would forever afterwards be called Joe. I do think that Joe's arrival rubber-stamped the decision to move to a new house, but maybe in the long run it was a trigger for our eventual decision to leave Donegal.

If we remained in Ardara, and Brendan was anxious that we would, we could not remain for much longer in Jim's house. The children were getting bigger and we were struggling for space. On the outskirts of town, set on a hill, was a large field overlooking the sea in the distance. The view was stunning. After much haggling, the owner agreed to sell us a plot, and we became the proud owners in 1984. Our first task was to plant trees at the bottom of the site. Our next was to design a house and find a builder. We ended up with a lovely house, with the most wonderful of vistas.

This whole process took some time, however, and it was after Joe's arrival in 1985 before we were ready to move in. We both loved the house and set about turning it into a home. We began to plant shrubs. Something someone had said to me, however, kept coming back to haunt me: 'You can't live on a view.' Fr Martin Brennan, who was still in regular contact with us, had made a similar comment when we'd departed for Donegal: 'I hope you'll be able to cope with the low clouds.' Even though we were happy in this house, there was something missing. In retrospect, I believe that in our hearts we had already begun to move on.

I continued to share the practice with Brendan. Increasingly, he was becoming interested in psychotherapy and was attending a course in Trinity College on a regular basis. On one occasion, I asked him what he was doing on the course. 'We are trying to learn what you already have,' he replied. I believe that he was referring to the concept of empathy, of listening emotionally to what the person was really saying. This was a skill that I think in retrospect I had naturally.

Shortly after moving into our new home, we had some surprise visitors. Peter, who had been such a close friend in Africa and who had assisted us with the vital project that helped children suffering from polio to walk again, had moved to London with his new partner, Sara. While they were with us, they became engaged. We were overjoyed. It was so exciting – to make a commitment to share their lives together and to do so while they were with us. They have remained dear friends and are now retired and living in Cornwall.

The Troubles in Northern Ireland were a constant backdrop to our stay in Ardara and were part of the decision to move from Donegal. There were known republican families in the town. For the most part, however, the Troubles impinged little on our everyday lives, apart from the influx of Catholics around 12 July each year.

There was one notable exception. We loved to go to Dublin for a few nights' break, leaving our children in safe hands. To get to Dublin, we drove through Pettigo and into the six counties, to exit at Butlersbridge in County Cavan. We were always on tenterhooks while in the North, aware of the risks of being in the wrong place at the wrong time. On this particular day, we were coming over the brow of a hill on our journey when the early-morning sun blinded us completely. It could have turned out so differently. Our children could have been left without their parents.

The British army had set up a road block, hidden from us by the blinding sun. The patrol was bristling with guns. Some of the troopers were hidden in the hedges. It was only at the very last second that we saw a flash of steel and screeched to a halt. If we had gone through the block, they would have assumed we were IRA volunteers and opened fire. In those days, if the IRA encountered a road block, they would often try to crash through it, with the soldiers opening fire to prevent this. It took us some time to calm down. I still feel apprehensive entering the North, even though the Troubles are long over.

It made us both realise, however, that we couldn't continue to live our lives like this, in fear of the journey through the North to get to and from Dublin. We were constantly on edge while passing through. Something would have to change.

There are times in our lives when we have to make critical choices – 'moments of truth', you might say. Sometimes these choices shape our futures. Life is, at the best of times, uncertain.

Often we must venture into the unknown, not really sure where it will bring us. This was one of those times.

I was sitting in the surgery when I happened to glance at the *IMT* and noticed that a major General Medical Services (GMS) post, which is in the public health system, was coming up in Drogheda. I returned home to lunch where Brenda had also seen the advert in a copy of the *IMT* sent to the house. She looked at me and I looked at her. Without the need for words, we knew. It was time to go.

On one level, it was sheer madness. We had just built a house and settled in. We had a new baby, along with two small children, one of whom, Lara, was already at school in Ardara. There was a mooting of a partnership agreement with Brendan. How could we even consider a move to the other side of the country and leave this rural tranquillity? But both of us knew, in that moment, that something had changed. Fate was intervening. Was it not Drogheda where the MMMs had been founded and where our journey to Africa had first been initiated? Somehow, the stars in the sky were aligning.

We were missing out on too much, even though we loved the area and its people. We were far from our family and friends. We missed being close to Dublin, which had played such a role in our lives. We realised that the adage was indeed correct: one could not survive on a view. All those realities were present, even if unstated. At the end of the day, it was a decision just waiting to be made.

To attain a major post in those days was amazingly difficult. I attended the interview in Kells, where the North Eastern Health Board was run from. I did so more out of hope than any real expectation. I did a good interview and the panel were deeply affected by my Tanzanian experience. I also had the Royal College membership, which made a major difference. But there were thirty-two other doctors vying for the post, so the chances of success were slim.

One question I always remember from the interview concerned remuneration. I replied that at the end of my time as a doctor, it would never be about how well I had fared financially that would matter to me, but how many people I had been able to help on the journey.

Subsequently, we were devastated to be placed second in the interview panel. However, we had made up our minds at this stage. We would be moving. The question was, where? Some months later, out of the blue, I received the phone call that would change our lives. The first person on the panel had turned down the post and I was now being offered the job. I will never forget the moment of joy when both of us realised that, after all of the hard work, we would be moving to the other side of the country to start our lives afresh. Our dream was about to become a reality.

Saying goodbye to Brendan, his family and all the patients and friends we had made over the previous five years was very difficult. There was shock and disappointment within the local community, and I could understand why. We seemed to have finally settled, especially after building our new house. The patients had come to know and trust me. It was hard to let them down in this way. There were hugs and tears and many goodwill gestures. Leaving them left a gaping hole in my heart.

How could I explain my reasons for leaving? They were so complex and personal. But our minds were made up and so the almighty task of moving us from one side of the country to the other began. What a task it turned out to be. There was one final decision to be made and that involved putting our new house up for sale, a decision which broke our hearts.

It was time then to begin a new phase in our lives, in the ancient historical town of Drogheda. I had learnt so much while in Donegal. What it meant to be a family doctor in an Irish setting. How to listen and emotionally empathise with patients in difficulties. The importance of caring, nurturing and bonding with them. The holistic nature of healing. Most importantly, it allowed me the time and space to reconnect with the feminine side of myself, preparing me for what would lie ahead.

But deep down, despite all these gifts, Donegal revealed to us both that we were urban creatures at heart. It was time to come home to the county where it had all begun.

PART SIX

*Coming Home*

CHAPTER 25

## *Drogheda*

Coming home. Back to where it all began. To County Louth – the 'wee county'. It is hard to believe that it will soon be forty years since our return. So many have come and gone in that time. Countless patients who have entrusted their physical and psychological care to me, a humbling legacy. A period during which our understanding of healing has also been totally transformed. Later, we will reflect more deeply on my own journey of discovery as to what this term truly means. Does it relate to physical wellbeing? Is it emotional wellbeing? Should it encompass both? What do we mean by the term 'holistic'? What is the role of listening? Little did I realise on arriving in Drogheda that four decades later I would still be grappling with these questions.

In the beginning, however, it was about survival. Our survival.

Little did we comprehend just how challenging the task of moving to Drogheda and setting up a new practice was going to be. Maybe that was for the best, or we might never have embarked on the project. But the years of hard work, from the hospital years, to our African adventures, to our time in Donegal, had prepared us for the task. These experiences had made us extremely resilient and accepting of hardship. We knew that hard work and perseverance were needed to achieve your dreams. In another sense, for both of us it felt as if we were finally coming home. We had first met the MMMs in Drogheda, and it felt like a natural decision to put down our roots there. After so many adventures, we had arrived at our final destination.

Back in 1986, the onus was completely on the GP to find a premises and set it up. It was also incumbent on them to find a place for their family and to hire staff to see the patients. In those days, many practices were run single-handed and it was only in major towns that several doctors might be working together in the same surgery. The original doctor whose practice I inherited wanted to work from his old surgery privately and did not want any interaction with us.

Luckily for us, a man called Colm Browne, whose son-in-law Joe was working in a one in two GP rota system with another GP in the area, contacted me and asked if he could assist us in setting up. He was anxious to help, hoping that I would join their rota and take pressure off his son-in-law. A former army commandant, he was now working with an estate agent in Drogheda. Colm was subsequently to become a close friend for life and we owe much to him for his kindness during this period.

There was only one practical problem. There were few suitable buildings available at the time to set up a new practice. There were also hardly any houses for rent or sale. Drogheda in the 1980s was, like the rest of the country, struggling with unemployment and recession. Despite the hard times, it was still a busy place with some family retail businesses in situ for decades. The hospital, which was situated in the heart of the town, was a major employer. There was a clear divide created by the River Boyne which flowed through the town centre. On the southside was the county and diocese of Meath. On the northside lay the county of Louth and the diocese of Armagh, in Northern Ireland. At this stage, there were no retail parks and so the town was always hectic, and car parking was free.

We eventually found one possible office building that might work. It was called Bells House and was a famous landmark in Drogheda. A well-known doctor, since passed, had once practised from there. Now it had been converted into an empty office building. There were stone steps leading up to the front door. There were two large rooms on the first floor with some sizeable rooms on the second floor. There was a toilet in the basement, but no bathroom, kitchen, bedroom or indeed any other facility in the building. It was totally unsuitable for a family, especially one with three small children, the youngest of whom was only ten months old. This really was where resilience came in. We did what you have to do to survive and this was all about survival. I'd lived without hot water in Thirty-Six for five years. I could cope. It was harder for Brenda and the kids. At least, unlike in Africa, we were able to access clean water to drink and food to eat. The rest was luxury.

Saying that, this was a crisis situation. We were due to open the doors of the practice within days, and there was nowhere else for us to go. We decided to rent the building and to squat/

live in the upper part of the house to get the ball rolling. Colm thought we were crazy.

We arrived with our possessions in a small truck and car on a Saturday morning in April in the pouring rain. Bells House faced the river and across the road was a car park which sometimes hosted a market. On the other side of the road lay a series of very old terraced houses. The first thing that hit us was the noise – the clamour of a busy town, so different from the quiet country idyll of Ardara. We were surrounded by buildings, shops, cars, fumes and the river. Despite this, we felt immediately at home.

We took over one of the rooms on the second floor and turned it into a temporary home. It was filled with boxes containing all our worldly possessions. In one corner we had a table and chairs where we ate; in another, some chairs where we sat and relaxed. We had an old examination table which served as our kitchen. A bed filled another corner. Eventually we took a pipe up from the basement to supply us with water. This became an all-purpose family room for the next six months. It was madness.

The two remaining rooms upstairs became bedrooms for the children, with a cot in the small box room for Joseph. Initially, before bringing the pipe up, we had to carry water up and down from the basement. There was no bathroom. It was a baptism of fire. We had left our lovely new home to arrive into this mess. Our resilience was once again tested to the full. You did what you had to do to survive.

Despite these challenges, there was a new sense of freedom. Nobody knew who we were. We could come and go as we pleased. Brenda rejoiced in being near shops and other amenities. We could bring in takeaways on occasion. We were near the sea so we could make some trips to the beach. It was hard for Lara, however, who had to begin in a new big-town school.

One of my most vivid recollections, and one often mentioned by patients in years to come, related to my barbecue. I had always loved cooking on this device and was determined, come what may, to continue. I took to placing my barbecue on the steps of Bells House at the weekend. There I would cook my meat, with the fumes drifting down to those onlookers who could hardly believe what they were seeing or smelling. To add spice to the occasion, the weather was often inclement, so I would have to erect an umbrella over the barbecue to keep it going. It was sheer lunacy, but I loved it.

On the Monday following our arrival, we opened the doors to our new patients. Clinics began at least an hour earlier than in Ardara. On that first morning the queue went around the block and the mayhem began. There were many challenges facing us. There were no medical records on any of the patients.

We had no means of checking whether the medical cards of those who presented were in date (many were not, but it would take months to discover this). Since the system at the time was a fee per one item, which you claimed retrospectively, this proved to be a costly exercise. If you saw a patient with a problem and dealt with it, this was classified as a visit and could be billed to the system. It would take at least a year to discover who my patients were, whether GMS or private. We simply absorbed the hit and moved on. Many patients were also on social welfare certificates, but we had no records of these either. It was a total mess.

For many years we simply saw whoever came on a first come, first served basis, so clinics were always packed. The waiting room was a busy place. Brenda initially tried to establish some kind of order, but it was difficult. At the start, she and I worked long hours, often late into the night, trying desperately to put some kind of structure on this chaos. We created new files for each person and their families, set up a working system for social welfare certs and began a long battle with the GMS to clarify just who our patients actually were. It was exhausting work, while battling survival at a domestic level. I also had to work out which patients needed to be seen for routine calls, as was the case in Donegal.

In time, we were able to employ Breda, my first receptionist, who did wonders to bring order to the chaos. This would free up Brenda to look after the children, which was a full-time task. The patients themselves were wonderful. Dr Moore, the outgoing GP, had been looking after a mix of true Drogheda natives and others who lived in more rural areas, especially around Dunleer. He had been a great man for hunting and fishing, and loved the country. All the patients were so supportive, and understood the challenges facing us. To this day, many still remember those early times with fondness, as do we.

In those days, all Drogheda doctors worked on a Saturday morning. I decided from the beginning that I would not do so. I was going to set up the practice the way I felt it should be run. Begin as you mean to continue. I never held clinics over weekends. The patients adjusted to this new situation. I also took every Wednesday afternoon off and continued this schedule until my retirement.

For the first decade or so, the main emphasis was on physical illness. After my years of training, I was well equipped to manage whatever came my way. There was so much pathology – heart disease, diabetes, hypertension, cancers, arthritis, strokes, neurodegenerative conditions such as Parkinson's disease and the usual childhood illnesses. In the beginning I had no practice nurse, so I managed my own vaccinations and midwifery. Most patients with fractures or lacerations were seen in the local MMM hospital, which was a bonus. There was little or no emphasis on mental health.

This made sense, as back then, smoking and poor diet were rampant and many of those we cared for had experienced hard lives. Unlike nowadays, we were less focused on prevention and more concerned with the diagnosis and management of physical conditions. It was a period when GPs were reacting to the illnesses presenting to them, rather than concentrating on prevention, which would come later.

The most important change in our lives related to being on call. It is the duty of a GMS doctor to cover all his or her patients, twenty-four hours a day, 365 days a year. I had spent so many years on a one in two rota. When I joined my two colleagues, Joe and Oliver, who both worked in different surgeries, we were able to move to a one in three rota, which was heaven. Later, we would add P.J. and Alan, and for many years were able to run a one in five rota. This meant, for example, that we would only work on-call rotas every fifth day and fifth weekend. On duty we each covered the patients of all five practices. It was extremely busy, especially in the days before mobile phones. But when we were off, we were off.

After six months or so, we grew weary of squatting in Bells House. It was also taking a heavy toll on Brenda and myself. We had to find a place to live before the winter set in. But, in the mid-eighties, the housing stock was low. We had sold our house in Donegal at a loss to enable us to acquire a home in Drogheda. All we needed was a break.

On summer evenings, we would regularly walk around the town, sussing out areas to live and hoping to spot a house for sale. We frequently passed one lovely old house in Greenhills, saying, 'If only a house like this came up.' There was usually an older lady out gardening and the grounds were a riot of colourful blooms.

Brenda kept scanning the estate agents, but nothing suitable was available. Then one day she came home excited. The house we passed by regularly was for sale, but there was no sign on the property. The lady vendor was particular about whom she sold the house to. Her husband had built the house himself, and following his death, she had run it as a B&B for years.

We made contact with the lady, who was called Mary, and developed a great relationship with her. She loved the children, and we began to visit her. It emerged that two of her sisters were patients and that I had helped one of them following an illness. As a consequence, Mary decided that we would be the people she would sell the house to. A deal was struck, and we moved in with a great sense of relief that at last we had found a home.

The house was ideally placed at the top of a hill. I could get into the surgery quickly, and yet it seemed as if we were in the country. It was close to the sea and near to schools. Someone up there was looking out for us. It also had a separate side entrance, ideal for seeing patients while I was on call. We are still here, almost forty years later. We have made many changes in that time. I loved the house from the start. There is an atmosphere of healing around it, and it has been the site of many mental health miracles over the years. I often think of this lovely lady, who has since left us for a better place, and hope that she would be happy with how matters turned out.

CHAPTER 26

## *Work and Play*

In 1986, a building was acquired by the charity Homeless Aid in North Strand, Drogheda. The charity was started by my dear friend Sr Cáit of the Daughters of Charity. With the assistance of many wonderful people like Sean O'Connor, Sr Florrie MMM and others, a hostel called St Joseph's was set up. It sheltered men who, through a combination of circumstances, often created by addiction, found themselves on the streets and living in terrible conditions. In the beginning there was opposition, but over time the local community got behind the project.

I became involved when I was asked if I would counsel some of the men who wanted to talk to a professional. I saw this as an opportunity to give something back to the community. There were few services available for them at the time. For a number of years, I went down to the hostel after dinner in the evening and met with some of the guys who needed help. It felt strange to be chatting to somebody about their difficulties with other men present in neighbouring rooms, but we did our best.

There were successes and failures. On the negative side, I can recall one terrible period when four men in a row, who were hopelessly addicted to alcohol, lost their battle and one by one died. One sat in front of me in the surgery, his eyes yellow from cirrhosis of the liver, and explained that he would never quit, no matter what. Sadly, he died not too long afterwards.

But there were also successes. One particular case stood out for me. I had spoken to this nice man, who had lost everything – his relationship, family, job and home – all due to alcohol. I felt he had the potential to make it. I gave him support and advice and soon afterwards he left the hostel.

Years later, in another part of the country, I was attending a wedding in a hotel when a well-dressed man approached me and put out his hand. I did not recognise him. He told me that I had once counselled him in the Homeless Aid hostel in Drogheda. It had taken time, but he had taken my advice and was now in a new place and had regained much of what he had lost. He simply wanted to say thank you. That one success story made all of the hard work worthwhile.

Sometimes it takes time for a seed to grow and flourish. My time with this wonderful group would come to an end. In 2000, a new homeless shelter was built on the site of the original hostel and is now run in a totally professional manner by a wonderful team. The dream of the founders has now become a reality.

After five years, the lease on Bells House ran out and we were faced with a dilemma once again: stay or move. Across the road in Leyland Place was a series of six old terraced houses, some of which were in very poor condition. By chance, number five was up for sale as the lady who had lived there had died. On my first visit, the state of the building was so bad that I walked out and dismissed it as an option. Later, I returned with a builder friend who reassured me that it could be turned into a surgery with some work. On his recommendation, we took out a mortgage on the building and set about its conversion. Eventually we were able to say goodbye to Bells House and set up surgery in 5 Leyland Place.

By this stage, we had settled into life in Drogheda and loved being part of the local community. It wasn't all work and no play for me, and I found a way to relax and unwind from the everyday pressures of work by playing golf. On first mooting the idea of writing this book, those closest to me inquired, 'Will you mention your obsession with golf?' I have loved the game since being introduced to it by old Jimmy Cassidy, the golf pro at Dundalk Golf Club. I have always been pretty useless technically, but made up for it with heart, competitiveness and a hot putter. I have a particular love of links golf. When I first arrived in Drogheda in 1986 I decided to join Laytown & Bettystown Golf Club, home golf course of the famous Des Smyth. My friend Colm and his son-in-law, my GP rota colleague Joe, also played on this great links. I have many wonderful memories of the years since.

Some of my fondest memories relate to the great Bobby Browne, the resident golf pro for decades and who was simply a character. We always got on well, even if he despaired of ever turning me into a golfer. He had coached many great golfers over the years, including the winner of the British Amateur Championship. No matter how hard he tried, however, he could not teach this obstinate doctor. Matters came to a head when he informed me that I had 'the worst swing in the club'. The following weekend, I went out and won his prize. To rub it in, I won it again during the club's centenary year. He finally laid out why I was unteachable. 'To become a great golfer,' he explained sadly, 'you must have nothing on top.' I do miss the old rogue. I played every Wednesday, for years, in a set four-ball – myself, Colm, Jimmy (who ran a local nursing home) and Michael (a retired bank manager) – and have fond memories of the fun we enjoyed on the course.

I won the club foursomes on this old links twice, once with my long-suffering golfing partner Arnie Brady, and then years later with his son-in-law, Dan Hughes. These were some of the happiest moments I have experienced on the links. They are both like golf brothers to me, even if I have shortened Dan's life by years as he tries to improve my game.

For me, the winners are the links and the game itself. There is something wild and free about the links, pitting yourself against constantly changing winds and weather conditions, and the sound of the club hitting the turf. There are two games that mimic life: chess and golf. Both teach you about the importance of winning and losing, and treating both the same, the unfairness of life, the importance of being strategic and most of all, how to handle adversity.

•

Have you ever met a bishop on a bike? It's an image that seems straight out of *Father Ted*. Well, we were fortunate to have made the acquaintance of one such bishop. Shortly after arriving in Drogheda, we were coming out of St Peter's Church (famous for being home to the head of St Oliver Plunkett) following mass. A tall, lean man with glasses awaited us. 'And who are you?' he inquired. We explained that we had just arrived in Drogheda and taken up temporary residence in Bells House, within walking distance of the church. He was intrigued and introduced himself as Bishop James Lennon, who lived locally on Fair Street and said mass regularly in St Peter's. 'I'll be down to visit you,' he promised.

Within days, Bishop Lennon arrived on his bicycle. This was his chosen mode of transport when doing his calls around the town. Up he came, into the one main room in the house. Frantically, we rumbled through the boxes to find clean cups and saucers and cutlery, explaining that we were not really set up for visitors. He was so easy to talk to. It was as if we were chatting to one of the White Father priests in Kabanga. His last words on departing were: 'You have to find a home on this side of the river.' Bishop Lennon had adopted us and wanted us to be part of his flock on the Armagh side. All we could do was try and obey his wishes!

Over the ensuing years, Bishop Lennon would regularly call to see us, even when we moved out of the centre of town. He was always on his bicycle and usually arrived late in the evening. He revealed that in his youth he had been a hardliner, but over the years his views had mellowed. He was a good friend to us. We were taken by his honesty and simplicity. On one occasion he said mass on the table in the front room, something we treasured at the time.

One morning during mass he dropped the chalice while leaving the altar and became distressed at his clumsiness. I thought no more about this until later in the day when I heard that he had died suddenly at home, most likely from a heart attack. No more would this lovely man grace us with his presence. To this day I have yet to see another bishop, archbishop or cardinal travelling on a bicycle. Hope springs eternal.

Apart from the bishop, I also inherited a number of religious orders when I took over the practice. At one stage, I was looking after the Mercy Sisters, the Presentation Sisters, the Dominican priests, the Franciscan Sisters and some MMMs. It was a privilege to have looked after them all. Nowadays, apart from parish clergy, there is only one order of active priests and one contemplative order of nuns remaining. But one of my favourite visits was to the Cistercian monks of Mellifont Abbey, based in Collon.

At the beginning, I visited the monks on a monthly basis. It was a visit I looked forward to. I was one of the few outsiders who had complete access to every part of the priory. On my arrival, I was greeted by the polished wooden floors and the smell of beeswax. I would be escorted down through the various corridors, by the church where the monks prayed at all hours of the day and night, before arriving finally in the infirmary.

Over the years, I had the pleasure of meeting some wonderful infirmarians who cared for the monks who were unwell. In the days when I first visited, the monastery was a vibrant, busy place. Some of the monks worked on the land, with others working in different sections of the monastery. Over the decades, numbers dwindled, as one by one age caught up with these special men, who had a wicked sense of humour and wore their spirituality lightly.

The infirmary was for monks who, through age or illness, had become bed-ridden. The care they got was amazing. I also held a clinic for more able-bodied monks who had minor illnesses. Every Christmas they would gift me jars of homemade honey and some beautiful poinsettias.

There were two infirmarians who stood out for me. The first was Fr Berchman who was, after Sr Kieran, probably the most spiritual person I have ever met. His eyes always seemed to be brimming with brightness and love, and his holiness shone through with his soft voice and caring touch. Like Sr Kieran, he seemed to have a connection with a world the rest of us struggled to access. His sudden death hit me hard.

The second person was Brother Brendan, a down-to-earth, completely pragmatic monk. He was a total contrast to Fr Berchman. He was so good to me for so many years. Together we were able to sort out whatever issues were ailing the congregation at the time. I continued to look after the monks until I retired full-time from the GMS. By then the numbers had dwindled to a handful. An era is now sadly coming to an end.

One never knows what the fates have in store for us, as we were soon to discover. When we make momentous decisions in life, we are never sure how matters will pan out. In our case, we were rewarded with a wonderful surprise. As I was appointed to Drogheda I learned that Sr Kieran had now been reassigned back from Tanzania to the MMM convent in the town, ostensibly to retire but still tasked with some responsibilities. Both Sr Kieran, now aged seventy-six, and ourselves were overjoyed that once again we would be together.

From the beginning, we were inseparable. She took an active interest in our work, our children, in fact everything about us. She became part of our little family group. She was to teach us much about life, retirement and spirituality in the process.

Every year she would join us for Christmas dinner; she would mindfully clear the food on her plate. Then we would head off to the sea, where arm in arm we would wander with the children along the beach. The day would always finish with her bringing us in to visit the convent crib.

During the spring and autumn, she would often accompany us on walks through the woods in Dún na Rí, County Cavan. I will cherish those moments forever. She was so filled with joy and loved living in the moment. In May, we would collect bluebells with her, something the children loved to do. Each walk was like entering into a spiritual paradise.

During the years that followed, she demonstrated how to retreat gracefully when one's active life was coming to a close. In the convent, she greeted everyone with that beautiful smile and looked after all those returning home for a break from their work in overseas hospitals. She also quietly visited homes where people were experiencing difficulties in the community.

Other than that, she lived such a prayerful life. Every time her protégé, namely me, was in trouble, she would do a Holy Hour and somehow things always seemed to work out. She was there for the First Communion and Confirmation of the boys. I would often see her walking quietly along paths around the town with her rosary beads in hand, in deep contemplation and oblivious to the world around her. How I envied her sense of joy and peace.

During those years in Drogheda, Sr Kieran conveyed to me in her usual quiet way that it was okay to finally accept that your days of being an active helper in the lives of others would come naturally to a close. This involved a major change in thinking. We are all so driven nowadays. She was demonstrating that sometimes we get to a stage where we have to be open to journeying inwards, to find peace and self-acceptance in the silence of our being. For someone like me, this has been the ultimate challenge. I have always found it easier to *do* rather than to *be*.

We had one other regular visitor to our home in Greenhills. Fr Martin, who had married us, loved to visit and would always bring a bottle of his home-made wine as a gift. The children were delighted to see him arrive and he was able to put up with all of their antics with good humour. I think he was secretly pleased that we had finally come home. He continued to grace our presence for many years following our arrival in Drogheda. Fr Martin, so beloved of our little family unit, has now sadly left us for a better place. Another of our support system had gone.

CHAPTER 27

## *Deaths of Loved Ones*

It comes to each one of us, the loss of a loved one. Loss lies at the heart of grief and brings with it waves of sadness and deep-seated emotional pain, with the knowledge that the person we loved is gone and will not be coming back in this life. It was now our time, Brenda and I, to experience these emotions and for our hearts to be torn into little pieces.

I had always loved Nicholas Lahart, Brenda's father. From the beginning, this tall, thin, slightly austere man with his bald pate and dark glasses took me under his wing. For decades after the war he and his wife Ciss ran a thriving general hardware store in the once bustling town of Eyrecourt. They had seven children.

It was the treatment of a peptic ulcer, twenty years before his death, which would prove to be his undoing. There was a myth at the time that peptic ulcers were caused by a combination of stress, genetic factors and lifestyle issues such as diet. We now understand that they are caused by a simple bacterium in the stomach, which can be cleared with a week's course of antibiotics. In his case, his ulcer eventually bled, and he had the standard surgical procedure of the time, namely a partial gastrectomy.

In 1993, this fine man and much-loved patriarch of the family began to feel unwell. Following tests, the diagnosis was a cancer at the site of the surgery. It soon became obvious that this was terminal. Typical of men of his time, he did not wish to discuss his condition, but bore the symptoms and diagnosis stoically. He was a deeply spiritual man who would visit the church beside him on a daily basis. Along with the love of his family and the support of his community, his deep faith sustained him through his final days.

He died in February 1994 and was buried in one of his favourite places, the cemetery overlooking the Shannon at Meelick outside Eyrecourt. It was one of the coldest days, with a Siberian wind whipping across the water. Somehow it was in keeping with the occasion. We were losing someone who had been a rock to us all, a quiet, good-humoured gentleman in the truest meaning of the word. To the very end, he despaired that his son-in-law would ever learn how to properly pack a car or be anything but a gentleman handyman around the house. Despite this, I feel he loved Brenda, myself and the kids deeply. We still miss him. He has passed the mantle on to us; it is now our responsibility to take care of those left behind and carry on his ideals.

Little did I realise when Nicholas died that, within a few years, death would come calling again. This time it was my dad. From the very beginning I'd had a complex relationship with him. The bond between a father and a son is unique. This is down to a mixture of personality, place in family, circumstances, life experiences and other factors. Each of my three brothers seemed to have an easier time relating to him than I did. However, he was a great father to all of us, especially when we were growing up. I feel that my decision to go to college and to become a doctor irrevocably changed our relationship. I was the only one of my family who went to college; all my brothers headed into banking and insurance, a world with which he was familiar.

I have already documented his disappointment when Brenda and I went to Africa, even though he did rally when we were there. A rift grew between us shortly after we returned, until much later, partly due to my choice to become a GP rather than a specialist, which was his preference. Ten years before he died, a lifetime habit of chain-smoking finally caught up with him, and he developed severe COPD, with an emphasis on emphysema. He also developed osteoporosis and suffered multiple rib fractures. Every winter he would descend into a crisis and Brenda and I would make a mad dash down to Thurles to assist my mother. But the rift remained. Then came that moment of healing.

It happened, unexpectedly, in a car park in Skerries, while overlooking the bay. He had come up to visit us on his own, a rare occurrence. He finally saw our little family for what we were, how we loved each other, and how we cared deeply about the work we were doing.

Men speak best to each other side by side, never face to face. He opened the window and breathed in the sea air. 'How I have missed this so much,' he admitted.

Then after a period of quiet had elapsed he said, 'I just want you to know how proud I am of you and Brenda, of the work you did in Africa, how you have carved out a life for yourselves in Drogheda, how you love each other so much.' It was as if a cloud had lifted and the sky between us became blue and clear. I gave him a big hug. There was nothing more to be said. The years of conflict were over.

His condition steadily worsened and he was admitted into the nursing home in Thurles to receive the care he needed. I was up and down to see him. He was acceptant of his situation and had lots of visitors. On the last occasion I saw him, he was becoming increasingly distressed. He had developed urinary retention and required a catheter. We were waiting for the local GP to come and insert one. He eventually held my hand and asked me to do it. It is such an intensely personal act. I found it difficult to isolate my emotions and perform the procedure, but I did. Little did I know at that moment, I would never see him alive again. I was back in Drogheda for a short period before he suddenly passed away. It was January 1997.

On the day of his funeral, the church was packed. I was asked to say some words at the end of the mass. I was filled with grief and confusion. I was surprised to hear my voice cry out in a loud voice, 'Father.' It was as if all of my interactions and struggles with him came to the fore in that one word. I somehow managed to finish the eulogy and was one of the pallbearers for his coffin. He was laid to rest in the cemetery in Thurles. All I can remember is crying in the arms of my golfing friend Jimmy, who had travelled down for the funeral.

Sadly, death was not finished with us yet. It was to come

again and this time to take the one person I loved most in the world, apart from Brenda and the children.

•

Sr Kieran was such a big part of our lives. It seemed as if she would go on forever. I should have known, however, that something heartbreaking was coming. In the spring of 1997 I had an unexpected visitor to my surgery. Sr Kieran had insisted on her return that I was to be her family doctor. This was easy, as she was never ill. So I was shocked when the door opened and in came my favourite person. 'What on earth are you doing here, Kieran?' I asked after giving her a big hug. She explained that she and some of the sisters had been chatting, and they told her that if something suddenly happened to her, and if she were to die, I might have to arrange a post-mortem. She knew that the idea of this would greatly upset me. She was now in to visit me professionally, to document the fact that I had seen her.

I examined her, but clinically she was asymptomatic and her routine checks were good. I gave her another hug. To the end, she was only thinking of others and not herself.

Towards the end of April, I was contacted by the hospital. Sr Kieran had taken a sudden heart attack in her room in the convent. I was told later that she was calling for me when the paramedics came, which nearly broke my heart. We were eventually allowed in to see her. She had been put on blood thinners following her heart attack, and although weak, she seemed to be recovering.

On May Day, I went in to visit her myself, when she made a strange request. 'Will you send Brenda and Joseph up to see me, as today is the feast day of St Joseph?' They arrived up that afternoon to see her. Shortly afterwards she fell into a coma following an intracranial bleed, most likely caused by the blood thinners.

We were devastated. On 5 May 1997 we decided to go to the woods in Dún na Rí to collect some bluebells for her and then call in to visit her on the way home. When we returned to the hospital we discovered that she had died. I often wonder if she passed when we were collecting those lovely blue flowers for her. Every time I see bluebells, I think of Kieran. The sisters invited us in to see her body laid out. We were inconsolable. Even the children were crying. We all loved her so much.

Subsequently, I learnt that Kieran had laid out the habit she was to be buried in. She sensed what was coming. She was buried in the MMM plot in Drogheda. How could she have left us? We have been bereft ever since. I have only met one saint in my life, and that was Sr Kieran; she taught me most of what I know. I can still feel her touch on my arm, see that beautiful smile and hear her words in my heart. I still try and help each person I meet, just as she counselled. If there is a heaven, she will definitely be letting us in the side door!

She truly loved our family and we loved her.

These deaths had a major impact on both Brenda and me. The loss of our fathers was the first real exposure for both of us to the reality of life. The pain of grief cuts deep and no more so than when we lose a parent. But we learn to carry this grief with us as we continue on through life. Those we have lost are still with us in our hearts.

The death of Sr Kieran, however, opened a chasm of grief in me. I truly loved this wonderful person and knew that there would now be a hole in my heart for decades to come, as has been the case.

None of us can escape loss, sadness or grief. It will come to each one of us. If we experience the joy, we will also on occasion feel the pain. Maybe this is the deal we make when we love someone.

## CHAPTER 28

## *My Journey into Mental Health*

My time as a GP in Drogheda can be divided into two distinct periods. The first dates from my arrival up to the new millennium. The second dates from the millennium up to the present moment. It was during this second phase when my interest in mental health really began to blossom. During that first period, the emphasis remained on physical health and well-being. Even then, I would frequently discover that underlying a patient's presentation of physical symptoms would be a human story of stress or distress. It was becoming increasingly obvious that separating physical health from mental health was impossible. They seemed to be two sides of the same coin. For true healing to occur, both would have to be integrated into one.

One of the greatest advances in the quality of lives of many GPs has been the arrival of out-of-hours services. This also gave me the space to focus on mental health. In 2001, after much consultation and not without concerns being expressed from senior GPs such as myself, North East Doctor on Call (NEDOC) was set up.

By then, I was on a one in five rota which was a massive improvement on those tough one in two rotas. But it was tiring when you were on call, and hard on your family. With the arrival of NEDOC, this would change. Now doctors would simply work on call shifts, some during the week and some at weekends. The whole north-eastern region was broken up into four areas, with a major call centre in each one, where patients could be seen and assessed. Calls would be triaged at a central location. There would now be professional drivers bringing the doctor to the patient in difficulty.

NEDOC was run by a board consisting of members from each area who would do a term and then move aside, to allow someone else to take on the pressure of the role. It was always chaired by a GP from one of the regions.

I did a stint on the board. I had already been on a board in Drogheda for many years, which helped run the Community Services Centre for the aged, and which organised the building of a new centre called the Dermot Kierans Centre, which is still actively running. I was also on the board for Aware, the national depression charity, for a decade, where I assisted in the modernisation of that wonderful organisation.

It was with some trepidation that I agreed to join the board of NEDOC. I was immediately made welcome by my old class colleague Jimmy, who was chairman of the board. He'd had his own brush with leukaemia, but his illness had gone into remission. He was his usual ebullient and kindly self. I do feel that I had some input during my time there, which lasted about five years.

The entire country is now replete with similar out-of-hours services. This has revolutionised the lives and careers of GPs, and especially the lives of their families. NEDOC was in many ways the prototype for this major change in how general practice would run. In retrospect, it was a privilege to have been part of this new revolution.

Another improvement in my working life came in the form of Nurse Brenda; one of the wisest decisions of my professional life was hiring her. Up to the millennium, the practice was run without any nurse input. This was about to change. Brenda, the daughter of a good friend of the family, was studying nursing in London. After she qualified, I persuaded her to return to the Lourdes Hospital to do midwifery, and then to begin working as my practice nurse.

She was a breath of fresh air. She was full of positivity and good cheer, and lit up the practice. I began to teach her everything I knew. She was soon taking over vaccinations, midwifery checks, suture removals, dressings, smear tests and ear syringing. She was like a sponge soaking up new information. The more I delegated, the more I could focus on more serious cases and, in time, on mental health.

Two years later, in 2003, I persuaded her sister Carmel to join Fiona, now my right-hand person on the secretarial front. Both Carmel and Nurse Brenda came from a farming background and had a wickedly funny turn of phrase. It was a joy to listen to their flow of conversation.

Bit by bit, we added more admin staff, Susan and Jane. We needed a practice manager, so Brenda, my long-suffering partner in crime, agreed to take over the role. She had taught for some time in a local primary school but ceased when the children were of a certain age. The whole team worked really well together for many years. It was a happy group, later nicknamed 'Harry's Angels' by Paddy, the local curate.

Nurse Brenda would train further and manage the Heartwatch programme. She was simply the finest practice nurse I have ever come across, a real natural. She would eventually marry Brian and years later have a lovely baby girl, Molly. As her dad was no longer with us, I remember Brenda and myself arriving the night before the wedding with a bottle of prosecco to celebrate. She was like one of the family. She remained with me until my departure in 2014. Without her input, and indeed the entire team's contribution, I would have struggled to find the time and space to develop my mental health interest.

As I carved out a new approach to mental health, the general practice carried on with the assistance of Nurse Brenda and my team. I grew to know all the families under my care very well, saw babies grow into children and then into teenagers, students and finally young adults, and have children of their own. At the same time, I was witnessing parents turn into grandparents and some of my older patients becoming unwell and passing on. The full range of family life played out in front of me. I knew them all by name. It was a privilege to serve them.

On one occasion I saw four generations of one family in my surgery on the same day. I found myself moved by this, and honoured that so many different generations were entrusting me with their physical, emotional and mental health. The term 'family doctor' really did apply.

It was normal to do regular house calls. This gave me a wonderful insight into the lives of many patients. These visits helped me to better understand individual problems. It is amazing how much one can learn from a single house visit. Every home has a different atmosphere. Home visits, however, are becoming a relic of the past. I still meet former patients who greet me with a hug; the bond created over decades carries on.

In an era where more and more practices are being run from busy centres and on a clinic-based delivery system, I fear that we are losing this intimate trans-generational knowledge. This has implications for both the doctor and the families being cared for. If we add in the current shortage of GPs, the modern spectre of specialisation, even within general practice itself, and an increasing tendency to cease seeing patients as holistic human beings, then one would have concerns for the future.

•

I regard Niall's story as the starting point of my mental health journey. I detail the story in my first book, *Flagging the Problem*, but will summarise it here.

On 15 November 2002, Niall left his home at 9.30 p.m. for a night out with friends. He got a lift in to town with his dad, John. Little did John know that he would never see his son alive again. The first warning signs came in the early hours of 16 November when a friend of Niall's rang him to ask if he wanted to share a taxi home, as they often did after a night out. Niall replied that he was down by the river. The friend rushed down to be with him as he sensed something was wrong. Niall appeared to be calm. While they were walking along, his friend tried to explore what was bothering him, when Niall uttered the final telling words, 'It's just me', and jumped into the cold, dark waters of the River Boyne.

The next six weeks were a nightmare for John, a much-loved figure in the town, and his wife Anne. The river refused to hand up Niall's body. Days and weeks passed but no body surfaced, despite heroic efforts by local search and rescue services. Then shortly before Christmas, the body was eventually discovered tangled in moorings, not far from where he had jumped in.

John and I tried to make sense of what seemed like a senseless suicide. We discussed how to prevent more families from having to experience such pain and hurt.

For me, Niall's death was the final straw. For years I had been increasingly frustrated with the way mental health was being discussed, understood and managed. There seemed to be only a psychiatric model. I am a total believer in the importance of having a proper mental health service for the management of serious mental illness. However, I could see that there was a gap in our knowledge of what mental health was all about. We were also falling into the trap of separating mental health from physical health.

I made a commitment to John and his family that I would write a book to highlight these issues. But as I couldn't type, I hand-wrote the text for *Flagging the Problem*, converted it to audio tape, then had it typed out and printed. It was an enormous undertaking that took years to bring to fruition. But first came the research.

Around the same time I was becoming increasingly interested in the growing area of neuroscience. We were at last exploring the brain as it pertained to mental health, and the findings were mind-blowing. So began my odyssey. I was to read thousands of papers and many, many books. I devoured all there was to know about neuroscience, psychology, mental illness, addiction and suicide. A clear blueprint emerged out of the mists. The article that transformed my thinking related to a scientist called Sapolsky who had demonstrated that severe stress could cause a part of the brain called the hippocampus (involved in memory storage and retrieval) to shrink, but that this area could also regrow and recover. The cells of the hippocampus were being directly affected by our stress hormone cortisol, which was often elevated in severe stress and during bouts of clinical depression.

This led me to explore the world of neuroplasticity, or the capacity of our brain cells to change. Our brain is composed of countless neural connections and pathways. We could weaken or strengthen these simply by changing our relationship with our environment. What was mind-blowing was the realisation that our minds themselves could play a critical role in changing these very same connections and pathways. We had the power within us to change ourselves.

This was the exciting, revolutionary concept that would underlie my whole approach to mental health from that moment on. We were not fixed entities, we could change. This opened up a whole new world of possibilities.

I also explored the difference between clinical depression and anxiety in its various forms. I had been frustrated with the constant merging of these two conditions. I had always believed they were different, and research was now backing this up. It became increasingly obvious that both conditions would therefore have to be managed differently. I was interested in how neuroscience could shed light on these conditions and on areas such as addiction and suicide.

Deep down, however, I was still a GP. We are, by nature, problem-solvers. We try to understand why a person is feeling the way they are and, if possible, make a diagnosis. You cannot treat what you cannot diagnose. Then it's all about what we can do together to manage the condition that is unveiled. This had always been my approach to physical illness. Why could we not apply the same approach to mental health? This brought me to the world of cognitive behavioural therapy or CBT.

My greatest concern on initially exploring the world of mental health was the over-medicalisation of the conditions. I was especially concerned about the use of strong medications in the management of anxiety. Surely there must be another way to manage this condition? I accepted that there was a definite role for medication in depression, but anxiety seemed different.

While researching my first book, I also attended training courses in CBT concepts in the Irish College of General Practitioners. Thus began my great love for this form of psychological intervention. At the heart of CBT lie two key concepts. The first is that it is not what happens to us in life that causes us distress, rather how we look at it. The second is that our thoughts control our emotions, which control our behaviours.

This seemed like a much more appealing approach to dealing with conditions such as anxiety and, in some cases, clinical depression. Over time, I began to see how many forms of emotional distress could be assisted by this type of therapy. I could visualise in my mind's eye the brain cells and pathways physically changing when CBT was applied effectively. Clearly, it was not the answer for complex family or social issues, which would require in-depth counselling or psychotherapy. For the rest, however, maybe it could unlock the puzzle. Maybe the real answer would be to combine neuroscience and CBT together, and that is what I proceeded to do. Thus began a journey that would finish with me, along with a number of other senior GPs, acquiring a master's in CBT in 2013.

I was especially interested in the concept of using CBM (cognitive behaviour methods), a simpler application of CBT principles that seemed to me to be ideal for use in a busy general practice. Some simple examples would be teaching the person how to manage panic attacks or phobias, or to deal with general or social anxiety. This could be done in fifteen-minute sessions over a period of time. CBM was becoming increasingly popular in the UK. It was unnecessary to spend years becoming a fully trained CBT therapist to manage many simple mental health difficulties in practice. Of course, there would always be a requirement for fully trained CBT therapists for more complex cases. In Tanzania, I had to frequently adapt to the situations I encountered. So, too, it was a simple adaption of CBT, combined with neuroscience, which would allow me as a GP to assist so many people in distress.

When I started to practise medicine in 1976, mental *illness* was the only game in town. Psychiatry looked after conditions such as schizophrenia, bipolar disorder, treatment-resistant depression, eating disorders and severe OCD. Mental *health* was not on the agenda. Nowadays, we are more aware of the importance of our mental health, equating it with physical health. Mental health has quickly become the new buzz word.

What had been overlooked, by many of us, was the world of emotional distress. There is not a person out there, including myself, who has not experienced this at some stage in their life. It affects us all. We should also remember that a significant number of suicides may have their origins in emotional distress, rather than in severe mental illness. In this scenario, the person is choosing to solve the problem causing them distress by ending their own lives. This followed on from the work of Edwin Shneidman who used the term 'psychache' to describe the phenomenon. This was one of the most important insights for me.

Emotional distress, which can be difficult to identify, is caused by a number of life-crisis situations that arise, sometimes in conjunction with common conditions that affect many of us. We may be mentally healthy, not mentally ill, but still struggle with periods of significant emotional distress.

There are a number of conditions commonly associated with emotional distress. Anxiety in all of its forms, toxic stress or routine bouts of depression are good examples. There are also other common unhealthy negative emotions that can give rise to this condition. These include hurt, frustration, depression (the emotion), shame, guilt and anger. Life-crisis situations include relationship break-ups, unemployment, family rows, debt, bereavement, suicide, road traffic accidents, a cancer diagnosis, caring for someone with dementia or some other neurodegenerative condition, and so on.

Sometimes a life-crisis situation combines with one of the conditions mentioned. At other times, they occur independently of one another.

This distinction between mental illness, mental health and emotional distress seemed to me to be critical. Serious mental illnesses should be handled by properly trained, resourced and funded mental health teams. From the beginning I have argued that we must fund and resource such teams properly. As the years have progressed, all of us are now realising and discussing the importance of mental health. Learning how to cope with emotional distress seemed to me, from the beginning of my journey, to be the missing link in the chain. My next task was to develop a blueprint to assist those struggling with this condition.

CHAPTER 29

# The Blueprint in Practice

It took me years to create such a blueprint, which would combine modern neuroscience with simple CBM techniques. The aim of this blueprint was to normalise many conditions underlying emotional distress and provide effective methods to deal with them. Such a blueprint would have to be solidly grounded in science and research, but also had to be simple to grasp and put into practice. I began to apply this combined blueprint to people who came to me struggling with emotional distress, whether from anxiety or from some other unhealthy negative emotion. I discovered that those struggling with the three main types of anxiety, namely acute anxiety (panic attacks and phobias), general anxiety and social anxiety, in particular, seemed to benefit from its application.

In a nutshell (and further outlined in a short appendix at the back of this book), the blueprint incorporated the application of CBM concepts (identifying the key emotion experienced, the triggering event, the underlying irrational or rational belief leading to the emotion, physical symptoms associated with the latter and finally the unhealthy negative behaviours triggered by it). It also explored the importance of neuroplasticity, the role of the right and left prefrontal cortex (the former being the source of catastrophising and the latter of rumination), the role of the amygdala (source of our emotional world and boss of the stress system) and finally our stress hormones, both acute (adrenaline and noradrenaline) and chronic (cortisol). It was the subtle weaving of these two worlds together that made the blueprint so effective.

I have dealt with the detailed mechanisms as to how to apply the blueprint to anxiety in previous books – such as *Anxiety and Panic* and *Emotional Healing* – so will confine myself here to some stories of people whose lives were changed as a consequence. In all cases I have altered names and key details of those involved to protect their confidentiality.

I found panic attacks especially amenable to the combined blueprint. This was where the person in question would suffer from crippling bouts of acute physical symptoms (heart pounding, rapid breathing, stomach in knots, etc.), often without warning. They could occur at any age, in either sex and in any occupation. There were, however, some cases which stood out for me.

*Tara* was seventeen, a Leaving Cert cycle student, who had been self-harming for years, unbeknownst to her parents. Her life was being taken over by panic attacks, which she did not understand or know how to manage. It was amazing to see how quickly on applying the blueprint she began to challenge her panic episodes and eventually succeed in banishing them completely. Her self-harm as a consequence also completely ceased. She was now free to get on with the rest of her life.

*Jim* was in his thirties and was holding down a stressful industrial job. He found himself paralysed with fear. Following at least twenty visits to A&E, where he was becoming increasingly distressed because he was told continuously that there was nothing physically wrong with him, numerous visits to see his GP, and a trial of both tranquillisers and anti-depressant medication, he came to see me. He had abandoned both medications, due to a combination of side-effects and a realisation that neither was helping him manage his condition. He was not mentally ill, but extremely emotionally distressed. At no stage had anyone ever explained to him what was happening to him physically, so he found the neuroscience part of the blueprint particularly reassuring. Following a series of visits and applying the blueprint to his life, he noticed a massive improvement. Without any medication, his panic attacks ceased, his visits to both the A&E and his GP stopped, and he took control of his life again. He was like a new person, now armed with both knowledge and skills to deal with any recurrence in the future. He also developed new skills as to how best to manage job-related stress.

I also found phobias to be extremely amenable to the application of the blueprint and discovered that it was possible to completely transform the lives of many by giving them control over their fears. It quickly became apparent that phobias often grew legs, so it was common to see someone with multiple fears. The good news was that if you could apply the blueprint to one phobia, you could apply it to them all, often transforming the person's life. I began to see patients with phobias around buses, trains, planes, motorways, crowded spaces, lifts, churches – the list just went on and on. The good news was that application of the blueprint produced massive changes for the better and often extremely quickly.

*Chantell*e came from a major European capital city. In her early thirties, her life was a mess. She had a myriad of different phobias that were completely ruining her life. Struggling with buses, trains, lifts and crowded spaces were the norm for several years. Eventually matters came to a head when her relationship foundered in the face of her fears. She attended my clinic and was delighted to discover that learning how to cope with one of her phobias would allow her to overcome the rest. I showed her how this would operate in practice and explained the exercises she would have to do to overcome her fears. She found the blueprint of great assistance and returned to her home city to put what she had learnt into practice. Within six weeks I was receiving videos of her in the different settings that she had spent years avoiding. She had control back over her life, her phobias fading into obscurity.

*Malachy*, who lived on the other side of the country, had spent at least four hours travelling to see me, rising at 6 a.m. to reach me by eleven o'clock. He had travelled every back road possible to avoid motorways, about which he had developed a major phobia. He was in his fifties and was finding his life increasingly restricted as he had ageing parents whom he had to visit regularly. His wife was also finding that his avoidance of motorways hampered their ability to visit her family. He had no other phobias, but this was paralysing him. By the time he came to visit me, he had spent years struggling with his fears, and his symptoms were deteriorating. He found the blueprint to be incredibly helpful, as for the first time, he began to understand that the problem was not the motorway, but the physical symptoms he would experience on the journey. He began to apply the blueprint by exposing himself to the motorway on a daily basis. Over time and a number of visits, he became increasingly comfortable. His final visit only took two and a half hours as he took the motorway. He had healed himself.

Another form of anxiety, namely general anxiety disorder, was also especially amenable to the application of our blueprint. Many, many people, the majority of whom were female, attended me over the years with this condition, which often led to significant emotional distress in their lives.

*Helen* was a classic example of this in practice. A primary school teacher in her forties, she simply could not handle the mixture of physical symptoms such as fatigue, sleep difficulties, sluggish cognition, teeth grinding, tension headaches and IBS (irritable bowel syndrome), and the constant worrying, foreboding, catastrophising and negative self-rating that accompany this condition. She was married with two children and was terrified of passing her anxiety onto them. She was also a regular visitor to her GP, who had tried medication but to no avail. By the time Helen came to see me, she was a wreck. She admitted to regularly using wine as a crutch to get her through the days.

I spent some time explaining the condition to her, which was the first time anyone had ever done so. She then agreed to use our blueprint to try and diminish her physical and psychological symptoms. Over the months that followed, with its use and regular exercises, Helen found her anxiety levels gradually begin to fall.

She ceased using wine as a crutch. She also became kinder to herself, less judgemental, and really challenged her catastrophising. She accepted that she would always have this condition, but with her new-found skills and techniques she would now be able to cope better with it. She also found most of her physical symptoms subsiding. Most importantly, she now realised that the best way to prevent her children from suffering from this condition was to manage her own anxiety. She was back in control of her life.

There was one other form of general anxiety that I encountered over and over again, namely health anxiety.

*Michael* was a classic example of this in practice. He was in his forties, married with one child and an engineer by trade. His father died from cancer when Michael was in his teens and he subsequently developed a full-blown health anxiety. No matter what condition or symptom he heard about from friends, family or work colleagues, within days he became convinced that he would develop it. For ten years he had been beating a trail to his poor GP, seeking reassurance that he did not have cancer, was not going to die of a stroke and in particular was not going to die of a heart attack. Despite numerous investigations, he remained convinced that he was going to develop some major illness. Following one particularly severe bout, he was referred by his GP to see me.

Once again, he had many of the physical and psychological symptoms of general anxiety. But it was his catastrophising that was lying at the core of his problems. A full explanation of the condition allied to a judicious use of our blueprint over the months which followed helped Michael to develop some insight into his anxiety. This, together with targeted exercises, gave him the skills and techniques to manage it better. He would always struggle with his health anxiety, but now at least knew how to challenge it. Just to note, he was completely banned from the beginning from using Dr Google, one of the prime drivers of this condition.

Finally, there was social anxiety. Over the years I have assisted countless male and female patients struggling with this condition to develop the techniques necessary to challenge and banish it from their lives. Some were incredibly emotionally distressed by the time they came to see me, with many feeling lonely and isolated.

*Simon* was a classic example of this in practice. He was in his early twenties, a college undergraduate who dreaded any form of social interactional situation, such as parties, meeting friends and strangers in a pub, even meeting friends in the college canteen. He was also struggling to socialise with girls due to his extreme anxiety. He had no history of acute or general anxiety. This was, in general, what I would have noted over the years. Social anxiety was often unrelated to the other two.

He took part in the usual ritual of avoidance and safety behaviours, such as rehearsing in front of a mirror and in his head before the event, avoiding it if possible, using alcohol as a crutch, staying at the edge of groups, not engaging in conversations and doing the dreaded post-mortem after the event. His life was slowly descending into a spiral of chaos, with fear of social situations dominating.

As with so many with this condition, he lacked a clear understanding of just what was happening with social anxiety. Providing the explanation, combined with our blueprint and a series of targeted exercises, transformed his life. Within three months, he was no longer anxious in social situations, was able to converse freely and, to his delight, had even met someone. He now had skills for life.

The results of applying the blueprint were amazing. Many people struggling with panic attacks, phobias and social anxiety seemed to be especially amenable to this approach and were able to heal themselves with appropriate advice and exercises. Many others struggling with general anxiety also seemed to find the concepts liberating and were able to get on with their lives.

I also began to apply some of these concepts to the clinical illness of depression, which I had always believed was a separate entity to anxiety. I have detailed the presentation, diagnosis and management of the illness in previous books.

But it was not only the management of anxiety and depression which benefited from applying our combined blueprint. I found that it was extremely useful in assisting those who were emotionally distressed from other negative emotions such as shame, guilt, hurt or frustration. Many of these patients found their lives transformed by its application. They learnt how to heal themselves by challenging their thinking and behaviour. None of those who attended were mentally ill, but many were severely emotionally distressed by the time they came to see me. It was lovely to see people learning, through the application of the blueprint, how to change their thinking and behaviour for the better.

That has always been my mantra: 'give the person the necessary skills and allow them to heal themselves'. This has to be the essence of healing.

# CHAPTER 30

## *Tragedy Strikes Again*

I was no stranger to grief by this stage, having already lost people very dear to me. One question kept recurring: can one truly heal following the loss of someone close to you? Are healing and grief not the most unlikely of bedfellows? If we accept that the sadness and pain of grief are often with us for life, is healing therefore impossible? I now realise that we only heal when we accept that the sadness and pain will always be there, but that we must learn to walk with the load on our back. That over time we become less aware of the burden. This acceptance eventually leads to peace. This insight has taken me many years to realise, and back in 2006 I was still struggling with the deaths of those I held dear at the time.

Then came the loss of David.

I often call my brother David the 'invisible sibling'. He performed this trick of remaining unnoticed following his bad fall as a child. He was so successful in this endeavour that we never really became close, something I deeply regret. He completed his secondary school education in the CBS in Thurles and joined the bank at the age of eighteen.

He was always the prankster in social situations, brilliantly disguising the fact that he, in reality, disliked them. He was very successful in the bank. Following a number of moves, he became involved in business banking in Cork. He was eventually moved to Listowel in County Kerry, where he became lending manager for the county. He was married to Una and had three children. He was a regular visitor to Thurles and had a special relationship with both my parents, especially my mother.

In November 2006, having returned from a week's holidays, I was feeling relaxed and looking forward to my first book being published the following April. Then the phone rang. It was David. In an emotional call, he told me that he had been diagnosed with terminal lung cancer and given a few months to live. He was only forty-nine, and his three daughters were in their teens. We were devastated.

Gerald and myself then made 'that trip' in December 2006. We arrived in Listowel, where David insisted that he cook for us. He was a red wine buff and proudly presented his impressive collection. I ruined his day by asking, 'Do you have any decent whites?' We had a great laugh, but he uncorked a special bottle of white wine that he had been saving for an occasion. After lunch, with great pomp and flair, he produced a bottle of vintage Armagnac, which he poured out in small measures. It was delightful. 'What the hell!' he then exclaimed, and poured another. It is a poignant memory.

Subsequently, I visited him in hospital in Cork. He knew he was dying, although he never really spoke about it. We talked about belief. 'I am not a great believer in formal religion,' he explained, 'but if there is a God, then I have lived my life helping others. I hope I have done enough to keep him happy. If there is nothing, then I will be a part of the universe and it will no longer bother me.'

He died at home in Listowel. He received the most wonderful care from the hospice team, community and his loving family. Una asked for my advice. She was a strong believer, but was now faced with a dilemma. David had expressed a desire to be cremated. Yet she felt that the community would want to show their respects to this much-loved man.

I thought for a while and suggested, 'Let's have a *Father Ted* moment.' We came up with a plan. We would have the wake at home, transfer David's remains to the church, have the funeral service, then we would go to the cemetery, where the priest would say a prayer of farewell and the coffin would be lowered. When everyone was gone, the coffin would be taken back up and proceed to Cork for cremation. A bit absurd, but it worked. The people of Listowel had a guard of honour for him. It was a beautiful ceremony.

A month later, we gathered around the grave again and buried his cremated remains. His wishes had been respected. But he was gone and our family would never be the same again. Death had once more ripped through our lives.

It didn't take too long for tragedy to strike again. This time death came for my mother.

It came on so subtly that I missed the signs. I'd always had a complex relationship with my mother, Dilly. Vivacious, a social butterfly who loved to be with people, popular with all of her friends, and yet someone that I struggled to form a deep connection or close bond with. She was a wonderful bridge player, had psychic skills at sensing where people were at, but was always difficult to get close to. She loved us children, but was not maternal. She'd always wanted a daughter, but got stuck with us four sons.

She experienced so much loss in her life, from losing her dad, her fiancé, her brothers and sister-in-law, her husband and finally even her own son, David. I feel this constant loss was, in large part, why 'dallying with Dilly' was so difficult for each one of us. She was disappointed in the direction my career had taken and could never understand my journey into mental health, the books I had written or why anyone would be interested in the area. Even though Brenda and I brought her away for breaks, she could never relate to the world we lived in. In some ways, I found this hurtful, but my mother was a product of her time and she was unable to leave her past. I think she always harboured some frustration that I had not gone down the specialist route.

In her eighties, however, there was a gradual change. Her behaviour became more extreme towards her children, their partners and her grandchildren. She became argumentative and difficult. It just seemed to family members that, as she aged, her behaviour was now becoming impossible.

It was only in her mid-eighties that the memory loss and periods of confusion began. Up to that, she had been mixing socially with friends, even playing bridge. This was masking an emerging vascular dementia. We now understand that dementia can present in many forms, and in some people, behavioural changes are the first warning signs. It was only later that the penny dropped. Her sudden change in behaviour had its roots in this subtly emerging dementia.

She had been living on her own with some limited help but was ferociously independent, refusing any form of assistance. My brother Kevin, a true Thurles native, who at the time was working and living in the town, kept a close eye on her, as did David before his untimely death. Gerald and myself were also regular visitors. As the periods of confusion grew, however, they were becoming more difficult to manage. I believe that it was the death of David that triggered her sudden deterioration. She then had a fall, suffering a hairline hip fracture. It became increasingly clear that she would need inpatient nursing care.

It was one of the most difficult decisions we had to make as a family, to place our mother in a nursing home. In retrospect it was the correct one. She settled in well and made many friends there. We would all visit her regularly. Then her hip collapsed and she required a hip replacement, but she never recovered or walked properly again. Her dementia deteriorated further, to the point where she ceased to remember our visits. The arrival of breast cancer did not help.

Finally, on 18 August 2010 she lost her battle. I got a call in the middle of the night from Gerald saying that she had gone into a coma and was dying. I got there by early morning. She was still alive, and my two brothers were with her. I held her hand and told her I was there. Shortly afterwards, she quietly slipped away. A part of me felt she had waited until I came, and then let go. We buried her beside my father and I pray that both are now at peace.

Death was not finished yet. Finally, it came for my mother-in-law Ciss.

My life has been shaped by three strong women: my wife

Brenda, Sr Kieran and Brenda's mum, Ciss Lahart. From the moment Ciss and I met in 1976 we were on the same page. She understood me, and I her. It was inevitable when Sr Kieran and Ciss met – and we have a lovely photo of the occasion – that they too would click instantly. Ciss was a deeply spiritual and immensely wise woman, who was always there for her children and their partners. She was such an important influence in our lives. She was the matriarch of seven children and a slew of grandchildren and was universally loved by them all. She retained a good-humoured cynical attitude to the 'princes of the church', but remained true to her faith till the very end.

The death of her husband Nicholas was a hammer blow, as they were so close. I always felt that the light went out of her eyes when he died. But she continued to live with her youngest daughter, Joan, for many years after his death.

In her mid-eighties she developed a serious illness called Guillain-Barré syndrome, and was placed on a ventilator for a long period, before making a slow recovery. Then in 2011 she began to show early signs of motor neurone disease, a not uncommon development following the earlier illness. She began a slow decline, which was hard for us who loved her to witness. Things came to a head when she lost her voice and was struggling to swallow any food. I was there when a surgeon wanted to put in a peg tube to feed her. I knew this would only prolong her suffering. She managed to write two words: 'no intervention'. Her wishes were fully respected.

She died in 2012, at home in Joan's house, in the arms of her loving family with the wonderful hospice team assisting her. She was ninety. She was buried in the cemetery in Meelick beside her husband Nicholas. How I miss her. Two of my rocks were now gone.

•

While all this was going on in my personal life, I was still engaged with my patients and the wider community. I am going to relay the story of *Paddy*, whose story profoundly impacted both me and Brenda. It all began with a simple house call. I arrived at Paddy's house and had difficulty gaining access. What I was to witness were the worst conditions I have ever seen, apart from Africa. Paddy was almost catatonic from severe depression. His hair and beard were down to his waist. He was filthy and the conditions he was living in were simply horrendous, almost beyond description. As for the dog! Paddy refused point blank to go to hospital. Where to start? My first task was to gain his trust. He agreed to begin taking medication and to accept help in terms of his living conditions.

I asked Brenda if she would take on the task. She arrived with Carmel, one of my team. They were shocked and horrified by what they saw, but rolled up their sleeves, put on their gloves and somehow began to clear out years of rubbish and make his living situation habitable. Over time, the meds began to take effect, and he came to life again. He agreed to accept help from the public health nurse and from Brenda.

Thus began a most beautiful friendship between Paddy and Brenda, which would survive until his death. Paddy's story was such an Irish story, of abuse and abandonment. He had never known his mother or father and was adopted but experienced an extremely harsh upbringing. He'd had a small business in Cork, but lost it following a serious accident. He ended up homeless in Drogheda. Without going into any further details, he eventually wound up living like a hermit in the small building we found him in.

We became the only people he would trust or listen to. Paddy was impossible; he was a chain-smoker, an isolate, but underneath, a real gentleman. We finally managed to persuade the council to move him to a lovely little house, where along with a new dog he began to do very well. He was still unmanageable, but friends and neighbours rowed in. Then illness struck. He developed lung cancer, which was operated on successfully in Dublin. Following a difficult period, he was just beginning to do well when a completely different lung cancer was discovered on the other lung. This one was not treatable. The palliative team were simply wonderful and everyone rallied to look after him.

I then began to get phone calls from social workers and public health nurses stating that his conditions were terrible and that he needed to be in a home. I knew Paddy, however. He was happy where he was. I explained that this was how he wanted things to be, and we should respect his wishes. This worked out really well. At the very end, he did agree to go into a nursing home for a short period before he died in 2014. What was lovely, however, was the community of people who were there to see him leave this world.

Brenda was distraught at his passing as she had come to know him so well. At least he knew love and care before he passed.

Depression was only part of Paddy's story. Poverty, social deprivation, loneliness, abandonment, combined with illness completed the tale. Like Paddy, we just need love and someone to care for us.

Grief for each one of us is so personal. I now understand we all have to travel our own unique journey towards healing. In my case, it took many years and much reflection before I was able to come to terms with the necessity of letting go of those I loved, while keeping a memory of them in my heart. It is in this letting go that we eventually find peace.

## CHAPTER 31

## *The Next Phase*

I had always promised that by sixty I would retire from full-time practice. I almost made it, retiring in 2014 at the age of sixty-one. The year before, we'd decided to have a party to celebrate my sixtieth birthday. Boy, did we have a party.

Everyone close to us was invited. My two brothers, some of Brenda's family, our children and their friends, nephews, my team from the surgery, their parents, along with many close friends all arrived at our home in Greenhills. Every room was filled with music, chatter and laughter. Food was plentiful and drinks were flowing. It was one of those magical evenings, never to be forgotten. It was an especially poignant moment for Harry's Angels, who knew that soon I would be gone from the surgery and their daily lives.

My brother Gerald, my son Daniel and the rest of my family had been up to mischief. They created a large newspaper front-page noticeboard called the *Evening Harold*, the *60th Anniversary Edition*, detailing in photos and paragraphs episodes from the previous sixty busy years. There were contributions from many members of my family, my golfing partner Arnie and Harry's Angels. To say that they were hilariously funny is an understatement. I stop regularly in front of the board if I want to have a good laugh. You would not want to take yourself too seriously amidst this lot. Finally, at some unearthly hour of the night, the party broke up and everyone went their way.

Nurse Brenda, one of the ringleaders in mischief on the night, came into my surgery room the following morning and slumped into a chair. 'Boss,' she said innocently, 'do I still have a job?' We both dissolved into a bout of helpless laughter. It was good to be able to share such love and companionship.

The hardest part of my farewell to full-time general practice was handing over the reins to my new GP partner, Dr Ruairi Hanley, and explaining to the patients why I was leaving. They were lovely and we received so many thank-you cards, letters and messages wishing us the best for the next stage of our journey. I still meet them and receive a hug or have a conversation with them about how their lives are going.

General practice was changing. There was too much emphasis on protocols, bureaucracy and endless filling-in of forms. The type of general practice that I and colleagues of a similar vintage had known was coming to an end. I still miss the patients, but knew in 2014 that it was time to finish this chapter of my life and begin a new one.

It was now time to take up a new challenge. I had requests to assist people with their mental health concerns. I decided to open up a clinic which would focus primarily on this area. Over the past decade I have had the privilege of assisting people, of walking the walk with them. I was now operating as a GP with a special interest in mental health. Many of my

GP colleagues referred patients to me or contacted me for advice as to how best to manage situations they were dealing with. Patients came from all over the country, some from abroad. We were regularly swamped with requests, so great was the need out there in the community.

Parallel to my clinical work, I was also becoming increasingly interested in the importance of emotional resilience skills and how these could revolutionise our lives. I was especially interested in how such skills could be taught to young adolescent students at school, to better equip them to deal with the world they were going to enter.

I had come to recognise that the adolescent brain was only being formed and developed between the ages of thirteen and twenty-five. If parents, students and teachers could identify the factors interfering with this development – such as lack of sleep, overuse of technology and social media and the damage done by illegal drugs – and combine this with acquiring emotional resilience skills, then many cases of emotional distress could be avoided. I was also drawn into the world of suicide prevention and the place of emotional distress in its causation.

I began to share concepts relating to emotional distress and emotional resilience with parents, teachers, students, business groups, doctors, dentists, nurses, therapists and many other interested parties, often in large settings. The response was extremely heartening. I found a hunger for real information in the area of mental health. I was also increasingly drawn into the world of self-care and its importance in preventing emotional distress. Were we ignoring the role of simple lifestyle changes in the generation experiencing so much mental health difficulties?

I have always believed that a GP visit to a house is worth multiple surgery visits. You can learn so much from a direct face-to-face interaction in a person's own sacred space. I found myself for the past decade doing 'house calls to the country' and visiting communities in various parts of Ireland, many of which I knew little about.

I travelled the length and breadth of the country, and I found it especially enlightening to visit towns such as Portlaoise, Longford, Westport, Ennis and Athlone. I realised just how Dublin-centric we as a country have become. How so many of these communities seemed to have fallen behind in our great rush to economic success. How they all need support and assistance.

What upset me the most was the hollowing-out of our towns, cities and communities. Clearly there is something going on in the heart of our planning system. We are busy building new houses, but have we forgotten the importance of building new communities? If we ignore this, will we pay a high price in the future in the form of our mental health?

What was immediately obvious, however, was that the life problems facing people in these areas were, at the end of it all, fairly similar. Difficulties with housing, the cost of living, childcare, drug abuse, the challenges of technology, poverty and lack of resources were clearly evident in most communities. There was also a yearning for peace, love, understanding and belonging. It was clear that emotional distress was just as prevalent as mental illness. What was lacking most was a blueprint for how to manage emotional distress.

I shared the blueprint I had put together, and was really heartened by the overwhelming response. I thank all those who invited me and those wonderful communities who supported the different talks, and I hope that some of the messages were helpful.

In 2016, I published the book I had been longing to write, the aforementioned *Anxiety and Panic*. In this book I was able to marry together all I had learnt from neuroscience and CBT to create a blueprint for how I felt this condition could be managed. The public response was amazing.

It's incredible how one phone call can change your life. It was from my agent, Vanessa, who suggested that the books, past and future, should be moved to a London publishing house, along with a new book I was writing called *Emotional Resilience*. I was fortunate to then begin working with Orion, an imprint of Hachette UK, and have never once regretted this decision. They have been a joy to work with. They re-published all of the previous books, including *Anxiety and Panic*. Further books followed. *Emotional Resilience* laid out many of the skills I felt we needed for good mental health. Increasingly I believe that our young people in particular are struggling in this area. Other books such as *Self-Acceptance*, *Emotional Healing*, *Embracing Change* and *The Power of Connection* flowed from this.

Being an author is a lonely occupation, and one that has taxed me to the hilt. I have loved the interactions with all of the editorial teams and thank them all for their belief and support in the whole project.

In association with the books on mental health, I was also able to put together a series of YouTube videos on how to manage panic attacks, phobias, social anxiety, general anxiety and depression. The video on panic attacks that is on my own site (drharrybarry.com) has been viewed over half a million times. A similar video filmed for an American website was viewed over a million times. This has allowed me to reach a much wider audience.

Just as it was never my intention to become a full-time author, it was also never my plan to become involved in the media world. Just before launching my first book in 2007, I was sent to a media guru to acquire some techniques to cope with the media onslaught which sometimes follows a publication. After two hours of video analysis, he finally suggested, 'Just be yourself.'

I am comfortable working on radio shows, making TV appearances and speaking to journalists. Even though it is not my natural medium, I found myself enjoying the experience. I have had the privilege of speaking to some of the finest broadcasters this country has produced, including Sean O'Rourke, Claire Byrne, Ryan Tubridy, Miriam O'Callaghan, Matt Cooper, Pat Kenny, Ivan Yates and Ray D'Arcy. I also found myself speaking to different local radio hosts on a regular basis. For over a decade, I have continued to do a monthly mental health slot, currently with psychologist and lecturer Dr Ann-Marie Creaven, on the RTÉ *Today with Claire Byrne* radio programme. This has given us a platform to explore a wide range of mental health topics. I have to thank Claire Byrne and her wonderful team for giving us this chance.

## CHAPTER 32

## *The Future*

It is hard for me to comprehend that in 2026 I will be attending my fiftieth class reunion. This will mean that I have been a doctor for fifty years. What an honour and privilege it has been to serve so many people during this time. It is, however, nearly time to put down my tools and rest.

At the beginning of my quest, I most of all yearned to find love. It found me and has never let go. In 2027, Brenda and I will celebrate our fiftieth wedding anniversary. What a lucky man I have been to have such a beautiful, strong and elegant lady by my side for all this time. What dreams we have shared. What adventures we have experienced. How many hearts we have touched. What special people we have met on the journey. Together, we have searched for healing, wisdom and meaning, each in our own separate way.

We have faced every challenge together, loving, caring and watching out for each other every step of the way. From that love has emanated three wonderful children and three beautiful grandchildren who enrich our lives so much.

What does the future hold in store? The answer lies buried in a veil of mystery. So many dreams still to be shared. So many adventures still lie ahead. So many places to visit, people to meet, hearts to be touched and wonders to be explored. All I wish for now is that Brenda and I (aka The Waifs, the poem I wrote back in 1976) are left to face this future together, as we have faced every challenge in life to date. May love continue to accompany us on the next phase of our journey. May joy, laughter and friendship be our constant companions.

If age or illness intervenes in this world, may we be there for each other. If one of us goes ahead, may they stop and await the arrival of the other. May we then set out together, hand in hand, on a new adventure into the Great Unknown, to be at one with those who have gone before.

In the meantime, may we never stop dreaming.

For maybe that is all that really matters.

That we continue ... 'To Dream'.

# *Reflections*

I have come to understand the true essence of love. But what about the rest of my quest? To understand the nature of healing. To seek out wisdom. To discover meaning. To be able to listen.

It has taken many decades for me to fully understand the importance of listening.

I believe that I was subliminally learning this skill at the feet of the master, namely Sr Kieran. She taught me the importance of actively listening to each detail, to recognise emotions but most of all to appreciate the nature of silence. I was absorbing this message without one word ever being spoken on the subject.

We live in a busy, noisy world, where everything and everyone is vying for our attention. Yet we seem to be increasingly unhappy and constantly stressed and anxious. Could it be that we have stopped really listening?

As I have had the privilege of listening to countless patients, initially as a busy family doctor and in later years as a GP with a special interest in mental health, I have come to understand the power of this special type of listening. We must learn to listen with our hearts, with full concentration on the emotions and details shared with us. This will unlock so many situations in life.

I have become increasingly concerned that, with the advent of technology and social media, we are losing this vital skill. There is so much noise and distraction that we are fast becoming bystanders in our own lives. Then came the pandemic. Suddenly, there was silence. All became quiet and we began to realise just how much we were missing one another. We began to value again those ordinary human interactions, which we had begun to dismiss as unimportant. We came to value the sounds of Mother Nature, finding ourselves silenced by its majesty and power. We were listening in a totally different way. Were we rediscovering what we were in danger of losing?

Now, the pandemic is over. The world is busy again. Noise is back. Our attention is once again fragmented and broken. We have once more stopped listening to each other. We have forgotten the importance of silence. Our distress levels seem to be climbing exponentially. We are being bombarded by false news, AI-driven bots, constant negativity and lies, and are back playing the rating game again. Do we ever truly learn?

In the autumn of my life, I now understand that an essential part of healing, wisdom and meaning is within reach of us all. We have to simply reclaim silence in our lives and learn to truly listen to each other. The rest will take care of itself.

## Healing

I have always been fascinated by the world of healing. This is why I became a doctor. The word 'heal' comes from the Old English word 'haelan', which means 'to cure or make whole again'. Healing is the process of restoring a healthy mind or body following a period of distress or illness. In this sense it is holistic.

Healing has, in the western world, been traditionally associated with physical illness, whether related to infection, trauma, cancer or some other bodily ailment, with the suggestion that when we are healed we are no longer experiencing significant pain or distress from the underlying ailment or condition and can return to normal functioning in our everyday lives. But human beings are not simply physical entities. We also have a psychological and, in the eyes of some, a spiritual dimension that too can be affected by illness or distress.

There has always been a difference between the West and the East in terms of how medicine and healing are perceived. With the advent of modern medicine and the multitude of discoveries over the past fifty years, the West has come down strongly in favour of a scientific, data-backed approach to healing. This has led to an increasing tendency to break the person down from a whole being into a collection of different organs and physical structures – which in turn has led to the gradual demoting of the 'whole person' in the eyes of modern medicine.

The East has tended to view healing in a different way, and many of the traditional healing approaches that evolved in China, Japan and Tibet incorporated therapies aimed at the total person – mind, body and spirit. I still believe that we in the West have a journey to travel before truly embracing this concept of healing. Both approaches have much to pass on to each other.

Throughout the decades of my life as a doctor, I have

gradually altered my own thinking as to what healing should be about. I now believe that we need to adapt our western thinking on the subject.

We need to see the human being as a whole person – mind, body and spirit. This concept, in my opinion, has to be the starting point for any form of true healing. We are holistic beings, and must be viewed as such when it comes to the management of physical and psychological illness and distress.

We have to cease separating the mind, body and spirit as though each entity was somehow operating on its own. Any condition which affects one will automatically have an impact on the other two. Healing must have the aim of restoring the mind or body, or in some cases both, back to wellness, following a period of illness or distress.

While we have made enormous strides and progress (and continue to do so) in our quest to heal many of the physical illnesses which affect us, the same cannot be said for mental illness. We are still struggling to find therapies for many of the serious mental health conditions that affect us as human beings. This should be a matter of concern to us all. Equally, we are finally beginning to realise that the side-effects of many treatments for mental illnesses may also on occasion be extremely damaging to our physical health and wellbeing.

The world of emotional distress has been either completely unrecognised or misunderstood, and often poorly managed. Yet this is an area where so many of us, with information and guidance, could be fully 'healed' in the truest sense of the word. I call this emotional healing. I have spent the last few decades of my life trying to highlight this gap and to demonstrate ways to fill it.

While physical medicine has finally grasped the importance of prevention of such illnesses as a cornerstone of healing, we have been slower to apply such approaches to our mental health and wellbeing. The latter must involve changing our lifestyles and also developing critical resilience and social skills to allow us to adapt to the challenges of life. This must include tackling areas such as technology and social media, which, along with an explosion in the proliferation of illegal drugs, form the greatest threats to the mental health of our children and young adults.

My hope is that in time we will, through a combination of genetic and molecular research, discover new therapies which, within the lifetimes of our children, may be able to offer genuine healing in almost all areas of physical health, including cancer, cardiovascular disease and neurodegenerative illnesses such as dementia and Parkinson's disease.

My dream is that we will also during this period discover new therapies for mental illness which might be transformative for the lives of many people. Perhaps these developments, combined with a whole new understanding of how to recognise and manage emotional distress, might lead to a new form of healing, namely emotional healing.

## *Wisdom*

What is wisdom and how does one acquire it? Is there a difference between knowledge and wisdom? Is it created when the emotional and rational parts of the brain and mind are in harmony? Is wisdom something we inherit or is it something we learn through years of life experience? Do we learn at the feet of masters, who in turn pass on their wisdom to us? Is there another way of looking at wisdom?

I have always been fascinated by these questions and even to this day I'm unsure of some of the answers.

Here are some of my own observations, after a lifetime of experience.

There is a deep chasm between 'knowledge' and 'wisdom'. The former relates to the acquiring of information or data. Wisdom is a much deeper concept and more difficult to define. If we are designated by others as 'wise', it usually means that we are skilled at making judgements about situations encountered in life, understanding the nuances, able to read people and giving sound or sensible advice to people in difficulty. Some might even use the term 'common sense' to define wisdom!

I have always believed that wisdom is generally something which we learn, acquired over many years of life experience. There are exceptions, of course, as some may demonstrate such traits from a very young age. Perhaps one could hypothesise that the latter trait is fertile ground for the seeds of wisdom to grow and develop.

I love the idea that wisdom is the result of perfect harmony between our rational and emotional minds and brains. We are rationally and emotionally tuned in to situations and people.

I have been fortunate in learning about wisdom at the feet of older, wiser men and women, who have gently, but firmly, directed me down the right roads in life. Sr Kieran was an example of such a person, and she has had a profound effect on me personally. Much of the wisdom I have gained comes from her. But there have been others along the journey who have added to my understanding.

At the end of my quest, however, I now believe that wisdom is simply another word for empathy. This is where we can first see into the emotional heart and mind of another person. We just 'know' emotionally where they are at. We call this emotional empathy. But true empathy or wisdom is being able to then join with the person using these cognitive empathy skills to assess what is really going on in any particular situation and come up with potential solutions. This concept lies at the heart of my approach to helping others deal with emotional distress.

To me, this pared-back understanding of wisdom makes most sense. We may inherit some natural traits but can also learn the skill. We can develop it with age and experience. We can encounter masters of the skill as we progress through life. Finally, we can use this skill to assist countless people in difficulty.

## *Meaning*

Meaning! What is life all about? Where have we come from? Where are we going? Is there life after death? Is the answer to be found in science or religion? I have had to cope with the loss of so many people I loved and cared for, leaving open the question 'Where have they all gone to?' This search for meaning has been a lifelong quest.

I began life with a simple child-like belief in Christianity in the form of Catholicism. God was in his heaven and all was right with the world. This was quickly blown away at college as science and the big bang theory destroyed those innocent ideas and understandings. Thus began a quest for the truth. I explored many avenues and approaches, seeking answers to the questions I posed above. I have read countless books on religion, spirituality, anthropology, history, geography, psychology, neuroscience, science, quantum mechanics, cosmology, string theory and M-theory. From the beginning I was open to all possibilities, and remain so to this day.

On the one hand, we have science, which is expanding its knowledge at an exponential rate, but which is focused mainly on the 'how' of existence. On the other side, we have religion and spirituality, which is focused on the 'why'. Meaning, I believed at the beginning of my quest, was to be found somewhere in the middle of these two opposing ways of understanding the world.

I have found myself torn in two when it comes to belief in the religious organisation I grew up in, namely the Catholic Church. On the one hand, some of the finest, most spiritual, beautiful people I have ever known, both in Africa and here in Ireland, have given their lives in its service. They have taught me all I know about being a truly loving, spiritual person. There are many wonderful men and women who work tirelessly and unseen to minister to their flock, not only spiritually but, in so many cases, practically. These are the real unsung heroes.

On the other hand, I struggle with the wealth and power of the Vatican and with some members (with the notable exceptions of Pope Francis and his successor Pope Leo) of the upper echelons of the church, their obsession with celibacy, their protection of the institution no matter the cost, their alienation of women and same-sex couples, together with the litany of horrific abuses and terrible deeds of commission and omission committed by priests, nuns, bishops and cardinals, all of which have emerged in the past twenty years. What a terrible past we in Ireland have to own up to. How many abuses, physical, sexual and emotional, carried out by priests, nuns and brothers have we uncovered? How often have the culprits been simply transferred to other areas by religious superiors or bishops, in full knowledge of their actions, to protect the order or the institution, no matter what? I, like so many others, have found all of this hard to stomach. The fact that these crimes often involved innocent children made them particularly reprehensible. When did love disappear out of the equation? When did Jesus become a bystander? Would he recognise the institution that he supposedly created? Is all of this not an insult to those wonderful men and women who have carried out (and still do) a vocation of love and caring for those in need?

There was little that I found in other religions that attracted me. All of them, despite positive traits, have their own dark histories. Are they all simply seeking the attention of a higher power, but through a different lens? I can fully understand the attraction of humanism for our young people, who have rejected all formal religions, but find it personally an unsatisfactory option. I also found myself, for similar reasons, rejecting the bleak landscape of atheism.

Science has identified the big bang as our point of creation, and evolution as the process by which humans came into being. It has even decoded the human genome. It strongly rejects the idea of a spiritual dimension, but is happy to accept that we may live in a quantum world of ten or eleven dimensions. It also postulates that the universe we reside in may be part of a giant multiverse. In some of these universes, scientists suggest, there may even exist a different version of ourselves, perhaps acting out in a completely different manner. The real problem for science is that it is unable to visit any of these alternative universes or dimensions to verify their existence. Scientists also believe that the universe is rapidly expanding and may in time be beyond our capacity to explore.

Science itself may struggle in the long run to answer the questions posed earlier. Despite amazing advances, some scientists believe that we may never know the answers to the major questions of our existence, especially the 'why'. It is also struggling with the idea of consciousness and whether something of the human person survives after death. Many scientists believe that it does not, but accept that there is no proof either way. Science therefore is extremely adept at explaining the 'how', but not so effective at the 'why' of our existence.

Then there is the state of the world we live in. I was born into a world still trying to come to terms with the horrors of the Second World War. I lived through the Cold War, the Rwandan inter-tribal massacres, the Balkan War where old scores and age-old grudges resulted in terrible crimes being committed. I have witnessed autocratic and religious regimes crush their own peoples worldwide, with their main aim being to hold onto power, no matter the cost. It should come as no surprise that it is men rather than women who have driven much of this death and destruction.

When we also look at the current carnage in the Middle East, the destruction of the lives, hopes and dreams of the people of Ukraine, and the armed conflicts and massacres in Africa, one would despair. The cries of women and children, innocent victims of evil men and regimes, should be loudly ringing in our ears, as they were for me in Tanzania. We seem as human beings destined to destroy each other, all for the sake of money, power and the total domination of one people over another.

If we add in the destruction of our planet, our oceans drowning in plastic, the plundering of our natural resources, with Africa in particular firmly in the headlights of many large countries and multinationals, together with a major biodiversity crisis, we know that all is not well on planet Earth. Then there is the reality of climate change, which will affect our children and grandchildren in years to come. Already it is making some countries in Africa and other parts of the world practically uninhabitable. We continue to put our heads in the sand and are denying what is to come.

All of the above challenges should sound the death knell for any quest for meaning. How can anyone find an answer to these important questions amidst such uncertainty and chaos? Yet, I find myself back sitting on the bed in Tanzania, with Sr Kieran's words of wisdom ringing in my ears. It was there that I discovered, in retrospect, the answer to my questions. It has taken the rest of my life to truly understand the significance of her words. It is only now, in the autumn of my life, that I feel I am reaching the end of my quest.

I now believe that there are two ways of 'knowing'.

The first is based on solid scientific evidence and/or strong religious and spiritual foundations. My approach to physical and mental health has been largely based on the former. Science definitively describes a way of 'knowing'. I find this form of knowing to be intellectually extremely satisfying, but emotionally barren. Equally, I have struggled to find solace in many of the religious and spiritual systems, including my own despite loving its ancient rituals. I do, however, still find myself at one with those men and women, lay and clerical, who have given of their lives to help others less fortunate than themselves.

The second way of 'knowing' is more subtle. It surpasses and bypasses all logical thinking. It is intuitive in nature and impossible to explain. Yet, deep down, in our very core, we 'know'. I believe that many great artists, musicians, poets, writers and spiritual masters take their inspiration from this hidden world. We can hear it in the words of the writer and poet John O'Donohue. I also sense it on encountering the majesty of Mother Nature and the wonders of the cosmos. I have found myself increasingly drawn to this way of knowing.

This is the form of 'knowing' experienced when one encounters someone intensely spiritual such as Sr Kieran. I always felt that she was in contact with some other power (we use the term God to represent this concept), which the rest of us struggle to reach. She was trying to teach me, without ever saying so explicitly, that the answer to the unspoken questions I was seeking might lie in a form of knowing that will never be found in books or science or in religious dogma but perhaps deep within the human heart and psyche. We just 'know'. I now understand that the biggest mistake of all has been our attempts to 'box' this form of knowing, as if by doing so we foolishly believe that we are still in control. True knowing, however, involves simply letting go.

This form of knowing brings many gifts:

You will find yourself embracing love, and wanting to share it with others on a one-to-one basis.

You will become wiser, more at peace with yourself and life.

You will find yourself listening in a totally different way.

You will cease to worry about what is to come or where you are going.

You will simply 'know' that at the end, all will be well.

You will be truly self-accepting of yourself and others.

You will also accept whatever life has in store for you.

You will, above all, know joy, as it will radiate from deep within you, as it did with Sr Kieran.

Others too will find themselves sheltering in your shadow, as they sense the joy, peace and love emanating from deep within you and seek shelter there from the storms of life.

I have found myself increasingly embracing this form of knowing and trying to practise it in my daily life. I can hear the wise words of Sr Kieran in my heart, see her gentle smile, bathe in her sense of joy. I can already sense the 'gifts' which this form of knowing has brought into my life. I certainly find myself feeling increasingly at peace. I have a long way to go yet, but I am finally on the right road.

Somehow, despite all scientific knowledge to the contrary, I now believe that I will see Sr Kieran again, that she will be waiting with open arms for Brenda, myself and the children. Maybe it will be in another dimension, where she can rejoice in introducing us to the entity that she seemed to reach so effortlessly. Maybe then all will be revealed, and we will truly understand and know. The Waifs will have finally come home.

Perhaps at the end of my quest, I have indeed found meaning.

# Appendices: Blueprints

## A Neuroscience Blueprint

My research led me to the following conclusions:

1. Our brains are composed of countless connections and pathways. These control our thoughts, emotions and behaviour.
2. The brain is neuroplastic. This means that these myriads of connections and pathways are capable of change. We can reduce the strength of negative pathways, whilst increasing the strength of positive ones.
3. Critically, we can use our minds to alter these pathways, a mind-blowing possibility. If we change how we think, we can change these pathways. This opens up the brain to cognitive bias modification (CBM) approaches. We can be in charge of our own destiny.
4. Two key structures are especially amenable to change from CBM, particularly in relation to our management of anxiety. One is the amygdala, the boss of our stress system and our emotional world. The second is the right prefrontal cortex, situated behind the right forehead. It is the main source of catastrophising, so common in general anxiety, and has a

straight line to the amygdala, which is why we get physical symptoms with this condition. These are caused by our stress hormones cortisol and adrenaline.
5. The amygdala can be reshaped viscerally to eliminate panic attacks and phobias. This was the biggest finding uncovered in my research. The right prefrontal cortex could be reshaped cognitively to manage general anxiety and social anxiety. These changes, in the main, would not require the use of medication.
6. The neuroscience findings relating to depression and how different therapies can change the relevant structures and pathways are too complex to detail here. If you are interested, you can find them in the relevant books of mine.
7. In relation to other common causes of emotional distress, such as hurt, shame, guilt, frustration, anger and depression (the emotion), it is likely that CBM approaches work by acting on the prefrontal cortex, where we store much of our unhealthy schema, and on other key pathways in the brain.
8. In relation to frustration and anger, CBM may indirectly involve the amygdala as well. Frustration, for example, may encourage the prefrontal cortex to activate the amygdala to trigger the stress system to release noradrenaline, our aggression hormone, into our bloodstream. This explains some of the physical symptoms we experience with this emotion. By using CBM to change the prefrontal cortex, we can indirectly calm down this process.

## A CBM Blueprint

My research led me to the following insights:

1. Our thoughts influence our emotions, which influence our behaviours.
2. We become emotionally distressed when these emotions are unhealthy and negative, such as anxiety, shame, guilt, hurt, frustration, etc.
3. Behind these emotions usually lies an irrational belief. All of us have rational and irrational beliefs. Irrational beliefs are the main reason we experience negative emotions when faced with challenges in life. We develop them as children and young adults and repeat them endlessly. Behind each negative emotion lies one of these irrational beliefs.
4. CBM begins always by identifying the negative emotion causing your distress, and from there identifies the underlying irrational thinking patterns and subsequent unhealthy negative behaviours.
5. This is best done by taking a simple example of this in practice and then, on paper, carefully mining it, until a clear picture emerges of how your thinking and behaviour is distressing you. Suppose, for example, you have social anxiety, believing incorrectly that others will be observing and judging you, then your behaviour might be to avoid the social occasion altogether.
6. CBM will then lay out a simple path to get you out of this negative loop and, using practical exercises, assist you in reshaping your thinking and behaviour.

7. At the heart of CBM lies the world of *self* and *other* rating. It was the father of CBT, Albert Ellis, who identified this as the source of so much of our emotional distress. We spend an enormous amount of our time under the harsh spotlight of self-criticism and of allowing others to do the same. Ellis identified unconditional self-acceptance as the pathway out of this world. This is where we accept ourselves unconditionally as being unique, special and loved, but where we also must take full responsibility for our actions.

This was the insight that was to have the greatest impact on my own thinking. We were not trapped. If we could cease merging who we were as human beings with the success or failure of our actions, then everything became possible. It was to become a cornerstone of my approach to emotional distress.

# Acknowledgements

I would like to start by thanking my editorial team in Hachette Ireland for all their wonderful assistance in publishing this book. I want to say a special thank you to Deputy Managing Director of Hachette Ireland Ciara Doorley, who has been so supportive in relation to the whole project. She has been hands on from the beginning. I am also indebted to so many members of her team. A special word of thanks to Claire Pelly for her invaluable assistance in reorganising the structure and flow of the text; to Stephen Riordan who helped to coordinate the team effort; to the copyeditor Aonghus Meaney; to the proofreader Emma Dunne; to Elaine Egan and Siobhan Tierney and all who helped in the publicity, sales and marketing areas. I have been so lucky to have you all on board.

I also owe a huge debt of gratitude as always to Vanessa Fox O'Loughlin, my agent, who has made this whole project possible.

There were so many people who assisted and advised me throughout the whole process of putting this book together. My brothers Gerald and Kevin; my cousin Katrina Molloy, who sadly lost her husband Franz during the year; my cousin Dr Michael Moran; and my GP and classmate Dr Martin

White. A special thank you to my sisters-in-law Patricia and Una for their input. It was also lovely to link back in with Tommy Mullen and his wife Maura and Peter Mumford and his wife Sara; both Tommy and Peter were such good friends in Africa.

I want to say a special thank you to the Medical Missionaries of Mary for allowing us the privilege of working with them in Tanzania, and for all of the wonderful work that these extraordinary frontier women have done. My time spent with you has formed the bedrock for this memoir.

I send the warmest of thanks as always to my good friend Cathy Kelly for her constant kindness and support throughout the years. I so value her assistance and advice. I have been so lucky to have you there. It is especially appropriate that you are one of the reviewers.

I am indebted as always to my dear friend and national treasure Sr Stan, founder of the homeless charity Focus Ireland and The Sanctuary Meditation Centre, for reviewing the book. She continues to be a light in the darkness.

I am also deeply indebted to broadcaster, author, book podcaster and radio presenter Ryan Tubridy for agreeing to review the book. I would also like to thank author, psychologist and neuroscientist Dr Sabina Brennan for kindly agreeing to also review the text. I was also delighted when my colleague psychologist Dr Ann-Marie Creaven, University of Limerick, agreed to be a reviewer. A special word of thanks also to Professor Brendan Kelly, Professor of Psychiatry at Trinity College Dublin, for his review.

I would also like to thank the *Today with Claire Byrne* radio show, especially Claire herself, a real lady, together with her wonderful team, marshalled by the excellent series producer Niamh Lyons, for allowing Dr Ann-Marie Creaven and I the opportunity to highlight key areas of mental health.

I say a special thanks to my sons Daniel and Joseph, and his wife Sue and beautiful granddaughter Saoirse, and to my daughter Lara, her husband Hans and my two much-loved grandsons Ciaran and Sean for all their love and support and for keeping me so well grounded! This book is my gift to you all.

As always, I reserve my biggest thank you to my wife Brenda. It has been your love, friendship, support and encouragement that has made the whole journey so special.

You will always have my back as I have yours. You are my light in the darkness, and truly my soulmate. *Mo ghrá, mo chroí.* My love, my heart.